Next Generation Communication Networks for Industrial Internet of Things Systems

This book presents Internet of Things (IoT) technology and security-related solutions that employ intelligent data processing technologies and machine learning (ML) approaches for data analytics. It presents practical scenarios from the industry for the application of the internet of things in various domains. *Next Generation Communication Networks for Industrial Internet of Things Systems* presents concepts and research challenges in communication networking for Industrial internet of things systems.

Features:

- Discusses process monitoring, environmental monitoring, control, and maintenance monitoring.
- Covers data collection and communication protocols in a comprehensive manner.
- Highlights the internet of things industrial applications and industrial revolution 4.0.
- Presents 5G-enabled internet of things technology and architecture.
- Showcases artificial intelligence techniques in the IoT networks.

It will serve as an ideal reference text for senior undergraduate, graduate students, and academic researchers in the areas of electrical engineering, electronics, and communications engineering, computer engineering, and information technology.

Future Generation Information Systems
Series editor - Bharat Bhushan

With the evolution of future generation computing systems, it becomes necessary to occasionally take stock, analyze the development of its core theoretical ideas, and adapt to radical innovations. This series will provide a platform to reflect the theoretical progress, and forge emerging theoretical avenues for the future generation information systems. The theoretical progress in the Information Systems field (IS) and the development of associated next-generation theories is the need of the hour. This is because Information Technology (IT) has become increasingly infused, interconnected, and intelligent in almost all contexts.

Convergence of Deep Learning and Artificial Intelligence in Internet of Things
Ajay Rana, Arun Rana, Sachin Dhawan, Sharad Sharma and Ahmed A. Elngar

Next Generation Communication Networks for Industrial Internet of Things Systems
Sundresan Perumal, Mujahid Tabassum, Moolchand Sharma and Saju Mohanan

Next Generation Communication Networks for Industrial Internet of Things Systems

Edited by
Sundresan Perumal
Mujahid Tabassum
Moolchand Sharma
Saju Mohanan

CRC Press
Taylor & Francis Group
Boca Raton London New York

CRC Press is an imprint of the
Taylor & Francis Group, an **informa** business

Cover image: Kom_Pornnarong/Shutterstock

First edition published 2023
by CRC Press
6000 Broken Sound Parkway NW, Suite 300, Boca Raton, FL 33487-2742

and by CRC Press
4 Park Square, Milton Park, Abingdon, Oxon, OX14 4RN

CRC Press is an imprint of Taylor & Francis Group, LLC

© 2023 selection and editorial matter, Sundresan Perumal, Mujahid Tabassum, Moolchand Sharma and Saju Mohanan; individual chapters, the contributors

ISBN: 978-1-032-39265-3 (hbk)
ISBN: 978-1-032-41038-8 (pbk)
ISBN: 978-1-003-35594-6 (ebk)

DOI: 10.1201/9781003355946

Typeset in Sabon
by SPi Technologies India Pvt Ltd (Straive)

Dr. Sundresan Perumal would like to dedicate this book to his father, Perumal Kannan, his mother, Pusphavalli Muniandy, and his sister, Mahaletchumy Perumal, for their constant support and motivation, and his family members, including his wife, Ms. Geetha Thorairajoo. I would also like to give my special thanks to the publisher and my other co-editors for having faith in my abilities.

Mr. Mujahid Tabassum would like to dedicate this book to his father, Mr. Tabassum Naeem Ahmed, his grandfather Md., Sharif, for their constant support and motivation, and his family members, including his wife, Ms. Ismat Mujahid. I would also like to give my special thanks to the publisher and my other co-editors for having faith in my abilities.

Mr. Moolchand Sharma would like to dedicate this book to his father, Sh. Naresh Kumar Sharma and his mother, Smt. Rambati Sharma, for their constant support and motivation, and his family members, including his wife, Ms. Pratibha Sharma, and Son Dhairya Sharma. I would also like to give my special thanks to the publisher and my other co-editors for having faith in my abilities.

Dr. Saju Mohanan would like to dedicate this book to all the stakeholders of the University of Technology, Muscat, Sultanate of Oman. Dr. Saju Mohanan is also thankful to the scientific members of the SITER – Society of IT Engineers and Researchers for the constant support and advice in the editorial works. I would also like to give my special thanks to the publisher and other co-editors for having faith in my abilities.

Mr. Yasin Genç, one of the authors of the book, would like to dedicate this book to his wife's beloved father Mustafa Tireli who passed away recently.

Contents

Preface   ix
About the Book   xi
Editors   xiii
Contributors   xvii

1 Fuzzy logic applications in healthcare: A review-based
  study   1
  AYUSH KUMAR, MANASVEE AND POOJA JHA

2 A comparative study of certificate and certificate-less
  cryptographic algorithm and its energy consumption
  analysis in WSN   27
  SHAILENDRA SINGH GAUR, C. M. SHARMA AND VARSHA SHARMA

3 A novel approach to indoor air quality monitoring by
  Cisco IoT-based toxic measurement system   41
  T. M. BHRAGURAM, R. K. RAJESH, SAJU MOHANAN AND MUJAHID TABASSUM

4 Babies' movement detection and constant monitoring in
  the crib by using Internet of Things (IoT): Ultrasonic sensor   67
  EMAN SAID AL-ABRI, AISHA NASSER AL-SALMI, MOHAMED AL-KINDI AND
  AHMED AL-NABHANI

5 Cloud security still an unsolved puzzle: A complete overview   89
  SHAIK KHAJA MOHIDDIN AND MOHAMMED ALI HUSSAIN

6 A layered architecture for delay tolerant networks and
  routing mechanism   103
  MOHAMMED ALI HUSSAIN, ARSHAD AHMAD KHAN MOHAMMAD AND
  THIRUPATHI REGULA

7 A lightweight identity-based authentication scheme using elliptic curve cryptography for resource-constrained IoT devices   113

YASIN GENC AND ERKAN AFACAN

8 Protocol stack in wireless sensor networks for IoT-based applications   145

R. DHANALAKSHMI, AKASH AMBASHANKAR, GANESH CHANDRASEKHAR, ARUNKUMAR SIVARAMAN AND MUJAHID TABASSUM

9 Secure communication in Internet of Things devices using steganography   169

MANJOT KAUR BHATIA, C. KOMALAVALLI AND CHETNA LAROIYA

10 Next-generation networks enabled technologies: Challenges and applications   191

UMESH GUPTA, DEEPIKA PANTOLA, ADITYA BHARDWAJ AND SIMAR PREET SINGH

Index   *217*

Preface

We at this moment are delighted to launch our book entitled *Next-Generation Communication Networks for Industrial Internet of Things Systems*. The notion of the Internet of Things develops an Internet environment in which numerous enabled heterogeneous items with varying intelligence and capacities are interconnected in various ways. It is impossible to overestimate the significance of heterogeneity and security in IoT-enabled networks. Due to the expansion and integration of IoT networks across businesses, massive data transfer and bandwidth consumption have become an issue. Consequently, researchers are faced with new challenges such as autonomous energy consumption, multimodal data processing, simple interaction between varied Internet devices, and effective Big Data analysis. A device capable of sharing data and communicating with other physical, digital, or electrical devices. The IoT domain's connected devices consist mostly of sensors and actuators that are Internet-connected via cloud or fog architectures. When paired with a range of network protocols and access strategies, IoT applications create a communication environment that is both extremely promising and demanding. AIML and IoT collaborate to create the most potent digital solutions and to solve the most difficult business problems. Consequently, this book will also focus on IoT and AI/ML applications in diverse domains/perspectives. It is an important source of information for academics, engineers, practitioners, and graduate and doctorate students in the same field. It will also be useful for graduate school and university faculty members. Approximately 25 complete chapters have been received. Ten chapters from these manuscripts have been included in this edition. All submitted chapters were evaluated by at least two independent reviewers and supplied with a comprehensive review template. The writers received the reviewers' feedback and incorporated their ideas into their updated articles. The recommendations from two reviewers were taken into consideration while selecting chapters for inclusion in the volume. The exhaustiveness of the review process is evident, given the large number of articles received addressing a wide range of research areas. The stringent review process ensured that each published chapter met the rigorous academic and scientific standards.

We would also like to thank the authors of the published chapters for adhering to the schedule and incorporating the review comments. We wish to extend my heartfelt acknowledgment to the authors, peer-reviewers, committee members, and production staff whose diligent work shaped this volume. We especially want to thank our dedicated team of peer-reviewers who volunteered for the arduous and tedious step of quality checking and critique on the submitted chapters.

Ts. Dr. Sundresan Perumal
Mujahid Tabassum
Moolchand Sharma
Saju Mohanan
Editor(s)

About the Book

Over the last decade, the networking of computers and digital systems, each unique identity and the ability to communicate data over a network without requiring human-to-human or human-to-machine interaction to increase network performance, is known as the Internet of Things (IoT). Artificial intelligence (AI) and its applications have risen to prominence as one of the most active study areas. In recent years, a rising number of AI applications have been applied in various areas. Agriculture, transportation, medicine, and health are all being transformed by AI technology. The IoT market is thriving, significantly impacting various industries and applications, including e-health care, smart cities, intelligent transportation, and industrial engineering. Recent breakthroughs in artificial intelligence and machine learning techniques have reshaped various aspects of artificial vision, considerably improving state of the art for artificial vision systems across a broad range of high-level tasks. This book will look at cutting-edge IoT technology and security solutions that employ intelligent data processing and Machine Learning (ML) methods. The book progresses on the topics in a step-by-step manner. It reinforces theory with a full-fledged pedagogy designed to enhance students' understanding and offer them a practical insight into its applications. Also, some chapters introduce and cover novel ideas about how IoT, 5G, and Industrial IoT have changed the world in the field of communication networks.

This book aims to bring together academic and industrial researchers to investigate the potential for next-generation IoT, evaluate its impact on the solutions to the difficulties listed below, and provide viable solutions. This book also provides a solid basis for the essential concepts and principles of Industrial IoT and Next-Generation Communication Networks, expertly guiding the reader through the fundamental notions. It contains chapters that introduce and discuss fresh ideas regarding how artificial intelligence, deep learning, IoT, and machine learning have impacted the world in various sectors.

Editors

Sundresan Perumal is an Associate Professor at the University Sains Islam Malaysia (USIM). He received his Ph.D. in Computer Science from the University Sains Islam Malaysia in 2012. He obtained his Technology Specialist (Ts) in 2018, which was awarded by the Malaysia Board of Technologists (MBOT). He has been attached to various software and hardware-based company since the year 2000. From 2019 to 2020, he was the Deputy Director at USIM Research & Innovation Management Centre. During his period, various innovation transformation work for the university have been proposed and implemented. Ever since his direction was focused on computer forensics in 2006, he has been involved in computer forensic investigation, and network security consultation, and is the noted authority on electronic evidence. He provides industry-leading secure information services, computer forensics, incident response, and technology consulting services to law firms, corporations, and government agencies. He conducts computer forensic investigations and provides insightful solutions and acumen to solve a wide array of matters involving electronically stored information (ESI). He assists clients in the assessment and analysis of their data and advises on issues relating to network security and engineering, penetration testing, risk and vulnerability assessments, incident response, data breach analysis, business continuity, and disaster recovery. His research interest is also in alignment with what he is doing where computer forensics, cybersecurity, and also Internet of Medical Things (IoMT). In 2021, he has published the book with a title known *Cybercops For Future Crime Readiness A Practical Guide for Cyber Crime Investigation*. This book has become the most notable reference book in law enforcement and computer forensic unit. He has also obtained numerous professional certifications, some of them are Network Security and Penetration Testing (NSPT), Certified Hacking Computer Forensic Investigator (CHFI), Certified Ethical Hacker (CEH), Certified Security Analyst (ECSA), Certified Network Penetration Tester (CNPT), and Certified Network Security Specialist. He has given various keynotes around the world and some of the most notable titles are on cyber terrorism countermeasure & IoT security policy, IoT forensic,

Immersive Security in the Information Warfare World, and Enmesh Humanizing Computing in Today Innovation. He always Inspires and motivates through action, his most inspiring security quote would be **"Expect the Unexpected."**

Mujahid Tabassum is a lecturer in Noroff University College (Noroff Accelerate), Kristiansand, Norway. He has completed Master of Science (Specialization in Computer System Engineering) degree from the Halmstad University, Sweden, and bachelor's degree from the University of Wollongong, Australia. He has worked in various International Universities in Malaysia and Middle East that makes his profile well reputed. He has managed and leads several students and research projects and published several research articles in well-known SCI journals and scopus conferences. He is a qualified "Chartered Engineer – CEng" registered with the Engineering Council, UK. He has 13 years of teaching experience. He is a Cisco, Microsoft, Linux, Security, and IoT-certified instructor. His research interests include Computer Networks, AI, Wireless Sensor Network, IoT, Security and Applications. He has published several Scopus papers, journals, and book chapters. He is a Member of IEEE, Member of Institution of Engineering and Technology, Member of IAENG, Member of Australia Computing Society (ACS), and Member of MBOT Malaysia. He is an active member of the Society of IT Engineers and Researchers, UK.

Moolchand Sharma is currently an Assistant Professor in the Department of Computer Science and Engineering at Maharaja Agrasen Institute of Technology, GGSIPU Delhi. He has published scientific research publications in reputed International Journals and Conferences, including SCI indexed and Scopus indexed Journals such as Cognitive Systems Research (Elsevier), Physical Communication(Elsevier), Intelligent Decision Technologies: An International Journal, Cyber-Physical Systems (Taylor & Francis Group), International Journal of Image & Graphics (World Scientific), International Journal of Innovative Computing and Applications (Inderscience) & Innovative Computing and Communication Journal (Scientific Peer-reviewed Journal). He has authored/co-authored chapters with international publishers like Elsevier, Wiley, and De Gruyter. He has authored/edited four books with a National/International level publisher (CRC Press, Bhavya publications). His research area includes Artificial Intelligence, Nature-Inspired Computing, Security in Cloud Computing, Machine Learning, and Search Engine Optimization. He is associated with various professional bodies like IEEE, ISTE, IAENG, ICSES, UACEE, Internet Society, and life membership of Universal Innovators research lab. He possesses teaching experience of more than 9 years. He is the co-convener of ICICC, DOSCI, ICDAM, & ICCCN springer Scopus Indexed conference series and also the co-convener of ICCRDA-2020 Scopus Indexed IOP Material

Science & Engineering conference series. He is also the organizer and Co-Convener of the International Conference on Innovations and Ideas towards Patents (ICIIP - 2021) & also the member of Advisory and TPC Committee of International Conference on Computational and Intelligent Data Science (ICCIDS-2022). He is also the reviewer of many reputed journals like Springer, Elsevier, IEEE, Wiley, Taylor & Francis Group, IJEECS and World Scientific Journal, and many springer conferences. He has also served as a session chair in many international springer conferences. He is currently a doctoral researcher at DCR University of Science & Technology, Haryana. He completed his postgraduate degree in 2012 from SRM UNIVERSITY, NCR CAMPUS, GHAZIABAD, and graduation in 2010 from KNGD MODI ENGG. COLLEGE, GBTU.

Saju Mohanan is currently a Faculty in the Information Technology Department at the University of Technology and Applied Sciences, Muscat, Sultanate of Oman. He also acts as the director of the SITER – Society of IT Engineers and Researchers. He has published scientific research publications in reputed scopus indexed International Journals and Conferences. He is also the organizer and chair of the International Conference on IR4.0 Innovative and Smart Industries Solutions (iCiiSiS) and the Program Chair of SNSIR4.0 – Student National Symposium IR4.0. He is the advisor and the founder member of the IJICSE – International Journal of Innovation in Computational Science and Engineering

Contributors

Eman Said Al-Abri
Department of Information
   Technology Higher College of
   Technology
Muscat Al-Khuwair, Sultanate of
   Oman

Erkan Afacan
Department of Electrical-
   Electronics Engineering, Faculty
   of Engineering
Gazi University
Maltepe/Ankara, Turkey

Mohammed Ali Hussain
KLEF (Deemed to be University)
Vaddeswaram, India

Akash Ambashankar
KCG College of Technology
Chennai, India

Aditya Bhardwaj
Department of Computer Science
   & Engineering
Bennett University
Greater Noida, India

Manjot Kaur Bhatia
Department of Information
   Technology
Jagan Institute of Management
   Studies
New Delhi, India

T.M. Bhraguram
Department of IT
University of technology and
   Applied Sciences
Shinas, Sultanate of Oman

Ganesh Chandrasekhar
KCG College of Technology
Chennai, INDIA

R. Dhanalakshmi
KCG College of Technology
Chennai, India

Shailendra Singh Gaur
BPIT, Guru Gobind Singh
   Indraprastha University
New Delhi, India

Yasin Genc
Department of Electrical-
   Electronics Engineering, Faculty
   of Engineering
Gazi University
Maltepe/Ankara, Turkey

Umesh Gupta
Department of Computer Science
   & Engineering
Bennett University
Greater Noida, India

Pooja Jha
Department of MCA
Amity University
Ranchi, India

Mohamed Al-Kindi
Department of Information
 Technology
Higher College of Technology
Muscat Al-Khuwair, Sultanate of
 Oman

C. Komalavalli
Department of Information
 Technology
Jagan Institute of Management
 Studies
New Delhi, India

Ayush Kumar
Department of MCA
Amity University
Ranchi, India

Chetna Laroiya
Department of Information
 Technology
Jagan Institute of Management
 Studies
New Delhi, India

Manasvee
Department of MCA
Amity University
Ranchi, Jharkhand, India

Arshad Ahmad Khan Mohammad
GITAM Deemed to be University
India

Saju Mohanan
Department of IT
University of technology and
 Applied Sciences
Shinas, Sultanate of Oman

Shaik Khaja Mohiddin
Lincoln University College
Malaysia

Ahmed Al-Nabhani
Department of Information
 Technology
Higher College of Technology
Muscat Al-Khuwair, Sultanate of
 Oman

Deepika Pantola
Department of Computer Science
 & Engineering
Bennett University
Greater Noida, India

R. K. Rajesh
Department of IT, University of
 technology and Applied Sciences,
 Shinas
Al-Aqur, Shinas, Sultanate of Oman

Thirupathi Regula
Information Technology
 Department
University of Technology and
 Applied Sciences
Muscat Al-Khuwair, Sultanate of
 Oman

Aisha Nasser Al-Salmi
Department of Information
 Technology
Higher College of Technology
Muscat Al-Khuwair, Sultanate of
 Oman

C. M. Sharma
BPIT, Guru Gobind Singh
 Indraprastha University
New Delhi, India

Varsha Sharma
BPIT, Guru Gobind Singh
   Indraprastha University
New Delhi, India

Simar Preet Singh
Department of Computer Science
   & Engineering
Bennett University
Greater Noida, India

Arunkumar Sivaraman
School of Computer Science and
   Engineering
Vellore Institute of Technology (VIT)
Chennai, India

Mujahid Tabassum
Noroff University College (Noroff
   Accelerate)
Kristiansand, Norway

Chapter 1

Fuzzy logic applications in healthcare

A review-based study

Ayush Kumar, Manasvee and Pooja Jha
Amity University, Ranchi, Jharkhand, India

CONTENTS

1.1   Introduction 1
    1.1.1   Fuzzy logic 2
    1.1.2   Structure of fuzzy logic 2
1.2   Applications of fuzzy logic techniques in medical domain 4
    1.2.1   Neuro-fuzzy system 4
    1.2.2   Fuzzy-based dynamic release of healthcare datasets 4
1.3   Internet of Things 5
    1.3.1   IoT in healthcare 5
    1.3.2   Internet of Things in monitoring the health 5
1.4   Implications and benefits of fuzzy logic in healthcare industry 7
1.5   A roadmap of fuzzy logic applications in healthcare 9
1.6   Some findings 9
1.7   Conclusion 23
1.8   Future scope 24
References 24

1.1 INTRODUCTION

One of the most significant components of our lives is medical analysis. In most circumstances, however, it is hard to provide precise definitions and symptoms of medical concepts, as well as the relationships between them. The lines between what is acceptable and what is not are blurry. Because of the unpredictable nature of the medical field, fuzzy logic (FL) or its conjunction with other artificial intelligence (AI) techniques provides an optimal solution.

Considering the case of cough syrups for the common cold: The cough syrups that we use in general have instructions on the back based on age group like: "Not to exceed 40ml for Adults and 20ml for children in 24 hours." More programming abilities and true/false assertions are required to process and model this statement in a computer system. The terms we need

DOI: 10.1201/9781003355946-1

to simulate this, that is, "Children," "Adult," and "time of 24 hours" are vague and fuzzy. For example, children as a variable is expressed such as the age group below 15, 12, or 10 years. In the same way here for time variables, we may go for different time chunks in the specified limit of 24 hours. As a consequence of this vagueness, approaches based on FL must be used in medical data processing applications.

1.1.1 Fuzzy logic

It resembles the decision-making process used by humans. The truth value of variables in FL, on the one hand, can be any real number between 0 and 1, making it a type of many-valued logic. It is used to deal with the concept of partial truth, where the truth value can be somewhere between true and false. The truth values of variables in Boolean logic, on the other hand, can only be the integer values 0 or 1. With Lotfi Zadeh's proposal of fuzzy set theory in 1965, the term FL was coined. Next, a description about Fuzzy set is discussed briefly.

Let "X" be a set of points (objects), with x denoting a standard element of X. As a result, X = x.

A membership (characteristic) function $f_a(x)$ is used to describe a fuzzy set (class) A in X. It associates a real number in the interval [0, 1] with each point in X, with the value $f_a(x)$ at x denoting the "degree of membership" of x in A.

As a result, the closer $f_a(x)$ is to 1, the higher is the grade of membership of x in A. The concept of FL is based on the observation that individuals make decisions based on inexact and non-numerical data. Fuzzy models or sets are mathematical representations of ambiguity and imprecise data.

These models are capable of reading, demonstrating, modifying, analyzing, and utilizing ambiguous and uncertain facts and information (hence the term fuzzy). From control theory to AI, FL has been used in a variety of domains. The structure of FL is discussed in the following sub-section. FL structure can be divided into the following four components or parts.

1.1.2 Structure of fuzzy logic

Definition 1: RULE BASE: This part of FL comprises of the experts' set of rules and IF-THEN conditions for governing the decision-making system based on linguistic data. Recent advances in fuzzy theory have resulted in several useful strategies for designing and tuning fuzzy controllers. Many of these advancements lessen the quantity of ambiguous regulations.

Definition 2: FUZZIFICATION: This is a technique for transforming inputs, such as crisp numbers, into fuzzy sets. Crisp inputs, such as temperature, pressure, and rpms, are the exact inputs detected by sensors and delivered into the control system for processing.

Definition 3: INFERENCE ENGINE: It assesses the degree of similarity between the current fuzzy input and each rule, as well as which rules should be fired based on the input field. The control actions are then formed by combining the fired rules.

Definition 4: DEFUZZIFICATION: This step converts the fuzzy sets generated by the inference engine into a crisp value. There are numerous defuzzification strategies available, with the optimal one being used in conjunction with a certain expert system to minimize error.

Definition 5: MEMBERSHIP FUNCTION: It is a graph that describes the way each point in the input space is mapped to a membership value of 0 to 1. The universe of discourse (u) or universal set (u) is a term used to describe the input space, which encompasses all the conceivable items of concern in each application.

In the previous example of age ambiguity in cough syrup instructions, FL can be applied as shown in Figure 1.1.

In the figure, for the Y-axis, the FL ranges between 0 and 1, and the X-axis shows the age groups, and the various polygons show the participation range.

Definition 6: LINGUAL VARIABLE: A lingual variable has a name, a definition domain, a set of values and an interpretation. The definition contains a set of lingual terms, which demonstrate the values that may take the lingual variable at different levels.

Lingual terms are defined as fuzzy sets, usually with a bell-shaped structure or a trapezoidal structure.

Consider the Lingual Variable "*Age*" as an example as mentioned in Figure 1.1 age described on a universe [0, 1] with linguistic terms labeled as {baby, toddler, child, teen, adult}

So, if we consider the age of subject as Age = 11 years, then as we can see in Figure 1.1, the participation of the subject in group for child is 0.6 and

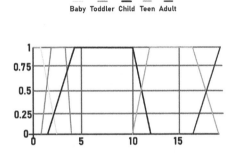

Figure 1.1 Fuzzifying the age ambiguity in cough syrup instructions as variable "Age."

for the group for Teen is 0.3, so the analogous lingual representation would be obtained as a linear combination: [0.6 Child + 0.3 Teen]; thus, by using FL, we have much more granular idea of which and how much into a category of age a subject falls in based on a number of years. FL has already been applied to many medical fields. The next section discusses about some of the work that has been done followed by the application areas.

The next section highlights most common applications where the concept is applied.

1.2 APPLICATIONS OF FUZZY LOGIC TECHNIQUES IN MEDICAL DOMAIN

This chapter presents two applications of FL in medical science.

1.2.1 Neuro-fuzzy system

Neuro-fuzzy system is a smart hybrid system that combines neural networks with FL. A neural network is a simplified mathematical model of a brain-like system that uses a network of distributed artificial neurons to execute concurrent calculation as well as pattern recognition; if we consider the brain systems, they are unsuccessful at articulating how they arrive at their judgments. Fuzzy inference systems, on the other hand, can reason with ambiguous data and explain their judgments effectively, but they lack the ability to learn the rules that are employed to make such decisions on their own. The disadvantages of each of these AI technologies have been overcome by combining them to create the smart hybrid systems known as NFS. [Kour, H., Manhas, J., & Sharma, V. (2020). Usage and implementation of neuro-fuzzy systems for classification and prediction in the diagnosis of different types of medical disorders: a decade review. Artificial Intelligence Review, 53(7), 4651–4706. https://doi.org/10.1007/s10462-020-09804-x]

1.2.2 Fuzzy-based dynamic release of healthcare datasets

There are three main steps in the proposed Fuzzy-DP method. The first phase entails utilizing FL to classify attributes. The next step is to allocate tuples to fuzzy boxes, and the final task is to integrate SAs (FBs) into the QIs table. [Attaullah, H., Kanwal, T., Anjum, A., Ahmed, G., Khan, S., Rawat, D. B., & Khan, R. (2021). Fuzzy Logic-based Privacy-aware Dynamic Release of IoT-enabled Healthcare Data. IEEE Internet of Things Journal, 1–1. https://doi.org/10.1109/jiot.2021.3103939].

After discussing about the FL and their applicability, the chapter moves forward to highlight and briefly cover some terms related with Internet of Things (IoT).

1.3 INTERNET OF THINGS

The IoT is a web in which numerous items are linked and may interact via a computer network. We may obtain information from sensors connected to this global network. We may obtain these data from anywhere in the globe by using a computer network. The IoT may link physical items to the Internet and enable the development of systems deriving from diverse technologies like near-field communication (NFC) and wireless sensor networks (WSN) sensors in a WSN to monitor their surroundings and transmit data to a base station. The utilization of the concept of IoT in healthcare is something which cannot be left behind in this chapter.

1.3.1 IoT in healthcare

In the healthcare sector, IoT provides intelligence for health monitoring. Sensors may be used to obtain health data with the aid of IoT. Healthcare is a structure that helps to enhance fitness and treat ailments. There are wireless systems in place in which various apps and sensors are fixed on to patients, data are acquired, and these data are related to medical personnel via an expert system. Clinical devices for the IoT may be accessed remotely, using equipment that are online and sensors and transmission devices that can monitor patient health. These devices enable the expert system to transmit patient data through a gateway to a secure cloud platform where the data are saved and may be evaluated. Nowadays in India, telemedicine is the practice of providing care to patients remotely when both the clinician and the patient are not physically present. Telemedicine can be described as "the delivery of healthcare services remotely." Figure 1.2 shows the plan of healthcare industry using IoT techniques.

1.3.2 Internet of Things in monitoring the health

The IoT may be employed to enhance patient therapy by using remote observation and communication, as well as follow patients as they travel through a healthcare institution. Sensors are used to capture extensive physiological data, which is then evaluated and stored by gateways and the cloud before being wirelessly transmitted for additional audit. It eliminates the need for a health expert to visit the patient at frequent periods to check their vital signs, instead of delivering a continuous automatic flow of information as seen in Figure 1.3.

As a result, it both enhances the nature of care via continual scrutiny and decreases the expenses by defeating the requirement for a caregiver to intently participate in data gathering and analysis. People all around the world may suffer because of the lack of readily available adequate health observation. However, compact, strong wireless options linked via the IoT

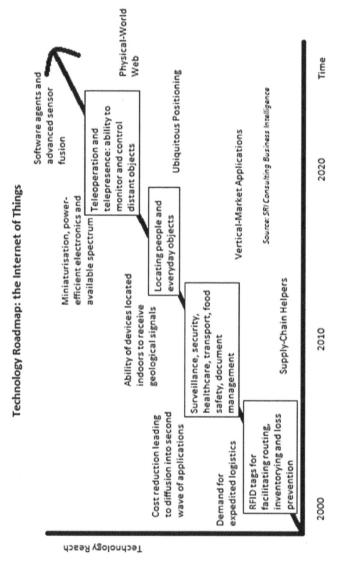

Figure 1.2 Plan of healthcare industry using IoT techniques.

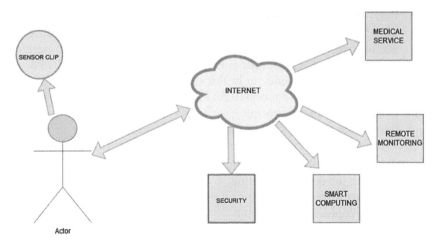

Figure 1.3 Structure of implementing IoT in healthcare.

are now allowing monitoring to be received by patients rather than the other way around.

Intelligence sensors, combining a sensor with a microcontroller, enable the IoT to be used for healthcare systems by precisely measuring, monitoring, and analyzing a wide range of health status data collected from patients. These can include vital indicators like heart rate and blood pressure, glucose levels, and oxygen (O_2) levels in the blood. Smart sensors can also be included in medicine bottles and linked to the connection to signal whether or not a patient has taken a medicine dose as prescribed.

Furthermore, the chapter discusses some of the applications of FL in the healthcare in the next section.

1.4 IMPLICATIONS AND BENEFITS OF FUZZY LOGIC IN HEALTHCARE INDUSTRY

This section aims to show some of the work done in this area and how the application of FL in healthcare has been benefited by providing accuracy and precision.

i. Healthcare system efficiency and management:
  To better capture the hazy inner workings of the patients' value evaluation, researchers used FL, a technology devised to simulate the fuzzy nature of the human mind. It was discovered that the most important factors for patients were quality of treatment and medical competence. [Frank F. C. Pan. (2011). Perceived values on hospital services: A fuzzy logic application. African Journal of Business Management, 5(11), 4465–4475. https://doi.org/10.5897/AJBM10.1626]

ii. Fuzzy-based risk evaluation models:

The effectiveness of a risk evaluation model established on FL principles was investigated. It was able to provide better care for patients by implementing the essential information system. [Ozok, A. F. (2012). Fuzzy modelling and efficiency in health care systems. Work, 41(SUPPL.1), 1797–1800. https://doi.org/10.3233/WOR-2012-0646-1797]

iii. Diagnostics and monitoring:

Fuzzy logic is used for various diagnostic and monitoring processes, which can be employed in the healthcare industry. To mention, some of them are as follows:

- Lung infection monitoring,
- Heart disease monitoring, and
- Schizophrenia monitoring

iv. Medical decision-making and supply chain management:

Fuzzy Logic is seen to be very helpful in medical decision-making, as it helps eliminate vagueness in diagnosis linguistics It helps to analyze the data in medical image-processing, information retrieval from medical databases, and medical data mining. [5]. [Fuzzy logic in healthcare. In Handbook of Research on Artificial Intelligence Techniques and Algorithms (pp. 679–707). IGI Global. https://doi.org/10.4018/978-1-4666-7258-1.ch022]

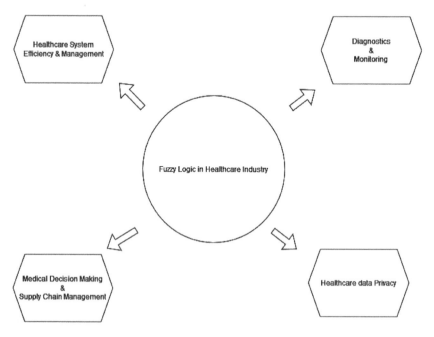

Figure 1.4 Applications areas of fuzzy logic in healthcare.

It also helps in decision-making in medical procedures as seen in the example of ICU [Bates, J. H. T., & Young, M. P. (2003). Applying fuzzy logic to medical decision making in the intensive care unit. In American Journal of Respiratory and Critical Care Medicine (Vol. 167, Issue 7, pp. 948–952). https://doi.org/10.1164/rccm.200207-777CP]. It also helps manage supply chains for the medicines.

v. Healthcare data privacy:

Healthcare data withhold sensitive personal data that must be safeguarded. A FL-based algorithm was demonstrated to preserve a subject's privacy in a dynamic data release situation with many sensitive features.

Attaullah, H., Kanwal, T., Anjum, A., Ahmed, G., Khan, S., Rawat, D. B., & Khan, R. (2021). Fuzzy Logic-based Privacy-aware Dynamic Release of IoT-enabled Healthcare Data. IEEE Internet of Things Journal, 1–1. https://doi.org/10.1109/jiot.2021.3103939

1.5 A ROADMAP OF FUZZY LOGIC APPLICATIONS IN HEALTHCARE

In the current state of the art, a substantial study has been performed in relation to the application of FL in healthcare (Table 1.1).

1.6 SOME FINDINGS

After the studies were conducted on selected papers, the various conclusions drawn are listed below:

a. According to the findings, patients who seek assistance, on the one hand, place the greatest value on timely and accurate emerging services, as well as the physicians' competency. Patients, on the other hand, were completely unaware of the intangible variables, which were even forced upon them by legal authorities. These did not contribute to a hospital's perceived worth in the least. The patients' hospital visits were prompted by concerns about their bodily and mental well-being. Any projects aimed at improving healthcare services, such as interior and exterior modernizations, as well as hardware and software upgrades, would be beneficial to patients if the services or medical results could be seen.

b. When the risk level and severity are combined in practice, the risk magnitude can be classified as negligible, minor, major, or severe. According to each, level one must take manufacturing engineering measures in a scientific and thorough manner.

c. Fuzzy logic is a good method to give the physician the help he/she needs in dealing with linguistic notions while avoiding accuracy loss.

Table 1.1 Application of fuzzy logic in healthcare

S. no.	Motivation in the paper	Methods	Parameters used

1	**Perceived values on hospital services [1]:**
	
	Patients who are loyal can be extremely beneficial to a hospital. The hospital's service quality was one of the driving reasons behind patient's happiness and loyalty; however, it was only a necessary but not a sufficient factor. Recent customer behavior research has shown that the perceived value is the most important factor in determining service loyalty. This is being analyzed using fuzzy systems
		The goal of this study was to find out what patients thought about hospitals. This study used fuzzy logic, a method developed to imitate the fuzzy nature of the human brain, to better capture the hazy inner workings of the patients' value assessment. This study was the first to use fuzzy logic in this setting, and it discovered that patients valued quality of care and medical competence the most. This was in line with earlier research, but it also disclosed some new information. To identify the two groups, the researchers utilized a proximity measure. This study employed a proximity index to separate the best hospital from the rivals, which were otherwise rated similarly by other methods. The hospital with the best operation performance also obtained higher levels of patient perceived value, according to the findings. The study had a number of managerial consequences, notably in terms of detecting and correcting marketing myopia.	**Parameters Considered:**
			
			• Weight of importance,
			• Ratings on perceived values such as:
			  • Quality,
			  • Emotion,
			  • Price,
			  • Reputation,
			  • Search

| 2 | **Healthcare system efficiency [2]:**

According to the American Medical Institute, approximately 50,000 people die each year as a result of medical mistakes.

Use of information systems in healthcare systems is critical for a safe and high-quality medical system.

Human error is reduced, and patient care systems are supported by health information apps.

Medical information system's applications, as has recently been reported, have a negative impact on all the medical integral parts.

Healthcare information organization account for around 4.6% of overall costs. | In this study, a risk determination model based on fuzzy logic principles is tested. It was able to provide safer treatment for patients by implementing the essential information system.

To reduce human mistake, the authors used fuzzy modeling as a study technique and generated sum fuzzy membership functions.

In a risk model, various procedures must be taken.

• First, the authors had to form a skilled panel, and then they had to define risk variables, according to these stages.
• Expert judgments are used to determine the weight of each component in the ANP Method.
• Experts evaluate the likelihood of risk, the magnitude of risk, and the significance of each variable.
• After that, linguistic variables are translated into standard fuzzy numbers, and expert judgment is used. Opinions are integrated.
• The risk levels were then calculated using fuzzy numbers and fuzzy inference. | **Parameters checked:**

• People's age
• Gender
• Educational level
• Skills
• Individual productivity
• Experience
• Training
• Communication 1
• Communication 2
• Organizational commitment
• User participation
• Level 1 coordination
• Level 2 coordination
• Ease of use of the system
• Usefulness
• Compatibility
• Impact
• Enjoyment
• Psychological elements in general

(*Continued*) |

Table 1.1 (Continued) Application of fuzzy logic in healthcare

S. no.	Motivation in the paper	Methods	Parameters used
3	**Pattern recognition in medical applications [3]:** The authors of this paper focus on the many ways that fuzzy architectures can be used in conjunction with fuzzy logic techniques to improve pattern recognition efficiency, with a particular focus on the many ways that can be used in conjunction with fuzzy logic techniques to improve pattern recognition efficiency. Despite the fact that medicine and control engineering are unrelated, accessible control options for online equipment are increasingly viable, especially in surgical procedures and intensive care units. Control engineering is being used in medicine in a variety of ways. Adaptive controllers range from basic dose prescription algorithms to very advanced adaptive controllers.	The usage of artificial neural networks and fuzzy logic systems to develop intelligent and adaptable systems is explored in this research, which allows for the depiction of real-world scenarios. Artificial neural networks can learn by adjusting the connectivity between layers. Fuzzy logic inference systems use fuzzy sets and rules, as well as fuzzy analysis, to give a computational framework. The aforementioned adaptive components are fused together to form a "Neuro-Fuzzy" system. This study focuses on the main aspects of the constructions discussed. This fusion, according to researchers, might be used for pattern identification in medical applications. Early detection has been shown to be quite beneficial in developing a more effective treatment approach. As a result, discovering a procedure that allows for early disease detection would be immensely valuable to patients. The major contribution of this research is to investigate several forms of fuzzy systems and their potential applications in early illness detection and disease categorization.	**Systems used:** • Neuro-Fuzzy systems • Fuzzy logic • Fuzzy neural networks • Biological and artificial neural networks

4 **Privacy in IoT-enabled healthcare data using fuzzy systems [4]:**
On the one hand, healthcare providers save healthcare data acquired from a variety of sources, which is important for patient diagnostics and crucial analytical study.

On the other hand, healthcare data contain sensitive personal information that must be protected.

Individuals' sensitive health information contains a variety of features, and linking them might result in a privacy breach. Such data are projected to be released on a regular and dynamic basis under increasingly complex situations, and the availability of personal data makes a privacy violation of individuals unavoidable.

The authors propose a privacy first system based on logic derived from fuzzy techniques to protect an individual's privacy in a dynamic data release situation with several sensitive aspects in this study.

The algorithms can be broadly described as:

1) **Fuzzy classification:** The initial stage in fuzzy classification is determining whether linguistic variables x (attributes) exist in a dataset.

Following the identification of the linguistic factors, each one is assigned a unique value and rated.

2) **Fuzzy assignment:** The fuzzy classification algorithm creates FBs from MFs.

The fuzzy assignment technique allocates tuples from tables to each bucket based on their values.

3) **Anonymization:** QIs and SAs are categorized and assigned into fuzzy-based buckets.

The final step is to assign FBs to tuple ids and add SA FBs to the QI fuzzy bucket table.

Algorithms used:

- **Fuzzy-DP algorithm 1:** Fuzzy classification algorithm
- **Algorithm 2:** Fuzzy assignment
- **Algorithm 3:** Anonymization

5 **Fuzzy logic in common medical procedures:**
The author presents a comprehensive study examining and explaining the fuzzy logic applications commonly used in the medical field. Medical image processing, information retrieval from medical databases, and medical data mining are examples of popular fuzzy logic applications.

The author cites that examples of fuzzy logic are used in healthcare computer applications because it can enhance the traditional Boolean logic of computer programs.

It links symbols and concepts to deal with the semantics of the connected domain, and it compares, constrains, extends, particularizes, and other concepts in the same way that humans do when reasoning.

Domains explored:

Fuzzy cognitive maps, fuzzy expert systems, fuzzy medical image processing, fuzzy information retrieval from medical databases, fuzzy medical data mining, and hybrid fuzzy applications are all examples of fuzzy applications.

(Continued)

Table 1.1 (Continued) Application of fuzzy logic in healthcare

S. no.	Motivation in the paper	Methods	Parameters used
6	**Fuzzy logic and diagnosis of risk of heart disease [6]:** In the most recent decade, this paper relied on clinical applications using Fuzzy logic being applied to distinct philosophies to produce keen Fuzzy demonstrative frameworks. In this audit, we will use Fuzzy frameworks to execute actual tasks. Because of the overlap of symptoms across numerous ailments, it is difficult to pinpoint a specific infection without consulting a research center, which takes time and money. To put this in context, the creation of hazy clinical finding frameworks was a desired prerequisite for serving the general public. Knowing whether or not a person will have a heart attack is not easy because a huge number of factors must be considered, some of which are well-known, such as cholesterol or disturbances in the heart pulse. Fifty percent of patients who had their first heart attack had never had any of these symptoms before.	**Fuzzify:** To convert each variable into fuzzy numbers, the first step is to specify the "membership functions" of each variable. The retrieved values must be converted into objects that belong to one or more sets with a degree of membership. **Inference mechanism:** The specification of fuzzy relationship rules underpins this method. "If your blood pressure is quite high, your danger is very high," for example. Each rule is given a weight, which determines its degree of validity. **Defuzzify:** It is important to defuzzify in order to acquire a result in the form of a percentage rather than a fuzzy variable, and the centroid method is employed for this. It is a straightforward approach for calculating the area's center after applying the rules to the supplied data.	**Parameters monitored:** • Age • Pressure • Cholesterol • Heart rate • ST segment depression • Risk (fuzzy)

(Continued)

7

Fuzzy set theory and medical field [7]:

To manage inaccuracy, uncertainty, and vagueness, fuzzy logic provides an intelligent peripheral for knowledge representation and reasoning. Because of their capacity to combine human expert knowledge and granular computing to represent the behavior of complex systems without having a precise mathematical model, fuzzy systems have found success in healthcare. This paper gives an overview of fundamental fuzzy logic and how it can be used into a variety of decision-making problems. It also underlines how FL tasks may be used to classify different sorts of medical data, classify a specific disease or diseased individuals, and build a decision support system. The goal of this study is to provide a general overview of FL and how it might be used in the healthcare business. This main aim of this paper is to provide a quick overview of fuzzy logic applications in various medical diagnosis systems.

We must specify language phrases and variables. Then, we must define a membership function for each linguistic variable. The next step is to create membership functions, and then to create fuzzy rules utilizing these membership functions. The database stores predefined global facts as well as expert knowledge. Then, there is fuzzification, which involves employing membership functions to turn crisp data into fuzzy data sets. The fuzzy inference system, which is responsible for decision-making, then begins by analyzing and combining the outcomes of each rule in the rule base.

The final phase is defuzzification, which involves converting output data into non-fuzzy values.

Tasks performed:

- Ranking analysis
- Clustering analysis
- Prediction analysis
- Classifications
- Pattern Recognition
- Feature Extraction

Table 1.1 (Continued) Application of fuzzy logic in healthcare

S. no.	Motivation in the paper	Methods	Parameters used
8	**Benefits of AI in fields of life, health** [8]: We provide a cutting-edge healthcare system that is both inventive and intelligent, based on the Internet of Things (IoT) and machine learning. This technology is intelligent enough to detect and process data from a patient's medical decision support system. This technology provides a low-cost option for those living in rural locations; they may use it to determine if they have a serious health condition and, if so, seek treatment at local hospitals. The results of the studies also show that the recommended method of delivering healthcare is both successful and sensible. The findings of this study serve as a proof of concept.	For health monitoring and health management system, the IoT technique is used. The capacity to monitor patients 24 hours a day, 7 days a week, which is practically impossible to achieve with human resources, is one clear benefit. The second goal of IoT-based system is to track critical metrics that may be used to determine a patient's condition, such as pulse rate, body temperature, breathing rate, body posture, blood pressure, ECG, and glucose level. An Arduino board is used to connect sensor networks and gather data from associated sensors. The data collected may be uploaded to a server and refined for use in decision-making or decision-support systems, which is nearly hard to do with human resources.	1. Unique notation of combining sensors with traditional telemedicine. 2. New and better diagnosis method based on fuzzy neural networks 3. Usage of decision support system to reduce the time constraints of traditional store-and-forward telemedicine in rural regions

9

Fuzzy logic and lung infection analysis [9, 10]:

Using a random number of inputs for a lung management system, the authors assessed the increasing risk of a lung infection.

The use of a fuzzy technique in the construction of such a self-operating system provides an innovative and specialized approach of detecting lung infections, particularly in high-infection areas.

We formalize medical items as fuzzy sets and analysis with rule-based systems in this study.

The use of fuzzy techniques in the construction of the diagnostic method described in this work is believed to be a safe and cost-effective way to treat lung diseases.

Furthermore, fuzzy logic implementation offers a number of approaches for generating consistent outcomes.

Computational intelligence has been widely used to solve a variety of complex problems due to its ability to manage ambiguity, ambivalence, proximate reasoning, and fractional truth.

Neural networks (NN), fuzzy logic (FL), and genetic algorithms (GA) are all used in soft computing.

In some form or another, all of these techniques work together to provide adjustable information processing capabilities for determination-making systems like expert systems and pattern categorization systems.

Symptoms that have a crucial role in the development of a lung infection include:

1. Cough (L, M, H)
2. Hemoptysis (L, M, H)
3. Probability of lung infection (scale 1–10)

(Continued)

Table 1.1 (Continued) Application of fuzzy logic in healthcare

S. no.	Motivation in the paper	Methods	Parameters used
10	A comprehensive assessment and classification of the literature on fuzzy system's applicability in infectious illness. Despite the fact that infectious disease outbreaks and their dissemination have a huge influence on global health and economy, a comprehensive literature review on the topic has yet to be completed. As a consequence, this is the first comprehensive review and categorization of fuzzy system approaches in infectious diseases that is systematic, recognizable, and complete.	**Research questions:** SLR was utilized to determine the impact of using fuzzy system methodologies in infectious illnesses. **Inclusive and elimination conditions:** Elimination criteria: studies not written in English language, animal sickness diagnosis, remedy, and follow-up, book, book chapter, letter to editor, brief reports, thesis, and review articles. **Search mechanism:** When searching databases, these arch strings should produce enough coverage of articles in an appropriate size. The keyword pertinent to the study topics, as well as the synonyms used to match the keywords, were used to determine the search string in this SLR. **Extraction of study characteristic:** A variety of approaches were utilized to extract the data. In general, a narrative combining strategy was used to solve various research problems.	1. Fuzzy inference systems are a type of fuzzy inference system that uses fuzzy logic to formulate the mapping from a given input to an output using FL. 2. A hazy mental map 3. Adaptive neural fuzzy inference system 4. Fuzzy set theory 5. Fuzzy reasoning based on rules 6. Hierarchical fuzzy analytic procedure 7. Neural network with Gaussian-fuzzy properties 8. Mining fuzzy association rules is number eight. 9. Neuro fuzzy classification 10. Fuzzy reed-frost model 11. Fuzzy decision-making assistance system 12. Fuzzy reed frost model 13. Fuzzy expert system

11	**Usage of neural fuzzy systems [11]:** NFS is a smart hybrid system that blends fuzzy logic and neural networks. A neural network, on the one hand, is a simplified mathematical model of a brain-like system that performs concurrent calculations using a network of distributed artificial neurons. However, brain systems are unsuccessful at articulating how they arrive at their conclusions. Fuzzy inference systems, on the other hand, can reason with ambiguous data and explain their choices, but they lack the ability to provide the rules that are used to make such decisions independently.	Researchers investigated numerous ways based on issue domain and study knowledge by merging NFS systems with other AI technologies for effective diagnosis of medical conditions. The most essential approach to the creation of medical diagnostic systems, according to researchers, ANFIS stands for adaptable neuro-fuzzy inference system. They can employ other neuro-fuzzy processes by implementing additional approaches based on their knowledge, interest, and study topic. As a consequence of combining feature selection methodologies similar to genetic algorithms with information gain, hybrid NFS systems have emerged.	1. Cancer diagnosis 2. CVD diagnosis 3. Depression and anxiety diagnosis 4. Diabetes diagnosis 5. Infectious and communication diagnosis 6. Kidney disorder diagnosis 7. Liver disorder diagnosis 8. Neurodegenerative disorder diagnosis 9. Thyroid diagnosis 10. Respiratory disease
12	**Fuzzy logic in TB diagnosis [12]:** Modern smart computing tools such as computer-aided diagnostics and radiography have enabled recent advancements in medical engineering. To determine the the stage of TB, a decision-based Fuzzy Expert System architecture was developed. This method has the potential to aid medical professionals and the healthcare industry in making timely decisions in the interim of TB diagnosis.	The main goal of this project is to create a mock-up of a warning system for clinical enterprise, established on the assumption that clinical issues can be broken down into many simple rules and that the physician's decision-making process can be modeled by sets of these rules. In a fuzzy system, each variable is declared by a fuzzy set of rules. The backbones of a fuzzy inference system are fuzzy rules and fuzzy reasoning, which convert system inputs (crisp integers) into fuzzy sets for determining the actual output stage. If A (antecedent) THEN C (consequent) Fuzzy if-then rules are production rules with antecedents and consequents of the form IF A (antecedent) THEN C (consequent), where A and C represent particular knowledge connected to input and output variables.	Outward signs of pulmonary tuberculosis include a persistent cough, chest pain, hemoptysis, and intermittent fever, as well as food aversion, tobacco dependence, BCG vaccination, lethargy, and weight loss.

(Continued)

Table 1.1 (Continued) Application of fuzzy logic in healthcare

S. no.	Motivation in the paper	Methods	Parameters used
13	New methodologies have emerged [13], and the fuzzy system has been widely used in medical institution as a result. The rationale for such smart systems-driven approach is that organic systems are so complicated that developing digital systems in such contexts is a difficult task. In reality, a definite model for organic systems may not exist or may be too problematic to construct. Most of the time, fuzzy system is seen to be an appropriate means since human minds operate with estimated data, important information, and provide sharp answers. The study examines the use of fuzzy system regulation and surveillance in medical science, as well as its potential future use.	Various fuzzy logic systems have been utilized, the first of which is a real-time expert system for advising and controlling (RESAC) based on fuzzy logic reasoning. A simple fuzzy logic controller, a self-organizing fuzzy logic controller, and hierarchical systems are some of the more advanced types. Cardiovascular indications such as systolic arterial pressure (SAP), heart rate (HR), and audio evoked response signals were used in a multisensor fusion system for anesthetic monitoring and control (AER).	1. Traditional disciplines 2. Invasive medication 3. Locally dined medicinal disciplines 4. Neuromedicine 5. Image and signal processing 6. Research laboratory 7. Rudimentary science 8. Healthcare
14	A framework was proposed for a fuzzy system [14], examine the applicability of artificial intelligence as a fresh soft paradigm, and review research for the creation of a medical diagnostic system from the literature. The newly presented method allows us to cope with diagnosability issues for both crisp and fuzzy input data values. By comparing expert knowledge and system generated responses, the accuracy of a proposed decision support system based on demographic data was assessed.	The integration of multiple computer paradigms, such as fuzzy logic, artificial neural networks, and evolutionary algorithms, has sparked intense research interest in artificial intelligence. All of these approaches work together to provide flexible information capabilities that can be transferred from one form to another in real-world confusing scenarios.	1. Coughing 2. BCG 3. Chest pain 4. Malaises 5. Fever 6. Loss of appetite 7. Smoke addiction 8. Hemoptysis 9. Weight Loss

(Continued)

15 | **Leanness of a supply chain using multigrade fuzzy logic [15]: a healthcare case study**

Lean ideas and practices, which focus on refining the effectiveness of business procedures by decreasing price, waste consumption, and exertion have been adopted by a wide range of businesses. Previous studies, on the other hand, have not looked at the supply chain's leanness in a healthcare scenario.

The purpose of this research is to make a recommendation of a way for evaluating the success of lean values and technologies in a supply chain. Additionally, the approach is validated in a healthcare setting in the publication.

This research begins with a complete review of the literature on leanness evaluation and fuzzy logic application.

Then, in order to quantify leanness, a theoretical model was developed.

The first version of the conceptual model was tested with a group of academic experts, notably those who work with leanness in healthcare organizations.

After replying to the experts' important remarks, the healthcare organization at the center of this case study was selected grounded on two conditions.

The capability of the organization to engage in the study was the first criterion, and the assurance to employing lean concepts was the second. These criteria were crucial in ensuring that the business had the appropriate basis for change projects like lean process improvements. Then, for leanness measurement, a multi-attributes fuzzy system was applied. The results were evaluated by professionals from the case study organization, who developed a leanness index.

Lastly, the weaker features of the organization's procedures were recognized in order to pave the road for future enhancements.

Table 1.1 (Continued) Application of fuzzy logic in healthcare

S. no.	Motivation in the paper	Methods	Parameters used
16	**Making medical decisions in the ICU using fuzzy logic [16]:** Making rapid decisions based on a large and diverse data set is common in intensive care medicine. When making medical decisions, ICU physicians frequently rely on conventional wisdom and past experience to come at subjective evaluation and conclusions. To create an ideal balance between clinical objectives that are frequently competing, this necessitates an intuitive, or non-explicit, weighing of numerous criteria. Physicians have recently been urged to follow more explicit criteria that are accepted by the whole medical community. These policies generally have a logical framework, which makes computer-implementable reasoning. As a result, in complicated clinical settings such as the intensive care unit, there is increasing interest in adopting computerized decision support tools to automate portions of medical decision-making.	A physician currently determines the rate at which intravenous fluids are supplied to a patient in the ICU. When determining the volume and pace of intravenous fluid administration that should be supplied to a patient, physicians consider a number of parameters. However, we will simply explore two variables to demonstrate how fuzzy logic control works: MAP and HUO. How should the intravenous fluid rate (IFR) be changed each time MAP and HUO values are taken, given the hourly measurements? The broad guidelines that apply to this situation is self-evident: if both the mean arterial blood pressure and hourly urine output are high, the IFR should be lowered; if both mean arterial blood pressure and hourly urine output are low, IFR should be raised. It is, however, more problematic to be exact about what the IFR ought to be for any particular pair of hourly urine output and mean arterial blood pressure values. If there was a scientific equation that gave an exact value of IFR for any provided amount of hourly urine output and mean arterial blood pressure, the problem could be solved. Unfortunately, there is no such formula. It may be impossible to come up with one. Another option is to model common ICU practice patterns in order to find a purely empirical equation. This is essentially what fuzzy logic accomplishes.	Fuzzy sets used: 1) MAP: mean arterial blood pressure 2) HUO: Hourly urine output Each of the two factors has been separated into three overlapping sets, namely, "Low," "Normal," and "High."

FL methods are used in every field of medicine and have proven to be effective.

d. Medical professionals have tested the system, and it gets close to simulating a doctor because the results are 94% accurate. The key benefit is that, with the input data, there is no need to visit an expert, and the user may determine his own risk of having a heart attack. It can also help a doctor with limited expertise make their first successful diagnoses. While this method was designed primarily for cardiac problems, others could be designed for any ailment. And, as noted in the Introduction, FL has a wide range of applications in medicine, including the ability to discern between distinct diseases based on symptoms.

e. The fuzzy inference system is a collection of methodologies that provide flexible information processing capabilities for dealing with ambiguous circumstances in real life. Its goal is to provide tractability, resilience, and low-cost solutions by leveraging tolerance for imprecision, uncertainty, approximate reasoning, and partial truth. In this study, we use a fuzzy inference system to diagnose TB in its early stages using subjective analysis. The suggested approach uses formalized reasoning in a rule-based framework to classify TB into four phases based on the severity of micro-bacterium infection.

1.7 CONCLUSION

This imprecision and uncertainty can be handled by FL. This chapter seeks to show how FL may help with this and enhance healthcare decision-making. As a form of review and creation of future research, prior studies and present methods of FL are chosen as the technique of study. Information of the patient, their medical history, physical examinations, laboratory test findings, and histology results are all crucial for proper patient therapy. For data modeling and control, FL is used in every sector of healthcare, including internal medicine, anesthesia, and radiography.

Also, by defining walking, running, standing up, setting down, laying, sleeping, and exercising daily activities of patients with insufficient cardiovascular disorder, asthma, diabetes, or Alzheimer's disease, for example, remote monitoring systems with a remote monitoring center can be used to collect data of patients. The system is an attempt to create an intelligent, adaptable, and integrated FL-based home healthcare system.

Due to hectic schedules in the current era, IoT-based health monitoring utilizing FL will assist individuals in maintaining and monitoring the health condition of old people and patients on a regular basis in order to keep track of their health.

This paper demonstrates how we can use IoT to create the finest health monitoring system possible. The values acquired by the sensors were analyzed using the FL technique.

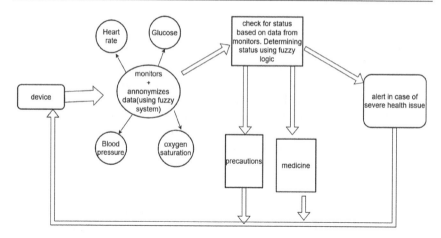

Figure 1.5 Expert system for healthcare industry.

1.8 FUTURE SCOPE

By combining IoT technology and the various applications of FL Systems used in Healthcare Industry, we can employ an Expert System that can drastically reduce the complexities of healthcare systems.

Using the IoT technology, we can obtain access to a user's health information and that data can be properly anonymized using the fuzzy algorithms before further processing.

We can employ various diagnostic techniques as discussed earlier to determine the status of the user. Using the processed information through the FL, we can properly assign flags such as precautions that need to be taken, or medicines that are recommended for the current health situation of the user, and in case the user is in a severe health issue, using the appropriate authorities and user's emergency contacts can be notified.

Here, the FL system can give the medical personnel the appropriate data well in time to provide proper care. This would be extremely difficult if standard Boolean logic was used to process the sensor information, and critical time would have been taken up in determining the cause of the issue. Figure 1.5 shows an expert system for healthcare industry.

REFERENCES

1 Frank, F. C. P. (2011). Perceived values on hospital services: A fuzzy logic application. *African Journal of Business Management*, 5(11), 4465–4475. https://doi.org/10.5897/AJBM10.1626
2 Ozok, A. F. (2012). Fuzzy modelling and efficiency in health care systems. *Work*, 41(SUPPL.1), 1797–1800. https://doi.org/10.3233/WOR-2012-0646-1797

3 Vlamou, E., & Papadopoulos, B. (2019). Fuzzy logic systems and medical applications. In *AIMS Neuroscience* (Vol. 6, Issue 4, pp. 266–272). AIMS Press. https://doi.org/10.3934/Neuroscience.2019.4.266

4 Attaullah, H., Kanwal, T., Anjum, A., Ahmed, G., Khan, S., Rawat, D. B., & Khan, R. (2021). Fuzzy logic-based privacy-aware dynamic release of IoT-enabled healthcare data. *IEEE Internet of Things Journal*. https://doi.org/10.1109/jiot.2021.3103939

5 Gürsel, G. (2014). Fuzzy logic in healthcare. In *Handbook of Research on Artificial Intelligence Techniques and Algorithms* (pp. 679–707). IGI Global. https://doi.org/10.4018/978-1-4666-7258-1.ch022

6 Iancu, I. Heart disease diagnosis based on mediative fuzzy logic. Artif Intell Med. 2018 Jul;89:51–60. doi: 10.1016/j.artmed.2018.05.004. Epub 2018 May 30. PMID: 29859751

7 Susmita, M., & Prakash, M. (2018). Fuzzy set theory (FST). *International Journal of Pure and Applied Mathematics*, 119(12), 16321–16342.

8 Hameed, K., Bajwa, I. S., Ramzan, S., Anwar, W., & Khan, A. (2020). An intelligent IoT based healthcare system using fuzzy neural networks. *Scientific Programming*, 2020. https://doi.org/10.1155/2020/8836927

9 Tiwari, S. K., Walia, N., Singh, H., & Sharma, A. (2015). Effective analysis of lung infection using fuzzy rules. *International Journal of Bio-Science and Bio-Technology*, 76, 85–96. https://doi.org/10.14257/ijbsbt.2015.7.6.10

10 Arji, G., Ahmadi, H., Nilashi, M. A., Rashid, T., Hassan Ahmed, O., Aljojo, N., & Zainol, A. (2019). Fuzzy logic approach for infectious disease diagnosis: A methodical evaluation, literature and classification. *Biocybernetics and Biomedical Engineering*, 39(4), 937–955. https://doi.org/10.1016/j.bbe.2019.09.004

11 Kour, H., Manhas, J., & Sharma, V. (2020). Usage and implementation of neuro-fuzzy systems for classification and prediction in the diagnosis of different types of medical disorders: a decade review. *Artificial Intelligence Review*, 53(7), 4651–4706. https://doi.org/10.1007/s10462-020-09804-x

12 Institute of Electrical and Electronics Engineers, Adhiparasakthi Engineering College. Department of Electronics and Communication Engineering, & Institute of Electrical and Electronics Engineers. Madras Section. (n.d.). *Proceedings of the 2017 IEEE International Conference on Communication and Signal Processing (ICCSP)*: 6th–8th April, 2017, Melmaruvathur, India.

13 Mahfouf, M., Abbod, M. F., & Linkens, D. A. (n.d.). A survey of fuzzy logic monitoring and control utilisation in medicine. *Artificial Intelligence in Medicine*, 21(1–3), 27–42.

14 Walia, N., Singh, H., Tiwari, S. K., & Sharma, A. (2015). A decision support system for tuberculosis diagnosability. *International Journal on Soft Computing*, 6(3), 1–14. https://doi.org/10.5121/ijsc.2015.6301

15 Almutairi, A., Salonitis, K., & Al-Ashaab, A. (2019). Assessing the leanness of a supply chain using multi-grade fuzzy logic: a health-care case study. *International Journal of Lean Six Sigma*, 10(1), 81–105.

16 Bates, J. H. T., & Young, M. P. (2003). Applying fuzzy logic to medical decision making in the intensive care unit. *American Journal of Respiratory and Critical Care Medicine*, 167(7), 948–952. https://doi.org/10.1164/rccm.200207-777CP

Chapter 2

A comparative study of certificate and certificate-less cryptographic algorithm and its energy consumption analysis in WSN

Shailendra Singh Gaur, C. M. Sharma and Varsha Sharma

BPIT, Guru Gobind Singh Indraprastha University, New Delhi, India

CONTENTS

2.1 Introduction 27
2.2 Information about network security 29
    2.2.1 Security in wireless sensor networks 29
    2.2.2 Digital signatures in network security 30
    2.2.3 ID-based encryption 30
    2.2.4 Related work in wireless sensor network 30
2.3 Algorithm used 31
2.4 Implementation 33
    2.4.1 ECC algorithm performed 34
    2.4.2 RSA algorithm 35
    2.4.3 Implementation of LEACH algorithm 36
    2.4.4 Implementation of PEGASIS algorithm 36
2.5 Analysis 38
2.6 Conclusion 39
References 40

2.1 INTRODUCTION

We are now surrounded by a network that can be wireless or physically connected and has become so dependent on sharing and communication that if a single step in the network of networks is interrupted, then it might leave everything in bane, and even if the pathway of the data is secure, we need to ensure that the end parties are secured. Therefore, network security should be present, which has its control over the connections as well as its authentications, such that with the development of science and its technology, there has been growth as well as advancement in the measures adopted in the algorithms used to keep everything with the pace and a validation technique is used for authentication and integrity of any message, software or digital-based document based on mathematics referred as digital signatures somewhat similar to a hand-based seal, which rather provides much more security for solving certain problems of tampering in communications digitally with added-on assurances and evidences of its development and status – acknowledgement consent of the signer.

The real-life based example of its usage is provided by the US printing office, which publishes various electronic forms of budget, laws and bills using the same. The digital signature is based on public key cryptography where cryptography refers to a hidden or secret form of writing and securing data and confidentially made available only to private members with rules and regulations through ciphers (text or algorithm for encrypt and decrypt of messages); the systems are basically of two types, namely, Symmetric and Asymmetric cryptography (Figure 2.1).

In the cryptography study, the asymmetric key algorithms are the most preferred ones because of the distinguishing approach, for hard to break in security provision it provides. The key has to be managed such that which keys are made to be distributed to the nodes on the network or which are to be erased is determined. The key management in WSN is much more difficult because lack of central-based authority occurs, where the resources are constraint, that is lack of availability of resources is present as well as nodes are vulnerable to physical capture by unfair means; where WSN (Wireless Sensor Networks) consisting of a group or a specific group made up of transducers spread all along collecting the data and storing the same with the help of nodes such that it can be again accessed and manipulated or processed for use just because the nodes are of small size and at low bandwidth/resource, which is constrained in that environment, the use of certificate might be undesirable. The certificate basically refers to the digitally certifying "public key" electronic document containing a digital signature as well.

It has been discussed as in [1] about the best and efficient algorithm that can be used with the WSN providing the security with efficiency based on computation, and as there are very limited resources and mostly protocols are based on the symmetric key because they are cost-effective but they

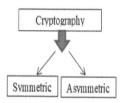

Figure 2.1 Basic classification of the cryptographic system as symmetric and asymmetric.

usually suffer from higher communication as well as memory overheads, for it to work efficiently, we first analyze certain algorithms and techniques discovered till now, which are being implemented in day-to-day life with their comparison for a better outcome, and have been presented with the possible best outcome accordingly as the most favorable approach for securing the network in a homogeneous environment.

2.2 INFORMATION ABOUT NETWORK SECURITY

A large number of small nodes form the WSN, which are highly intrinsically vulnerable to the active and passive attacks such as eaves dropping activities, DDoS, Denial of services or Sybil attack due to limited resources available and the employment environment wireless sensor networks are susceptible to these attacks, thus leading to the vulnerability to lose any confidential data across the network.

2.2.1 Security in wireless sensor networks

Several improvements have been made over implementations and its low power-consuming devices help making ubiquitous computing easier, which helps to lead the networking through devices much more easily as in [2]. The basic algorithms involved like LEACH (Low Power adaptive Clustering Hierarchy [3]), a homogenous environment-suitable algorithm managing WSN cluster head nodes between the base stations by dividing the cluster head or central node in between the group of clusters, and therefore, the base station after being received data are transferred to the base station consumed less power in four stages, but because of its conventional way and certain problems, it has been evolved to LEACH-C(LEACH-Centralised) applying threshold algorithm and centralized cluster algorithm improving check over the amount of energy as well as distribution of a cluster head nodes throughout the network. Then, there comes a concept called HEED known as Hybrid, Energy Efficient and Distributed Clustering Approach as mentioned in [4, 5] providing a prolonged lifetime by energy consumption and distribution along with the forward processing of the data using clustering method or technique of aggregation or not in a given constant iterations such that cluster overheads are minimized. In another method called PEGASIS, known as Power efficient gathering in Sensor Information System, difference lies to its reduction in energy consumption by the communication in neighboring nodes that are very close to transmitting, and as in [6] shows that it has greater and much better performance of about 100–300% such that when it is around 1–100% of the nodes that are dead for using variable sizes and topologies. Thus, again the problem is to achieve a more secure and efficient network.

2.2.2 Digital signatures in network security

As digital signatures are formed by the asymmetric cryptographic verification through its attribute based on the validation of the integrity of the data as established such that using the signer's public key and the hash values can be decrypted, and if there is no match, it concludes that it has been tampered within or maybe the signature has been created with a public key that has no correspondence to any public key that has been presented by the signer.

2.2.3 ID-based encryption

ID-based encryption is formed over the verification of the identity of the recipients and public key certificates are correspondingly issued, and the sender, using a known identity, generates a public key certificate of the intended recipient. The encryption provides a method for verification of the public parameters, that is the identity of the intended recipients, which can be generated locally by the sender such that a trusted authority is checked as soon as the sender receives the private key allowing it to decipher the secret key or accessing any confidential information, as explained in [7]. It provides us with a CLAE method (Certificate-less cryptography introduced by AI-Riyami and Paterson) that works on the same basis of verification before the transmission of an encrypted message. The process goes with the authentications provided to the sender for initiating the process of deciphers checking private key received locally from the trusted party. The approach of being certificate-less remains the same using an asymmetric algorithm, which is used for managing the private key by generating and distributing the user key and the scheme that is proposed based on ID is managed by the Key Management service, but no permission is given to the third party and is performed in a single simpler manner of two-party system.

2.2.4 Related work in wireless sensor network

In [8], the author addressed the various types of WSNs, which are similar in [9] in terms of their security issues and their countermeasures, and which can be implemented to improve the level of security of various military operations. The paper suggests countermeasures, which involve many cryptographic algorithms, Multi-Parent Routing Schemes and various key management protocols. Secure WSN was also proposed for battlefield inspection.

In [10, 11], the main purpose of the author was to transmit data in a secure manner while consuming least power possible. In order to consume less power for efficient transmission of data energy, LEACH algorithm is used with the association of Certificate-less Authentication Encryption (CLAE) to transmit data. Encrypted bit strings of long length are used as a secret key for highly sensitive data and CLAE is used as a scheme to protect the secret key. Public Key Cryptography (PKC) and Identity-Based Encryption (IBE) are used as the basis for PKC to cipher the secret key and IBE is used as an authentication of secret key, which provides flexibility in the delivery of secret key.

2.3 ALGORITHM USED

According to the comparison obtained through literature review and related studies, certain analysis factors in the algorithm still prevail and are identified as costs occurring in communication and higher computations. "ECCSI (Elliptic Curve Based Certificate-less Sign for identity based cryptography): based on asymmetric cryptographic algorithm i.e. ECC (elliptical Curve Cryptography)" [11].

The equation of Elliptic Curve Cryptography is defined by using finite field with an equation mentioned below (Figure 2.2):

$$y^2 = x^3 + ax + b \tag{2.1}$$

In certificate-less cryptography, the receiving end will be set to an inactive state, and simultaneously, we will assume that the two-party signers with verifiers have a trust maintained through services provided by the key management system (KMS) such that the receiving end does not need to be in an active state. "Before the deployment of the network happens, the base station generates all the parameters registering those nodes into the members list as (n, N, F, E, B, G, q) and generates the KSAK (KMS secret Authentication Key) and further derives the KPAK (KMS Public Authentication) from KSAK and signatures are created such that each signer has its SSK (integer), PVT (elliptic curve point) and need not to be kept as a secret as to KMS and SSK do and every signer ID has to be assigned with a different (SSK, PVT)" [11]. The formulation of the algorithm (Figure 2.3):

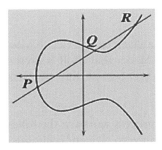

Figure 2.2 Equation of elliptic curve cryptography [11].

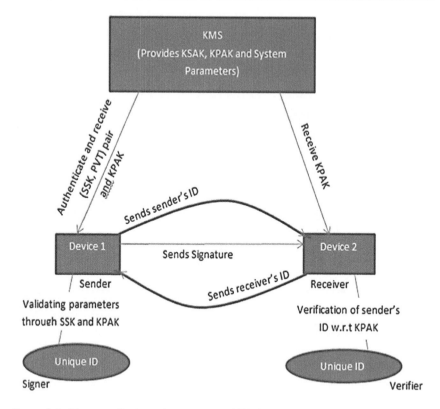

Figure 2.3 Diagram displays the process of KMS maintaining and managing security in the network.

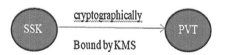

Figure 2.4 The identifier is with the Signer and SSK (Secret signing Key), which is cryptographically bounded by KMS with the PVT (Public Validation Token) as shown in image.

Consisting of a Key Management Service (KMS) bounding a PVT (Public Validation Token) to the Signer that itself is present with the identifier and its corresponding SSK (Secret Signing Key) is given or attached (Figures 2.4 and 2.5).

A. The certificate-less process works in the following phase:
  (i) The random non-zero element is chosen, represented as v.
  (ii) Computing PVT and HS, using an N integer.

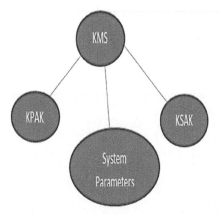

Figure 2.5 The figure displays the components that KMS produces and selects when required.

   (iii) Then compute SSK, a Secret Signing Key.
   (iv) Obtain the pair values of SSK and PVT.
B. The received value of SSK has to be verified:
   (i) The PVT has to be verified if lying on the elliptic curve E;
   (ii) Compute and store the SSK;
   (iii) Validate the KPAK [11]
C. The message is then signed:
   (i) A random non-zero value is chosen.
   (ii) Compute the value of J=(Jx, Jy), as affine cords.
   (iii) Re-computing the value of HS and comparing it.
   (iv) If verification fails, restart again with a fresh value.
   (v) Computing the value of s using the equations = q − s.
   (vi) Signature = (r ‖ s ‖ PVT).
D. Verification of the algorithm:
   (i) PVT is checked and verified;
   (ii) Compute both the values of HS, as mentioned above.
   (iii) Compute Y = [HS]PVT + KPAK.
   (iv) Compute the value of "J= [s] ([HE] G + [r] Y)" [11]
   (v) Verify the value of J, before accepting the Signature as not equal to zero.

2.4 IMPLEMENTATION

The execution of the algorithm is done by the Java, Matlab, and other programming tools for encryption and decryption of information or data and its testing is done so as to obtain the desired outcome.

2.4.1 ECC algorithm performed

ECC key generation, agreement, and signature are executed with the help of Java programming language [12] (Figures 2.6 and 2.7).

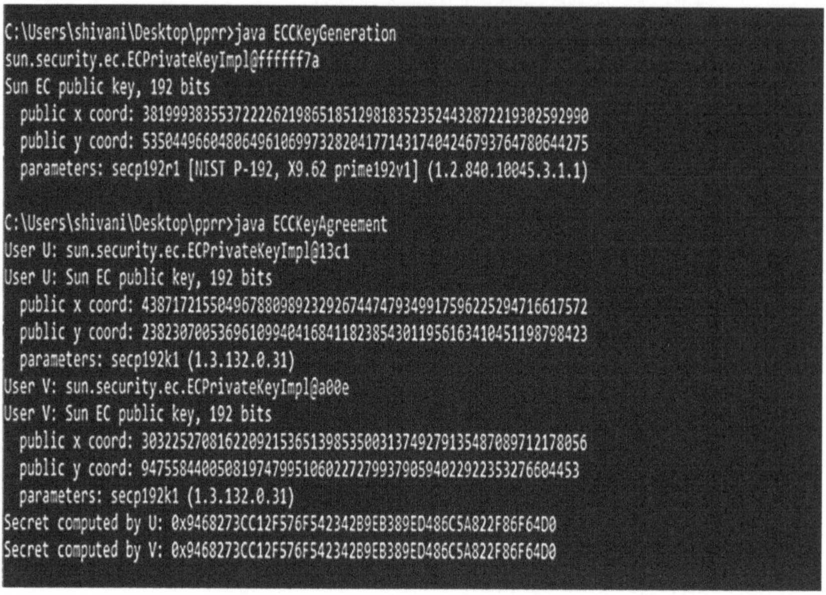

```
C:\Users\shivani\Desktop\pprr>java ECCKeyGeneration
sun.security.ec.ECPrivateKeyImpl@ffffff7a
Sun EC public key, 192 bits
  public x coord: 3819993835537222262198651851298183523524432872219302592990
  public y coord: 5350449660480649610699732820417714317404246793764780644275
  parameters: secp192r1 [NIST P-192, X9.62 prime192v1] (1.2.840.10045.3.1.1)

C:\Users\shivani\Desktop\pprr>java ECCKeyAgreement
User U: sun.security.ec.ECPrivateKeyImpl@13c1
User U: Sun EC public key, 192 bits
  public x coord: 4387172155049678809892329267447479349917596225294716617572
  public y coord: 2382307005369610994041684118238543011956163410451198798423
  parameters: secp192k1 (1.3.132.0.31)
User V: sun.security.ec.ECPrivateKeyImpl@a00e
User V: Sun EC public key, 192 bits
  public x coord: 3032252708162209215365139853500313749279135487089712178056
  public y coord: 9475584400508197479951060227279937905940229223532766044453
  parameters: secp192k1 (1.3.132.0.31)
Secret computed by U: 0x9468273CC12F576F542342B9EB389ED486C5A822F86F64D0
Secret computed by V: 0x9468273CC12F576F542342B9EB389ED486C5A822F86F64D0
```

Figure 2.6 Key generation and agreement is obtained in an ECC algorithm.

```
C:\Users\shivani\Desktop\pprr>java ECCSignature
sun.security.ec.ECPrivateKeyImpl@b6d
Sun EC public key, 163 bits
  public x coord: 9561770026556720672462095077552118938174728455541
  public y coord: 271979041108226540651055730378257441068131882086
  parameters: sect163k1 [NIST K-163] (1.3.132.0.1)
Text: Elliptical curve cryptography
Signature: 0x302C02144900C8BB522F714FBBD30E4167141323E4A8954902140AE4D617812757B1F3D82FA034AA5D293691811C
Valid: true
```

Figure 2.7 Signature is obtained in an ECC algorithm.

2.4.2 RSA algorithm

The execution of RSA algorithm has been done in Java programming language with two examples shown in the following (Figure 2.8).

The Diffie-Hellman algorithm is also executed in Java Programming Language (Figure 2.9):

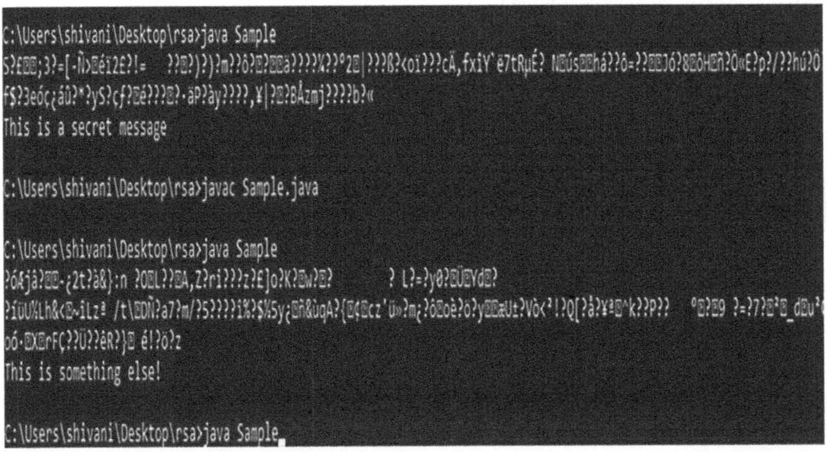

Figure 2.8 Encryption and decryption of message using RSA algorithm: Implementation of Diffie-Hellman algorithm

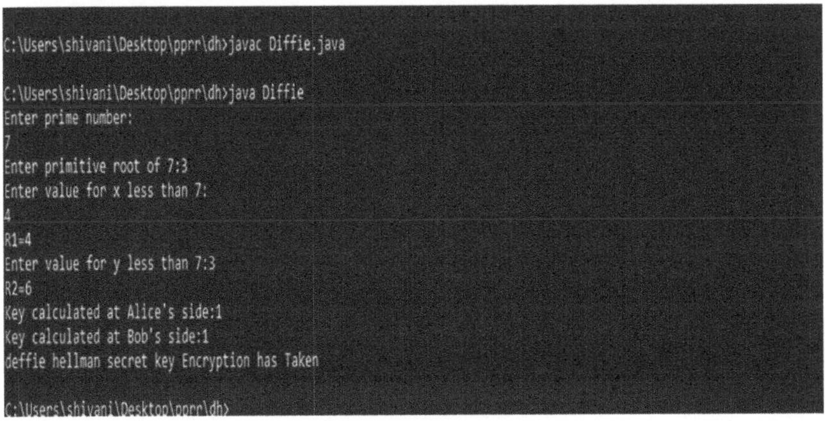

Figure 2.9 Execution of Diffie-Hellman encryption algorithm.

2.4.3 Implementation of LEACH algorithm

The execution of LEACH algorithm using Clustering is done in the MATLAB tool as given in Figure 2.10:

2.4.4 Implementation of PEGASIS algorithm

Compared to LEACH, the PEGASIS algorithm is also implemented in Matlab tool (Figures 2.11–2.14):

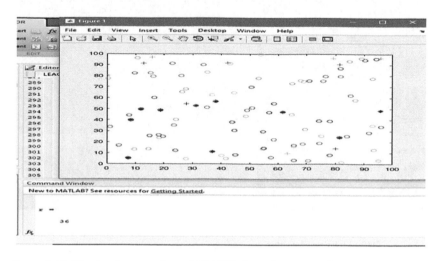

Figure 2.10 The implementation of LEACH algorithm using clustered nodes.

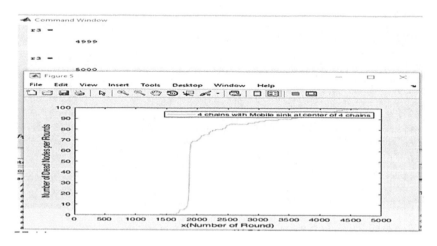

Figure 2.11 Number of dead nodes w.r.t. number of rounds.

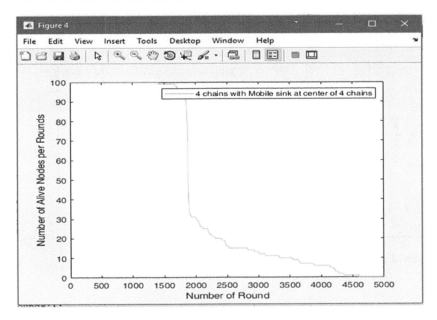

Figure 2.12 Number of alive nodes w.r.t. number of rounds.

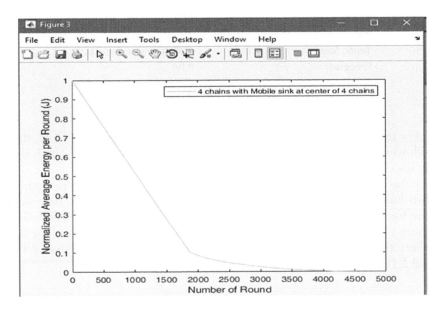

Figure 2.13 Normalised average energy-level w.r.t. number of rounds.

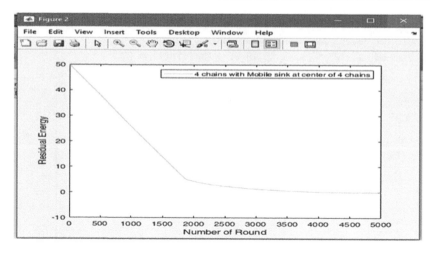

Figure 2.14 Execution of residual energy w.r.t. number of rounds.

Table 2.1 Adapted data for simulation parameters as in [15]

Simulation Area	500*500m
Simulation Time	150 sec
Size (Packet)	512bytes
Radio Range	250m
Traffic Source	CBR (Constant Bit Rate)
Processor	P IV
Key Length Size	128 bits

For the usage and implementation of the proposed approach ECCSI, the following method is performed using Network Simulator 2 (version 2.35) on the O.S Ubuntu 14.04.64 bit.

It has been assumed that 11 nodes that are being used are in a randomly distributed manner such that the nature of nodes is homogenous. Base station has to be in contact with every node so that it should be present in the center of the location or region. Every node present has its own unique ID where the resources being provided are limited (Table 2.1, Figures 2.15 and 2.16).

2.5 ANALYSIS

The proposed approach will enhance the improvements as well as the integrity and confidentiality in protection of the data being transferred through the network. The improvement in secured data transmission by implementing

Side-A
Side-B
Base_Station
1
2
3
4
5
6
7
8
9
10

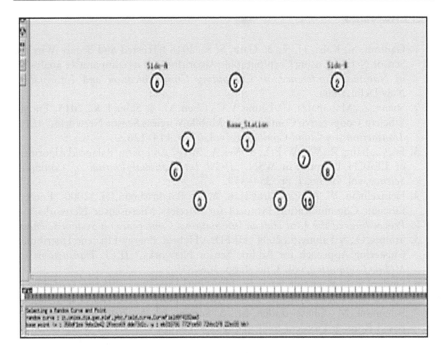

Figure 2.15 Selection of random curve and B.P.

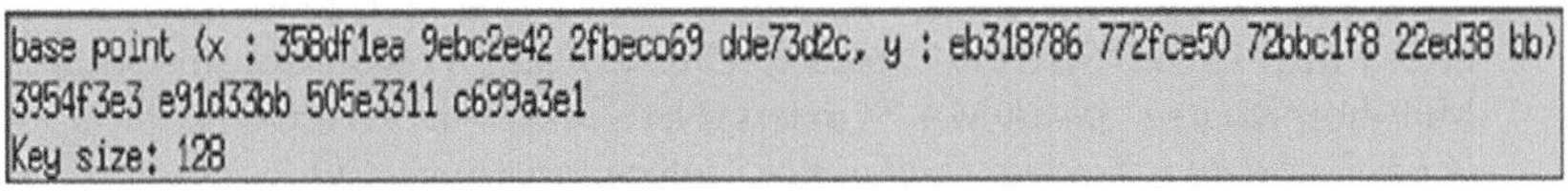

base point (x : 358df1ea 9ebc2e42 2fbeco69 dde73d2c, y : eb318786 772fce50 72bbc1f8 22ed38 bb)
3954f3e3 e91d33bb 505e3311 c699a3e1
Key size: 128

Figure 2.16 Key generation of ECC.

the certificate-less approach with a reduction in energy cost associated with the communication from base station to cluster heads by using an efficient algorithm makes the approach more resilient against node compromises or cloning or any other eavesdropping active or passive attacks.

2.6 CONCLUSION

The proposed approach of using ECCSI, which uses certificate-less scheme, proves to provide more security to both end parties without being verifier party to be in an active state and end parties need not to check or store certificates either. Due to limited availability of resources, the energy-efficient LEACH algorithm proved to be best in the homogenous environment of clusters of nodes in wireless sensor network.

REFERENCES

1. Gautam, S., Kalsi, H. S., & Gaur, S. S., 2018 "Trusted and Secure Wireless Sensor Network using Cryptographic Algorithm and its comparative analysis," in *National Conference on Computing Communication and Informatics*, New Delhi, India.

2. Sheng, Z., Mahapatra, C., Leung, V. C., Chen, M., & Sahu, P. K., 2015 "Energy Efficient Cooperative Computing in Mobile Wireless Sensor Networks," *IEEE Transactions on Cloud Computing*, vol. 6, pp. 114–126.

3. Fu, C., Jiang, Z., Wei, W. E. I., & Wei, A., 2013 "An Energy Balanced Algorithm of LEACH Protocol in WSN," *IJCSI International Journal of Computer Science*, vol. 10, no. 1, pp. 354–359.

4. Heinzelman, W. R., Chandrakasan, A., & Balakrishnan, H., 2000 "Energy-Efficient Communication Protocol for Wireless Microsensor Networks," in *Proceedings of the 33rd Hawaii International Conference on System Sciences*.

5. Younis, O., & Fahmy, S., 2004 "HEED: A Hybrid, Energy-Efficient, Distributed Clustering Approach for Ad-hoc Sensor Networks," *IEEE Transactions on Mobile Computing*, vol. 3, no. 4, pp. 366–379.

6. Lindsey, S., & Raghavendra, C. S., 2003 "PEGASIS: Power-Efficient Gathering in Sensor Information Systems," in *Aerospace Conference Proceedings*, Los Angeles.

7. Soleimani, M., Ghasemzadeh, M., & Sarram, M. A., 2011 "A New Cluster Based Routing Protocol for Prolonging Network Lifetime in Wireless Sensor Networks," *Middle-East Journal 2011 of Scientific Research (MEJSR)*, vol. 7, pp. 884–890.

8. Azzabi, T., Farhat, H., & Sahli, N., 2017 "A Survey on Wireless Sensor Networks Security Issues and Military Specificities," in *International Conference on Advanced Systems and Electric Technologies (IC_ASET)*, Hammamet, Tunisia.

9. Ettus, M., 1998 "System Capacity, Latency, and Power Consumption in Multihop-Routed SS-CDMA Wireless Networks," in *RAWCON 98. 1998 IEEE Radio and Wireless Conference*, Colorado Springs, CO.

10. Gaur, S. S., Kumar, A., & Mohapatra, B. K., 2018 "An Optimal Lightweight Cryptographic Approach for WSN and its Energy," *International Journal of Intelligent Engineering and Systems*, vol. 11, no. 3, pp. 59–67.

11. Suhag, D., Gaur, S. S., & Mohapatra, A. K., 2019 "A Proposed Scheme to Achieve Node Authentication in Military Applications of Wireless Sensor Network," *Journal of Statistics and Management Systems*, vol. 22, no. 2, pp. 347–362.

12. Hamed, A. I., & El-Khamy, S. E., 2009 "New Low Complexity Key Exchange and Encryption Protocols for Wireless Sensor Networks Clusters Based on Elliptic Curve Cryptography," in *2009 National Radio Science Conference*, New Cairo, Egypt.

13. Lavanya, M. B., 2012 "Comparison of RSA-Threshold Cryptography and ECC-Threshold Cryptography for Small Mobile Adhoc Networks," *International Journal Advanced Networking and Applications*, vol. 3, no. 4, pp. 1245–1252.

14. Ramanathan, R., & Rosales-Hain, R., 2000 "Topology Control of Multihop Wireless Networks Using Transmit Power Adjustment," in *IEEE INFOCOM 2000. Conference on Computer Communications. Nineteenth Annual Joint Conference of the IEEE Computer and Communications Societies*, Tel Aviv, Israel.

15. Jafri, M. R., Javaid, N., Javaid, A., & Khan, Z. A., 2013 "Maximizing the Lifetime of Multi-chain PEGASIS using Sink Mobility," *arXiv e-prints*.

Chapter 3

A novel approach to indoor air quality monitoring by Cisco IoT-based toxic measurement system

T. M. Bhraguram, R. K. Rajesh and Saju Mohanan
University of Technology and Applied Sciences, Shinas,
Sultanate of Oman

Mujahid Tabassum
Noroff University College (Noroff Accelerate) Kristiansand, Norway

CONTENTS

3.1   Introduction..41
    3.1.1   Affected criteria for indoor air quality..............................43
    3.1.2   Leading carbon monoxide sources 45
    3.1.3   Technological impact on Covid-19 pandemic.....................45
3.2   System measurements and problem...46
3.3   Specification and the measurements 47
3.4   Literature review..50
    3.4.1   House observations of microbial and environmental
           chemistry (HomeCHEM) project 51
    3.4.2   Indoor air pollution study: NO, CO, CO_2 51
    3.4.3   Indoor air quality and coronavirus disease.......................51
    3.4.4   Indoor air quality: carbon monoxide and carbon
           dioxide (AEN 125)...52
3.5   Cisco Internet of Things based toxic measurement system 52
3.6   Methods of proposal...52
3.7   Experimental setup 54
3.8   Results and discussion 55
3.9   System performance analysis...59
3.10 Conclusion..63
References 64

3.1 INTRODUCTION

THIS Novel approach gives an effective method to improvise the quality of home quarantine by considering various atmospheric measurements. The home quarantine is very important during Covid-19 period and it must be executed in a very effective manner. The Internet of Things (IoT) boosts up this execution at a high-performance level by incorporating various measurements and criteria. Covid-19 has been declared as a pandemic by the World Health Organization [WHO] [1, 2, 6, 9], and many people are affected by this fast-spreading virus. Most of the countries declared home isolation and quarantine systems to prevent the fast spreading of this disease. Today, our technical world also supports to prevent this pandemic situation by developing more technical products used in medical domains. Still, most of the countries in the world are under the threat of this disease and more affected disease cases are being reported every day. The only most effective method is to prevent this disease from its spreading, as no vaccine has been discovered till now. The prevention takes us to home isolation or quarantine by maintaining a good health and individual immunity power. Most of the countries implemented this by increasing the awareness about the disease and also by maintaining of individual hygienic plans.

Home isolation with improper ventilation leads to a serious situation where more health-related problems such as physical symptoms, skin irritation, some respiratory problems and heart-related problems may lead to a dangerous disease like cancer. Home isolation must aim for complete separation from the society, but it may affect the quality of the indoor air movement. The isolation or quarantine situation becomes more serious once the air quality is affected in a poor manner. During the isolation period, most of the people spend 93% of time inside the isolation chambers, and sometimes, it becomes 100%, which may increase the rate of low-quality air inside the rooms. The owners of the home can improve the air IAQ [1–3] by some activities like regular filter maintenance, proper maintenance of cooling and heating systems, and also by opening windows/doors to allow fresh air inside the premises. Many studies have shown that proper air ventilation is important, and at the same time, the disease transmission is also highly associated with it and we must take care of this to avoid the infectious diseases such as respiratory syndrome (SARS) [2, 3, 5] and influenza. IAQ is highly dependent on indoor as well as outdoor factors, which may rise due to the building crack, ventilation systems, and open windows/doors. Many studies show that the air inside a chamber is more dangerous and around 93% more contaminated than the outside air. Some recent studies demonstrated that the Covid-19 virus may sustain its persistence in the air for around 3 hours. This leads to a fast spreading of Covid-19 virus in some individuals. This proves that nowadays social distancing is more important than before. Some people are not allowing fresh air inside the rooms by timely opening of windows/doors, and this will always boost up the disease transmission level. It is important to maintain a proper home isolation/quarantine in family housing, senior citizen homes, labor camps, and other organizations where the number of living individuals is higher. More occupancy means we need to improve the ventilation structure.

Lack of information, misleading information, unfamiliar information about Covid-19, and human perception are the factors affecting human behavior. Apart from the risk involved and other conditions that may influence the possibility of Covid-19 transmission, human inception is also an important factor in this. So, if we do not have sufficient information about Covid-19, in terms of transmitting the disease, its persistence or its movement direction, the message we are passing to public must be avoided. The various indoor air pollution sources are depicted in the figure below with its rate of existence (Figure 3.1).

3.1.1 Affected criteria for indoor air quality

As discussed earlier, during quarantine period, most of the people spend their time inside the rooms, so it is important to give more attention to the factors, which are increasing the air pollution like smoking, burning candles, frying foods and other strong chemicals used in a closed cabin. If there is any indication of foul or suspicious smell like mold, we must take proper precautions to find its sources and how this affects the entire chamber. Some organic compounds may produce new odors causing serious body infections and also the fumes/odors emitted from adhesive materials, vanishes and plastic materials are also seriously affecting the air quality of the premises. Gas stoves emitting several potentially severe toxic gases and fumes, including carbon monoxide and nitrogen dioxide, may increase the respiratory problems for adults and children. Cooking gas increases nitrogen dioxide level, which may exceed the standard air quality of the outdoor air. According to the World Health Organization, pollutants like carbon

Indoor Air Pollution Sources

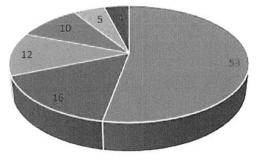

- HVAC Systems
- Indoor Contaminants
- No Problems
- Outdoor Contaminants
- Biological Contaminants
- Building fabrics

Figure 3.1 Indoor air pollution sources.

monoxide, formaldehyde, naphthalene, nitrogen dioxides and polycyclic gases [1, 2, 5] are found to be more toxic and its concentration level reaches to a threshold leading to serious health issues. The most affected pollutant is carbon monoxide due to its high emission level and the fast damage done to many human tissues. The restriction of this toxic material is difficult, but the increasing level of this pollutant is seriously affecting unhealthy people very badly. Once the increased level of this material reaches to a threshold level, reduce the amount of oxygen in red blood cells. The most vital organs like brain, nervous tissues and the heart do not get enough oxygen to work properly.

Carbon monoxide (CO) [4, 7, 9] is the vital role player in this study to consider the flow execution in the system and this might be the most demanded criteria while implementing a study like this. CO [4, 6, 7] is an odorless and colorless gas, which seriously affects the human body and it is a compound mixture of carbon-based materials. The CO level in the blood must be measured accurately and the high production of this gas can take the control over the hemoglobin metabolism (Figure 3.2).

Carbon monoxide level is measured in almost all respiratory-based problems and the death rate due to this toxic material is very high according to the studies that were conducted in the past 5 years. The recovery from this disease is also increasing and it gives a new hope while developing the new systems for disease recovery. We have different carbon monoxide measurement procedures, but the measurements taken from the most affected parts in every hour will give a high sampling rate and the diagnosis may provide accurate result while developing the systems. Hourly mean concentration of CO from a particular location was reported first. The threshold value of the carbon monoxide concentration is measured as 24.75 ppm with a low level value of 17.17 ppm and an average value of 13.3 with a low-level value of 13.1. This concentration may vary depending on the factors affected in that particular area.

Carbon monoxide is a highly poisonous mixture, which brings a drastic effect on both healthy and unhealthy people. It may reduce the oxygen content in the indoor air and leads to severe lung-related diseases. The hemoglobin

Figure 3.2 Carbon monoxide poisoning sources.

content in the red blood cells might be affected due to this. More vital organs like brain, nervous tissues and heart in the body do not receive proper oxygen, which leads to some severe health problems.

3.1.2 Leading carbon monoxide sources

Tobacco smoke, gas stove, pilot lights, wood stoves, fireplaces, gas and kerosene fueled space heaters, gasoline engines, camping lanterns and stove, attached garage and street level intake vents are the major identified sources of carbon monoxide emission. The level of CO increases drastically once these things are overused. The level of CO should not reach to a threshold value, as it measured at the low level.

Levels of CO exposure range from low to dangerous:

- Low level: 50 PPM and less
- Mid-level: Between 51 PPM and 100 PPM
- High level: Greater than 101 PPM if no one is experiencing symptoms
- Dangerous level: Greater than 101 PPM if someone is experiencing symptoms

In a quarantine environment, most of the people spend the time inside a closed cabin with limited ventilation facilities. As the quality of air inside a closed cabin reaches very poor and leads to drastic variation in air structure variation, this leads to a situation where most of the human body organs are affected as concluded from 10 clinical studies. So, a quarantine system is not always good for the human health, but the government officials and health people are forced to advise it for a better prevention of diseases like Covid. The human body expects a pure air circulation atmosphere, as it is needed for the normal functioning of body. In order to maintain this proper body health for a human being, it is recommended to maintain a good air quality always inside the living cabin like atmosphere. Once any of the pandemic situation arises, the human living condition becomes varied, and the human body should adapt with these new environments where the mediums of ventilation are less. The air modules should detect toxicity in a timely manner and take the proper actions, as it is necessary to maintain good quarantine environment for human life to prevent fast spreading of diseases. Some toxic agents like CO and carbon dioxide require more attention and a timely reaction once it reaches to a particular threshold level.

3.1.3 Technological impact on Covid-19 pandemic

The artificial intelligence and related tools are emerging during the pandemic for improving the human job efficiency and other social related activities. Telehealth options are at its peak level during the disease spreading time and it ensures the decreasing level of social contact and the health-related activities like secure video appointments, secure messaging system, online prescription and billing and doctor schedule. The risk of social and surface contact must be reduced using special contactless smartcards and the spreading of disease from an infected person can be tackled by these technological improvements. Contact tracing and surveillance also made a big impact on these latest technological associations.

3.2 SYSTEM MEASUREMENTS AND PROBLEM

Most of the indoor air quality checking methods require a detailed study on the contaminated air and can measure the quality of air. Once the quarantine period is started, the isolated place gradually moves to a sensitive area where more measurements can be carried out. The existing systems failed to provide a proper action according to the measurements detected and its further processing. The Internet of things based systems is capable of automatically detecting all these sensitive measurements and the processing unit can take proper action without any delay in time. A genuine sensing unit is needed to satisfy these requirements and must be modeled with high accurate measurement values. Various sensor units may take different dynamic values without the threshold time delay, and this can help to provide a high-quality quarantine facility without prediction of any wrong value.

The problems detected during quarantine lead to various health problems for a human being and they severely affect the unhealthy people. The system must respond with a proper result, which will reduce the effect of such severity. To develop a method in order to take necessary actions according to the time frame is a complex task, as many of the existing systems failed to do this. In this context, the procedure should start with indoor air quality checking according to various parameters and then take necessary actions according to the variations of the measurements detected by the sensor unit. The diagram in the figure below depicts some detailed IAQ problems, which cause health-related severe problems according to the National Institute of Occupational Safety and Health (Figure 3.3).

According to the said depiction, most of the IAQ problems arise due to inadequate ventilation [4, 6, 7]. A wrong ventilated quarantine place is the big source of contaminated CO mixture. The measurements taken by the system are very critical, as this may affect status of the entire system once the action is being taken. Various measurements affect the IAQ, but the most effective air preservation values are considered for the system. Carbon monoxide, carbon dioxide, gas or air mixture values are pointing to the system measurements.

In the implementation aspect, we can adopt various technologies like Wireless sensor technologies (WSN) [4, 7, 8] and Internet of Things (IoT). As per various policies, many of the government firms and organizations are

Causes of Indoor Air Quality Problems

- Inside Contamination
- Outside Contamination
- Building products
- Unknowns causes
- Inadequate Ventilation
- Bioaerosols

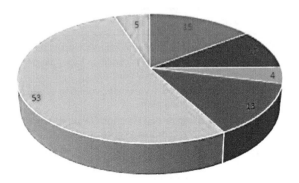

Figure 3.3 Causes of indoor air quality problems.

adopting IoT as the master implementation scheme, as it provides many smart sensor technical concepts. When the IoT systems are combined with new age information and other communication channels, it promises a high-end reliable solution for a complex problem. According to the IoT service technologies, any of the monitoring systems include both hardware and software. The degree of pollutant levels and its calculations always depend on the smart technical code and also the quality of the hardware used to measure the values. It includes the correct selection of the sensors, micro-controllers and other gateways and it becomes a crucial factor for the next level of action.

3.3 SPECIFICATION AND THE MEASUREMENTS

In this research, we have used indoor air quality index (EIAQI) [1, 2, 4, 7] as the main reference index status level that contains three indoor air pollut-ants (IAPs) and three thermal comfort pollutants (TCPs). The measurements are detected based on the IAQ circuit systems and the thermal comfort. The input elements taken for this consideration include CO_2 [1, 2, 3, 16, 23], CO [2, 3, 5, 6] and Nitrogen oxide (NO_2) [2, 3, 4]. These elements attain their thermal comfort by incorporating organic compounds, particulate matters, temperature and humidity. The output signals are based on the concentra-tion of these materials and will be the tabulated based on the particular criteria (Table 3.1).

The said parameters provide the necessary detection values based on the response in a specific time frame. After gathering data from sensors, the first stage is to check all input values for further processing on the monitoring block and then move to the next level for the purpose of data storage, analysis

Table 3.1 Indoor air quality parameters

Indoor air quality parameters	
Parameter name	*Health-related argument*
CO_2	Psychic problems, cardia-related issues, cerebral disease for trauma patients, performance loss, pulmonary and corona disease, respiratory infection
CO	Headache, weakness, vomiting and loss of consciousness, fetal circulation
NO_2	Respiratory infections (asthma, emphysema, bronchitis), skin cancer, pneumonia, bronchial reactivity, chronic respiratory diseases
Particulate matters	Asthma attack, chronic bronchitis, cardiovascular diseases, diabetes
Temperature	Perspiration, eye strain, accelerated respiration, accelerated heart rate, and warm discomfort
Humidity	Eye becomes dry and irritated, skin gets flaky, and dries out the mucous membrane.

and data visualization. The air quality parameters fall under the following categories based on the threshold value set for a high-level pollution.

- Worst: This takes the value below 1 and it initiates a health status indication, and the quarantined people may encounter their health impacts genuinely. For every critic and crisis condition, it will receive a notification for this parameter measurement.
- Bad: When the measurement value falls under the category of 1 and 3, it indicates that the individual members of a particular group may encounter severe problems. But it likely indicates that the health is influenced at lower levels compared to public variants.
- Good: The range indicates the values between 3 and 5 and shows the status as the air quality is in an accepted level. But some parameter values have medium health concerns for a small number of individuals. Respiratory side effects at a low level are one of the medium-level concerns in this case.
- Excellent: The range indicates values under 5 to 6 and the air quality range is satisfactory and the pollution content is at very small level, which has no risk for the individuals.

The development of the system needs a good construction of integrated air quality analysis; it is highly significant to assess the pollutant values independently. The concentration level depends on the individual health condition and their characteristics. The accuracy of measurements for a group of people and individuals is different according to the standard health checking reports.

In this regard, it is critical to recognize how each pollutant may create various adverse impacts on individuals. One of the best options to solve this issue is by defining an uncertainty value where a particular pollutant may take different concentrations in different conditions.

The air pollution values [11, 12, 13] given in this framework take the reference values from the scoring system of IEQ index [7, 8, 10] and the measurements taken depend on the sensor Harare modules used in the system. The base of Index scoring system is taken into consideration and has the highest impact values from various IEQ parameters [7, 8, 10]. The scoring system is furnished in the following table, and the parameters taken into consideration in this study also take the best scoring standard according to the national level scoring index (Table 3.2).

After the deep excavation of IEQ index score system, the measurements and parameters selected are based on the standard quarantine places. The threshold values are also considered according to the pollution average value by deeply examining various quarantine places. The table mentioned below depicts various air pollution threshold values considered in this research (Table 3.3).

According to the standard IEQ score [7, 8, 10], the thermal comfort is one of the most effective pollutant forms, which may lead to an increase in air pollution. It gives all the necessary measurements and threshold values, which can be handled by the system in an effective manner. Both the air pollutant criteria and thermal comforts are working independently and are also measured at a constant threshold level. Every time, the process takes the values from both parameters and are processed separately. This procedure is taken into consideration and the research also focuses on these parameters and the values taken into consideration are depicted in the following table.

Table 3.2 IEQ index scoring system

IEQ parameter	"Good"	"Average"	"Poor"	"Bad"
Humidity	40–50%	50–60%	60–70%	70>H>40%
Temperature	20–24°C	16–20°C	24–26°C	26 > T > 16°C
PM2.5	0–10 µg/m³	10–15 µg/m³	15–35 µg/m³	>35 µg/m³
PM10	0–50 µg/m³	50–80 µg/m³	80–150 µg/m³	>150 µg/m³
Total VOC	0–200 ppb	200–350 ppb	350–500 ppb	>500 ppb
CO_2	350–500 ppm	500–1000 ppm	1000–5000 ppm	>5000 ppm
CO	0–3 ppm	3–8 ppm	8–10 ppm	>10 ppm
Indoor air quality	0–10 ppm	10–25 ppm	25–50 ppm	>50 ppm
Illuminance	300–500 lux	200–300 lux	100–200 lux	<100 lux
Sound levels	0–40 dB	40–70 dB	70–80 dB	>80 dB
Scoring impact	0	0.2	0.5	1.0

Table 3.3 Threshold air pollution values

Threshold values of air pollution				
$CO_2(ppm)$	$CO(ppm)$	$NO_2(ppm)$	Index value	Status
0–606	0–2	0–0.025	2–3	Good
580–1020	1.8–8.5	0.02–0.2	1–2	Moderate
800–1520	7–10	0.09–0.4	0–1	Unhealthy
1480–5000	9–50	0–3.5	0–(−3)	Hazardous

Table 3.4 Threshold thermal comfort values

Threshold values of thermal comfort				
Particular matters(gm/m^3)	Temp(oC)	Humidity (%)	Comfort index	Comfort status
0–0.023	18–25	40–70	2.25–3	Most Comfort
0.02–0.15	22–29	60–80	1.5–2.25	Comfort
0.042–0.18	26–39	70–90	0.75–1.5	Not Comfort
0.54–0.6	32–45	80–100	0–0.75	Least Comfort

The parameters, measurements and the threshold values are furnished according to the standard categorized labels from the IEQ Index score [7, 8, 10] (Table 3.4).

Major contributions of this research study are as follows:

(i) The research proposes the use of Internet of Things (IoT) based systems for the precise monitoring of indoor air quality.
(ii) The research proposes the effective implementation of an IoT for smart implementation of real-time data.
(iii) The research proposes the adoption of IEQ-based index score to categorize the parameters and to generate rule-based models of IAQ.
(iv) The research developed an application by incorporating various parameter-based rule programs with IoT.
(v) The application has been tested for reliability of the data and the framework has been implemented in various quarantined places to test its feasibility.

3.4 LITERATURE REVIEW

In this section, we provide a short overview of the relevant work on IAQ monitoring system based on IoT. Since our novel framework is based on

IAQ parameter processing, we also provide a short overview of this research area. In recent years, many studies have been reported in the area of IAQ monitoring [1, 2, 3, 4] and many of these studies are based on the standard parameter values without considering the region-based measurements.

3.4.1 House observations of microbial and environmental chemistry (HomeCHEM) project

This study was published in the year of 2020 by Farmer and Marina Vance, mechanical and environment engineering graduates at the University of Colorado Boulder, and they have documented that the pollutants are generated from cooking in a clean atmosphere.

They have identified and observed a serious of experiments, which were under the controlled level to learn more about the various chemical reactions and substances produced in a home environment. Special cooking types include roasting a pan of Brussels sprouts in a gas oven, which can generate more particulate matters [3, 5, 9] and it is around 250 micrograms per cubic meter of air, and these cases have been reported in the most populated cities in the world. They have reported that some of these particles are produced by the gas stove combustion and some others are from the food itself. Gas stoves emit more particulate matters than the electric ones. This emits more potential toxic gases, including CO.

3.4.2 Indoor air pollution study: NO, CO, CO_2

The research work was proposed by W. Michael Albert and Md Tampa from Florida with a detailed report of incompletion of combustion mixture and its various effects in blood. This study focuses on CO and other toxic reactions to the level of CO in the blood and it is determined by the gas production and is also based on the catabolism of hemoglobin [1, 4, 26] and other hemoglobin-containing mixtures with the intake of low ambient CO levels. The identified major CO produces include tobacco smoke, gas stove and pilot lights, wood stoves and fireplaces, and kerosene compounds. The documented content includes a detailed report of the various measurements of the blood-affected pollutants and its various symptoms.

3.4.3 Indoor air quality and coronavirus disease

This work has been initiated by Mohammed Yehia Zakaria Abouleish by the background of information dissemination lagging with the people regarding the spread of disease. Some measurements have been proposed to improvise the air quality and the quality of the air is detected for a particular threshold level. The deterioration of the air quality can be measured and with the help of certain criteria-based values, the system can generate the supporting values, which can be then processed for generating an accurate value. Various disease levels and the causing factors are measured, and human perception is attached with these conditions to improve the accuracy. Misleading information [15, 25, 26] or conflict level information gathering, unfamiliarity and human behavior are the main factors considered in this research methodology and the studies had published a good source of factors analysis.

3.4.4 Indoor air quality: carbon monoxide and carbon dioxide (AEN 125)

This article found in ISE extension Pub No. AEN 124 by the author Tom Greiner from IOWA State University states various reasons and factors that affect the air quality. The toxic agents produced on the top of CO and carbon dioxide are measured and processed with various threshold values and documented at its toxic severity [22, 23, 24]. The causing factor like fossil fuel burning, cigarette smoke, human and animal respiration are the factors identified here and categorized as deadly poison modules and how they can affect the human body at various disease levels. The quantity measurements are focused on the levels of the toxic agents and the solutions are developed to tackle the generated modules. Warning signs of heating trouble and excessive levels of moisture in the home take into the account the addition of more processing modules at the time of decomposition of various particles like fossil fuels.

3.5 CISCO INTERNET OF THINGS BASED TOXIC MEASUREMENT SYSTEM

The suggested system proposes a sensor-based network framework, which can accept the simulation modules, and based on the characterized data, it can measure the toxic content in an indoor environment. This work simulated IoT based modules by the help of various sensor modules, micro controller unit, email server, gateway router, and health authority end machine units. The simulation proves to coordinate with a high-end module system, which will direct the concerned people to prior alert of the various crucial situations.

3.6 METHODS OF PROPOSAL

The system hardly produces a framework, which can initiate the module descriptions at each level of data processing. At the quarantine center or home, we can continuously monitor the indoor air quality with the help of CO detector. It detects the CO value, and the connected microcontroller unit with the sensor can process the data with the help of various factors and threshold values. Once the basic processing is finished, the microcontroller can analyze the processed output values and take the necessary actions based on this. Here, the system uses Cisco IoT concept and the simulations incorporate with the Cisco packet tracer tools. The topology proposed here contains the following sensor modules:

carbon monoxide sensor setup, micro controller unit, e-mail server, gateway router and health authority end machine.

The topology contains nodes, which are locally arranged and the ISP switch systems [24, 26, 27] are connected to pass the parameter values detected in a dynamic environment. For each place, we can setup client and server modules, which are active locally to process the local data values and pass to the remote machine. A LAN (Local Area Network) [21, 22, 25] always communicates with the sensor modules where it handles all the sensor components. The CO alarm modules are responsible to produce a threshold alarm warning for the CO level. The humidity sensor can detect the atmospheric humidity value with the help of a sensor controller unit and produce the alarm warning for each detection time frame.

Then, the health department modules are responsible to take the necessary actions and various measurement precautions based on the local ISP processed values. A switching module is placed in the system topology to connect to the health department server and also to the health monitoring system.

This system framework is easily accessible to the local and remote setup users and highly scalable with high reliability. The portable sensor component can be reused for local and remote areas where we need more attention on the air quality indicators.

The underneath system flow makes it more reliable with the necessary requirements. The flow expresses the detailed system running status and the procedures to apply in each module configuration.

The system makes the initiation of client server module immediately after the initiation of sensor switching module. The data storage module is active for the entire duration of sensing and the toxic content detection is evaluated based on the preinstalled criteria. System can check the CO threshold level [20, 18, 22] and then it detects the next level of humidity with the help of a sensor. The integration operation of humidity and CO value moves to the comparison of the threshold value. The analyzed content is checked for the relationship status. When the threshold level reaches its maximum value and the relation content is correctly processed, an alarm can be pop up to the second level CO and humidity level sending as well as the server module. The second phase is also initiated for checking the CO level and humidity [12, 14, 17, 19] values according to the threshold measurements. Once the measured value becomes degraded in accordance with threshold value, the system tries to maintain the first threshold level again. Humidity level alarm popup might be active in the next step and the measured data and alarm

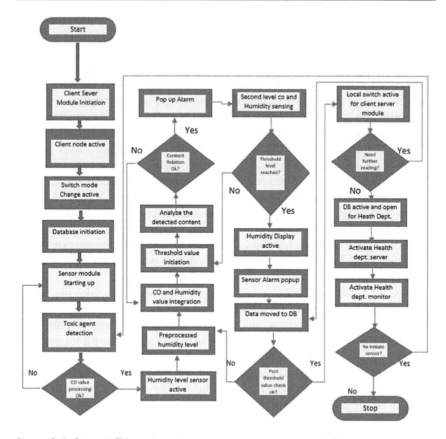

Figure 3.4 Cisco IoT-based toxic measurement system workflow.

status are moving to the data storage module. Post value integration is checked and the system fails to detect moves to the preprocessed content once again. This analysis process leads to the local switch activation for client machine and the storage module is now open for the health department end user. The health department server is able to handle different measurements and make a decision regarding this. Reinitiating the sensor module can be done in the final stage (Figure 3.4).

3.7 EXPERIMENTAL SETUP

The Cisco topological module constructs the configurations for toxic measurement system. The client server system communication initiates all the switching modules and sensor setup. The measured values can pass to the next level in the microcontroller module for the checking of system threshold value. The configuration contains various CO sensor modules [11, 13, 14] to check the toxic content [19, 24] measurements and humidity sensor parts to verify the measurements detected by the corresponding module. The server modules are active and responsible to act with the proper decision and value storage task. Each location has its own client and server system setup, and the health department may take the actions for respective precautions according to the threshold values and initiate a new sensing operation (Figure 3.5).

The system may read the CO value in the room by using the CO detector and will measure the humidity of the room using the Humidity Sensor. The coding has been activated under the MCU module. The code will initiate the setup action, and once the CO level is greater than the threshold value (here the threshold value may be detected as 50) and humidity of the room is greater than the corresponding value (here the value is set as 70%), then the popup alarm will be ON, and a new alert message will be displayed, which moves to the storage module for further actions. The health authorities can take an immediate action based on the measurement of processes.

The sample pseudo code [9, 10] has been initiated under MCU [17, 12, 10] and can be active for the entire duration of the sensor module detection operation. The code has been executed under the variation of client and server machine separately and every time it is able to make an e-mail notification based on the sender preferences. The delay time frame is sufficient to make the sensing module active and reinitiate the needed modules (Table 3.5).

The execution code may have pushed to the MCU [17, 12, 10] and the system is set from the start once the client and server modules are active. The code is set in the flexible model, as it can be reused during attachment of other devices and or new sensor module activation. This scalability is an advantage of this setup and more reliable during system enhancements.

3.8 RESULTS AND DISCUSSION

The following system results show the accuracy of measurements and the high-level impact of several toxic detection levels in the room environment. The resultant screen shows various communication parts and its respondent modules at the time of system activation. The configurations and modules might be regenerated and we receive the resultant component and data for each successful sensor detection case. Moving to the resultant cases, the below screen represents the sender preferences with the corresponding subject's line. The date and time frame of [3, 4, 6] content detection of each sensor module and its preprocessed steps can be viewed through this output module and the sender can compose the decision part according to the analyzed data part. The e-mail preferences can be configured and the indoor air quality measurement status can be displayed for each successful execution.

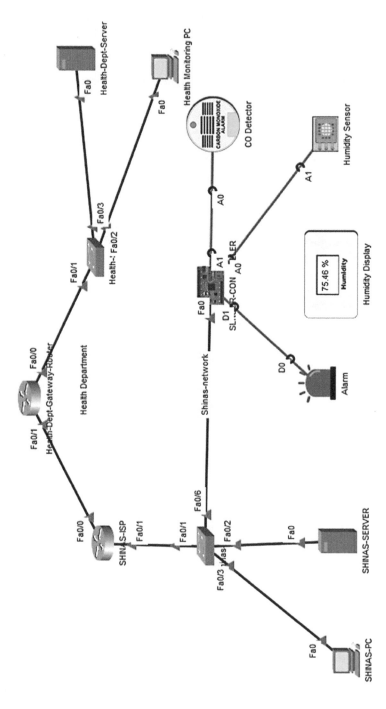

Figure 3.5 Cisco IoT-based toxic measurement system topology.

Table 3.5 Sample system pseudo code under MCU

```
function setup () {pinMode (1, OUTPUT); pinMode (A1, INPUT); pinMode (A0, INPUT);
EmailClient.setup("admin@omantel.com", "omantel.com", "admin", "admin");
}
function loop () {
    EmailClient.receive();
    var Colevel = analogRead(A1);
    var humid=(analogRead(A0)/10);
    Serial.println("Carbon Monoxide level:" + Colevel);
    Serial.println("Humidity" + humid);
    if ((Colevel > 50) &&(humid>70)) {
        digitalWrite (1, HIGH);
        Serial.println("Critical situation - Carbon Monoxide and Humidity values are more
than allowed value, Alarm is ON and email alert sent to Health Authorities:");
    EmailClient.onReceive = function (sender, subject, body) {
        Serial.println("Received from: "+sender);
        Serial.println("Subject:" + subject);
        Serial.println("Body:" + body);
    };
    EmailClient.onSend = function(status) {Serial.println("Sent: "+ status);};
    EmailClient.send ("pc@omantel.com", "Indoor air quality is poor", "Humidity level is
\t" + humid);
    EmailClient.send("pc@omantel.com", "Indoor air quality is poor", "Carbon Monoxide
level is \t" + Colevel);
    }
    Delay (10000);
}
```

Knowledge of the CO level is important information and this sensor-detected content can also be viewed through the mail browser. The old data content can be deleted, and the new sensor analyzed data can occupy the required space.

The below screen modules represent the configuration window modules and the desktop viewed module (Figure 3.6).

The below output specifications represent the threshold value comparison model and e-mail modules wake up for each value detection time. All the mail configurations regarding the decision convey that the CO threshold values have been modified according to the environment factors and dynamic environment. The model layout is suitable to represent the decisions in a user-friendly way and the represented decision items are saved in the storage area available in the server machine (Figures 3.7 and 3.8).

The decision notification window may be active during the mail configuration and the same communication is transferred to the health authority people and can be moved to the storage area. The appropriate actions can

Figure 3.6 (a) E-mail configured window module.

(Continued)

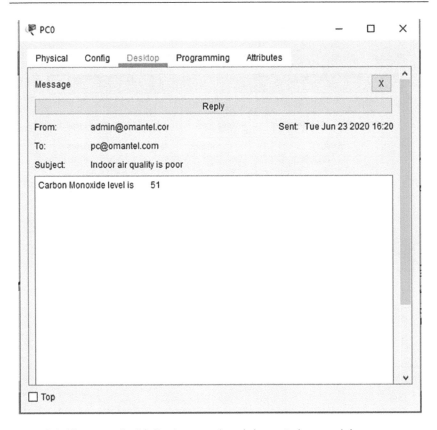

Figure 3.6 (Continued) (b) Desktop analyzed data window module.

be modeled and disseminated in an effective manner once the decision part is sent as a mail notification (Figure 3.9).

3.9 SYSTEM PERFORMANCE ANALYSIS

The system is benchmarked with other IAQ monitoring systems available in the market. The system procedure indicates the reinitiation of the sensor part whenever the system is expected to run. The levels of CO and humidity are the important criteria to apply in the execution of each step. The system shows high accuracy level compared with the other existing models and we obtain the measurement statistics accordingly. The ppm value of CO factor [1, 2] is analyzed as part of the decision making and the humidity-level measurement can also be taken as the next predecessor part for measurement value analysis.

According to the graph representation, it indicates the high level of IAQ pollution as the time increases based on the CO value. The time is

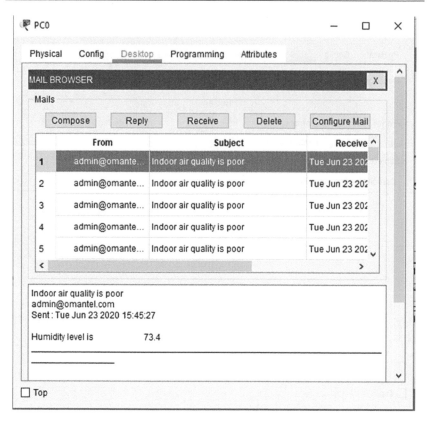

Figure 3.7 Desktop analyzed data comparison module.

represented in hours and the sensor modules are active during the running time of entire system. The threshold value comparison of CO [5, 7, 12, 13] is active for each system cycle and also at the time of reinitiation of the sensor (Figure 3.10).

The threshold value comparison of concentrated carbon monoxide and the decision level status in a particular room environment [25, 26] are represented with the corresponding time frame. As the time progresses, the carbon monoxide concentration increases drastically and affects the room environment in a dangerous manner. According to the graph representations provided below, the gas concentration touches the range of 140 seconds and crosses 250 seconds above the time frame. This fast change in concentration increases the pollution level and the alarm status is more critical. This alerts the healthy people immediately based on the fast decision making (Figures 3.11 and 3.12).

Figure 3.8 Desktop analyzed data comparison module.

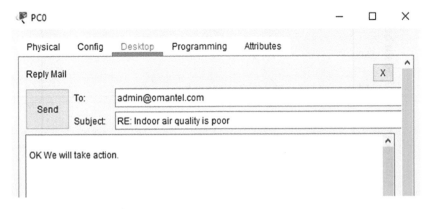

Figure 3.9 Desktop analyzed data window module.

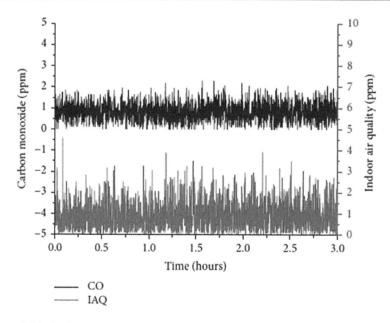

Figure 3.10 Carbon monoxide and IAQ measurement status.

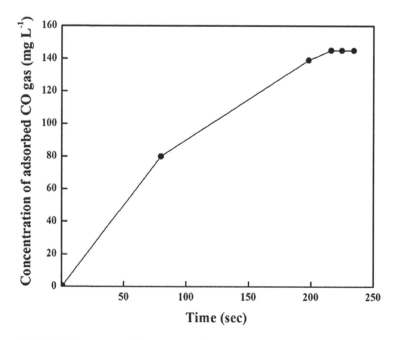

Figure 3.11 Carbon monoxide concentration status.

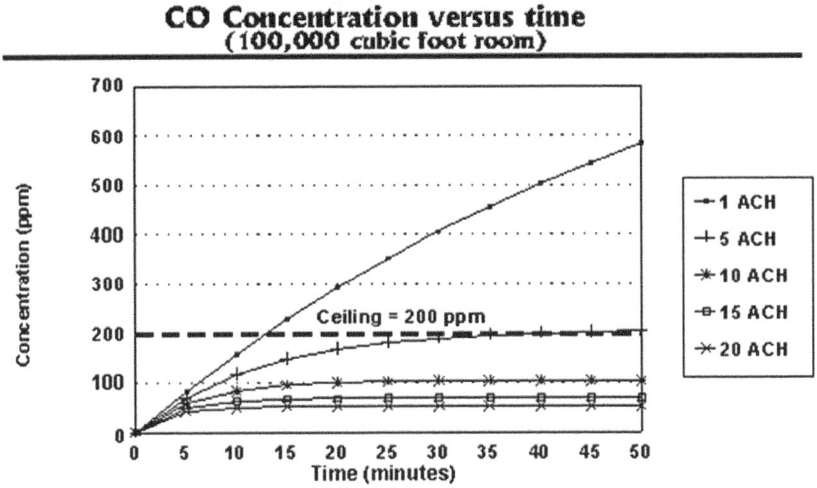

CO Concentration versus time
(100,000 cubic foot room)

Figure 3.12 CO concentration decision-making status.

3.10 CONCLUSION

The IoT-based toxic measurement system is capable of detecting various environment factors like carbon monoxide and humidity level for then effective calculation of IAQ. The system used IoT-based configurations with CO sensor detection and humidity model as well. The suggested system is capable of handling various measurements through the sensor detecting data and analyzes the data effectively after the preprocessing operation. The CO and humidity level measurements are checked with the threshold system measurements and the result is moved to the storage area after a detailed analysis operation. The Client server system initiated in this framework can popup the specific operational and decision-level information dissemination to the specific ports. The alarm-based warning is the indication to the health authority people and it might be the data for the responsible authorities to take proper actions once the analyzed data are crossing the threshold value level. The system has a specific setup model for e-mail notification and the data collection is done through IoT-based sensor mechanism. This pervasive model setup can be reliable, as this system is adapted for the environments where more household or devices are in an active state. This system is highly scalable, as the framework or modeled part can be reinitiated in any of the supportive environment. The micro controller unit of this framework is capable of handling various sensor-based data, and for each test data, the corresponding analysis may take place and the decisions can be generated according to the analyzed content. The IoT-based toxic measurements system is a good reference system for the basic toxic elements present in our environment and the same can be applicable for other toxic contents in the surroundings.

REFERENCES

1　M.N. Mohammed, Investigation on carbon monoxide monitoring and alert system for vehicles, in: *2019 IEEE 15th International Colloquium on Signal Processing & Its Applications (CSPA)*, March, 2019, pp. 239–242.

2　A.A. Hapsari, A.I. Hajamydeen, M.I. Abdullah, A review on indoor air quality monitoring using IoT at Campus environment, *Int. J. Eng. Technol.* 2018, 7, 55–60.

3　F. Stazi, F. Naspi, G. Ulpiani, C. Di Perna, Indoor air quality and thermal comfort optimization in classrooms developing an automatic system for windows opening and closing, *Energy Build.* 2017, 139, 732–746.

4　S.M. Saad, A.Y.M. Shakaff, A.R.M. Saad, A.M. Yusof, A.M. Andrew, A. Zakaria, A.H. Adom, Development of indoor environmental index: Air quality index and thermal comfort index, in: *AIP Conference Proceedings*, Vol. 1808, August, 2017.

5　A. Aggarwal, T. Choudhary, P. Kumar, A fuzzy interface system for determining Air Quality Index, in: *2017 International Conference on Infocom Technologies and Unmanned Systems (Trends and Future Directions) (ICTUS)*, January, 2018, pp. 786–790.

6　S.L. Fong, D.W.Y. Chin, R.A. Abbas, A. Jamal, F.Y. Ahmed, Smart city bus application with QR code: A review, in: *2019 IEEE International Conference on Automatic Control and Intelligent Systems, I2CACIS 2019 – Proceedings*, October, 2019, pp. 34–39, http://doi.org/10.1109/I2CACIS.2019.8825047.

7　M.N. Mohammed, H. Syamsudin, S. Al-Zubaidi, S.A. Karim, E. Yusuf, Novel covid-19 detection and diagnosis system using IoT based smart helmet, *Int. J. Psychosoc. Rehabil.* 2020, 24, 2296–2303.

8　A. Jamal, D. Kumar, R.A.A. Helmi, S.L. Fong, Portable tor router with raspberry Pi, in: *Proceedings of the 2019 8th International Conference on Software and Computer Applications*, 2019, pp. 533–537, http://doi.org/10.1145/3316615.3316694.

9　I. Zurida, S.L. Fong, S.C. Shin, SMART KPI management system framework, in: *2019 IEEE 9th International Conference on System Engineering and Technology, ICSET 2019 – Proceeding*, 2019, pp. 172–177, http://doi.org/10.1109/ICSEngT.2019.8906478.

10　M.A. Ali, N.M. Tahir, A.I. Ali, Monitoring healthcare system for infants: A review, in: *Proceedings – 2018 IEEE Conference on Systems, Process and Control, ICSPC 2018*, December, 2018, pp. 44–47, http://doi.org/10.1109/SPC. 2018.8704143

11　E.D.L. Patino, J.A. Siegel, Indoor environmental quality in social housing: A literature review, *Build. Environ.* 2018, 131, 231–241.

12　M.N. Mohammed, S. Al-Zubaidi, S.H.K. Bahrain, M. Zaenudin, M.I. Abdullah, Design and development of river cleaning robot using IoT technology, in: *IEEE International Colloquium on Signal Processing & Its Applications (CSPA)*, 2020.

13 A. Takian, A. Raoofi, S. Kazempour-Ardebili, COVID-19 battle during the toughest sanctions against Iran, *Lancet* 2020, 395(10229), 1035–1036, Accessed date: 28 March 2020.

14 M. Filonchyk, V. Hurynovich, Validation of MODIS aerosol products with AERONET measurements of different land cover types in areas over eastern Europe and China. *J. Geovis. Spatial Anal.* 2020.

15 J. Griffiths, A. Woodyatt, *China goes into emergency mode as number of confirmed Wuhan coronavirus cases reach 2,700.* CNN, 2020, January 27. https://www.cnn.com/2020/01/26/asia/wuhan-coronavirus-update-intl-hnk/index.html

16 A. Schütze, T. Baur, M. Leidinger et al., Highly sensitive and selective VOC sensor systems based on semiconductor gas sensors: How to?, *Environments* 2017, 4(1), 20.

17 F. Salamone, L. Belussi, L. Danza, T. Galanos, M. Ghellere, I. Meroni, Design and development of a near able wireless system to control indoor air quality and indoor lighting quality, *Sensors* 2017, 17(5), 1021.

18 J. Kang, K.-I. Hwang, A comprehensive real-time indoor air-quality level indicator, *Sustainability* 2016, 8(9), 881.

19 S. Sun, X. Zheng, J. Villalba-Díez, J. Ordieres-Meré, Indoor air-quality data-monitoring system: Long-term monitoring benefits. *Sensors* 2019, 19, 4157.

20 J. Saini, M. Dutta, G. Marques, A comprehensive review on indoor air quality monitoring systems for enhanced public health. *Sustain. Environ. Res.* 2020, 30, 6.

21 T. Parkinson, A. Parkinson, R. de Dear, Continuous IEQ monitoring system: Context and development. *Build. Environ.* 2019, 149, 15–25.

22 F. Salamone, L. Belussi, L. Danza, M. Ghellere, I. Meroni, How to control the indoor environmental quality through the use of the do-it-yourself approach and new pervasive technologies. *Energy Procedia* 2017, 140, 351–360.

23 H. Liu, L. Zhang, K.H.H. Li, O.K. Tan, Micro hotplates for metal oxide semiconductor gas sensor applications—Towards the CMOS-MEMS monolithic approach. *Micro Machines (Basel)* 2018, 9, 557.

24 P. Kumar, C. Martani, L. Morawska, L. Norford, R. Choudhary, M. Bell, M. Leach, Indoor air quality and energy management through real-time sensing in commercial buildings. *Energy Build.* 2016, 111, 145–153.

25 H.-R. Wang, C.-Y. Hsu, T.-R. Jian, A.-Y. Chen, On the design and implementation of an innovative smart building platform, in: *Proceedings of the 2016 International Conference on Networking and Network Applications (NaNA)*, Hakodate, Japan, 23–25 July 2016, pp. 404–409.

26 Y. Jeon, C. Cho, J. Seo, K. Kwon, H. Park, S. Oh, I.-J. Chung, IoT-based occupancy detection system in indoor residential environments. *Build. Environ.* 2018, 132, 181–204.

27 R. K. Nath, R. Bajpai and H. Thapliyal, "IoT based indoor location detection system for smart home environment," *2018 IEEE International Conference on Consumer Electronics (ICCE)*, 2018, pp. 1–3, doi: 10.1109/ICCE.2018.

Chapter 4

Babies' movement detection and constant monitoring in the crib by using Internet of Things (IoT)

Ultrasonic sensor

Eman Said Al-Abri, Aisha Nasser Al-Salmi, Mohamed Al-Kindi and Ahmed Al-Nabhani

Higher College of Technology, Muscat Al-Khuwair, Sultanate of Oman

CONTENTS

4.1   Introduction... 67
4.2   Literature review... 68
4.3   Background 69
     4.3.1   Ultrasonic sensor.. 70
     4.3.2   Breadboard 71
     4.3.3   NodeMCU ESP8266 71
     4.3.4   Temperature and humidity sensor (DHT11)........................ 71
     4.3.5   Blynk mobile application 72
     4.3.6   RTSP IP camera application 73
4.4   Experimental set-up 73
     4.4.1   Design of a transmitter... 74
     4.4.2   System flowchart... 75
     4.4.3   Design of receiver 77
4.5   Result and discussion.. 77
     4.5.1   Simulation environment experiment.................................... 77
     4.5.2   Real environment design 80
4.6   Conclusion and future work 83
Notes 84
References... 84
Appendix: System configurations 85

4.1 INTRODUCTION

Parenting a child is a big responsibility. This means that taking care of the baby at an early age is essential to reducing the risk of injuries [1]. However, the most difficult challenge for parents is to care for their children using popular existing monitoring solutions, such as audio or video monitors. According to [2], many of the existing monitoring devices do not provide a

DOI: 10.1201/9781003355946-4

sufficient set of data or the appropriate type of data to the parent. This is due to the fact that the data stream should be monitored by the parents, and they should also be able to identify any future issues by providing the data feed.

For these reasons, this study introduces a new prototype made up of various components controlled by NodeMCU. This main sensor of the prototype is UltraSonic (HC-SR04), which is used to calculate the distance between the baby and the end of the bed. If the baby attempts to get out of his or her bed, the sensor will send a notification to the parent's phone. In addition, the device will emit an alarm sound. The prototype also includes a temperature sensor (DHT11) for measuring the temperature of the room. As a result, the parents will know the temperature of the room and will be able to turn the air conditioner on or off or change the temperature of the air conditioner to make the baby much more comfortable. The prototype also includes live streaming for the baby to monitor and record his movements for safety and to determine whether the baby is still awake or asleep.

The remainder of the chapter is structured as follows. Section 4.3 describes the proposed embedding and extraction algorithms. Section 4.5 presents the experimental results. Section 4.6 contains concluding remarks.

4.2 LITERATURE REVIEW

Various remote monitoring devices have been designed for monitoring babies [3]. One of these systems is to identify the exact location of the subject within the crib and identify three different activities of the subject and give out an alarm in case a risky location or behavior has been encountered. Such alarms are displayed on the screen of a display panel and on a mobile phone [1]. Another system devised by [4], has been designed to perform different activities, in which the baby will get the mother's response automatically (like cradle swing and mother's voice). This system senses the sound of baby cry and triggers the mp3 module to play an audio having mother's voice, which is stored in the SD card in an mp3 format, and simultaneously, the servomotor starts moving the cradle with a gentle swing and all the sensed data are sent to the parent's mobile phone with the help of a Bluetooth module or they are sent to the attached PC/Laptop through USB cable for continuous monitoring. This type of system has been designed to assist the working mothers to get information about their babies.

A study by [5] has emphasized the advantage of using ultrasonic sensor techniques for monitoring. Its ultrasound facility has the capability to spread through any type of media such as solid, liquids, and gases. The study has used the ultrasonic sensor to build a monitoring system to detect the water level in a river and provide an early warning for a flood in the area. Another study which utilized the IOT technology to monitor the baby is IoT–based baby monitoring system for smart cradle [6]. This study focused on the sound of the baby and the crib wetness. In their system, they used Node MCU, sound sensor, soil moisture sponsor and *Blynk* application. Sound sensor has been used to detect the baby cry and then the system will play some music to calm down the baby.

The soil moisture sponsor is used to detect the wetness of the baby diaper and sent an alert to the parent for a need of diaper change. All the alert and data were sent to the *Blynk*[1] app, which allowed the parent to take an action. A study by [7] has designed a smart baby cradle to create a comfortable environment for the baby and make the parent prepared for control. The system employed multiple sensors and devices, which are setup around the baby cradle. A sound sensor is utilized to detect the baby cry and then automatically swaying the cradle. In addition, the study hooked a mini fan to work as a ventilation system in the cradle. The swaying and the fan can be switched on and off by the sensor or remotely using the MQTT server. The authors also attached a web camera externally to provide extra control and mentoring.

The [8] have proposed a system using IOT devices to monitor infant in an incubator. They used multiple sensors to gather the data; the pulse rate sensor is used to detect the heartbeat, which continuously records the baby pulse per minute. Another sensor used is the humidity sensor utilized to measure the humidity inside the incubator. The data which are gathered in these two sensors are send to a computer for more analysis.

More researchers have proposed an E-Baby Cradle [9], in which they designed their cradle to swing at a specific speed based on the sound of the baby's cry. The system includes an alarm that detects two conditions, namely, wetness of the bed and continuous baby crying. The proposed cradle includes a microphone that detects the baby's cry and converts it to an electronic signal that is fed into an amplifier. The microcontroller will use the amplified signal's output to start the motor that rocks the cradle.

4.3 BACKGROUND

This section contains a summary of the essential characteristics of Internet of Things (IoT):

1) Internet of Things (IoT)

The Internet of Things is a popular term in the field of information technology (IoT). The Internet of Things will transform real-world objects into intelligent virtual objects in the future. The IoT aims to unify everything in our world under a common infrastructure, giving us not only control of the things around us but also keeping us informed of their status. The phrase "Internet of Things," also abbreviated as IoT, is derived from two words: the first is "Internet," and the second is "Things" [10]. The Internet is a global network of interconnected computer networks that serve billions of users worldwide by utilizing the standard Internet protocol suite (TCP/IP). It is a network of networks composed of millions of private, public, academic, business, and government networks ranging in size from local to

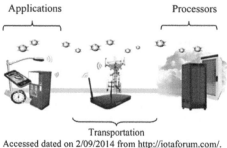

Applications   Processors

Transportation
Accessed dated on 2/09/2014 from http://iotaforum.com/.

Figure 4.1 Internet of things architecture.[2]

global in scope and linked by a diverse set of electronic, wireless, and optical networking technologies [11]. According to the IoT Forum, Internet of Things Architecture is divided into three categories, namely, Applications, Processors, and Transpiration, as depicted in Figure 4.1.

2) **Hardware used for prototyping**

The IoT prototype is made up of smart, self-configuring sensors called objects, which is linked to an active, global network infrastructure. Things refers to any object, from a communicative gadget to a non-communicating dull thing [10]. To accomplish the aim of research, some of the hardware needed to design the prototype of the devices is proposed. The following section will discuss each of hardware components used.

4.3.1 Ultrasonic sensor

HC-SR04, as shown in Figure 4.2, is commonly used as a module for non-contact distance measurement for distances ranging from 2 to 400 cm.

Figure 4.2 HC-SR04.

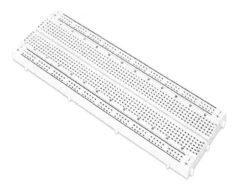

Figure 4.3 A breadboard.

The sensor transmits sound waves and receives a sound reflected from an object. If the object is very close to the sensor, the sound waves return quickly. Hence, if the object is far away from the sensor, the sound waves take longer to return [12].

4.3.2 Breadboard

A breadboard, as shown in Figure 4.3, is a tool used to connect wires and other electronic elements when building circuits. The Breadboard has two main sections—the outside rows and the middle columns. The holes or contact points in the row sections are only electrically connected to contact points in the same row [13, 14]. The contact points in the column sections are only electrically connected to the contact points in the same column.

4.3.3 NodeMCU ESP8266

The NodeMCU module, as shown in Figure 4.4, is the best suited for IoT at its low cost and low power consumption capability, as it requires 3.3 V power. In addition, it has a built-in WiFi module, and an integrated TCP/IP protocol stack, which makes it easy to flash and erase firmware. The module is USB powered [15, 16]. Most of the IoTs application modules can be deployed in home automations, home appliances, industrial wireless network, and sensor networks fields [17].

4.3.4 Temperature and humidity sensor (DHT11)

There are many sensors in the market, which can measure the humidity and temperature. For the purpose of this project, DHT11 sensor was utilized as shown in Figure 4.5. This sensor can be used to monitor the temperature and humidity levels in a surrounding area. DHT11 operates with a NodeMCU

Figure 4.4 NodeMCU module.

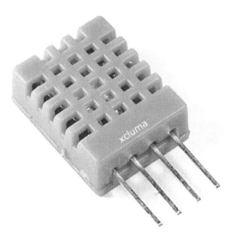

Figure 4.5 Temperature and humidity sensor (DHT11).

module and can provide immediate results [18, 19]. The project uses this sensor to monitor and record the variation of humidity and temperature levels in the room where the baby sleeps [20].

4.3.5 Blynk mobile application

Blynk, which is shown in Figure 4.6, is a platform with iOS and Android apps to control Arduino, NodeMCU and the likes over the Internet. It is a digital dashboard where you can build a graphic interface for your project by simply dragging and dropping widgets. It is really simple to set everything up and you will start tinkering in less than 5 minutes. *Blynk* is not tied to some specific board or shield. Instead, it is supporting hardware of your

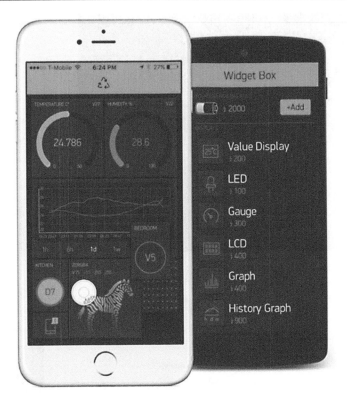

Figure 4.6 Blynk mobile application.

choice. Whether your Arduino or Raspberry Pi is linked to the Internet over Wi-Fi, Ethernet, or this new ESP8266 chip, *Blynk* will get you online and ready for the Internet of Your Things [21].

4.3.6 RTSP IP camera application

RTSP Server, as shown in Figure 4.7, is a mobile application, which is able to serve live or recorded camera view to the RTSP clients. It works in the background as a service and supports the different camera resolutions and fps. They have the ability to specify duration of record from a specified time.

4.4 EXPERIMENTAL SET-UP

The proposed system is designed with two main sensors, namely, HC-SR04 Ultrasonic sensor and DHT11 sensor. These sensors are connected with the Wi-Fi module, which is the NodeMCU ESP8266. Moreover, the data collected from these sensors can be monitored by using a *Blynk* Application.

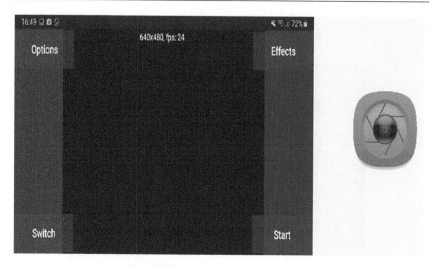

Figure 4.7 RTSP IP camera application.

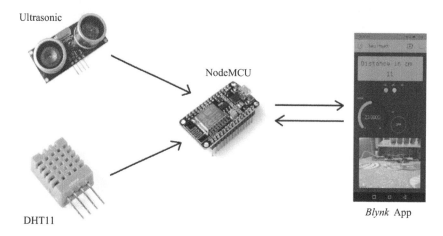

Figure 4.8 Blueprint of the proposed system.

Figure 4.8 shows the blueprint of the proposed system. It is the system design of IoT implementation for a baby crib. The abovementioned system is powered by a battery for safety reason. Table 4.1 shows the setting of a device.

4.4.1 Design of a transmitter

Transmitter design used in this study is the NodeMCU ESP8266 module connected with the sensors, namely ultrasonic sensors, DHT 11, and phone camera (using RTSP IP camera application to provide live streaming). Figure 4.9 shows the system design of IoT implementation at the transmitter.

Table 4.1 Setting of a device

Distance (cm)		
Simulator environment	*Real environment*	*Color*
30–21	90–81	Green
20–11	80–71	Green, Yellow
10–0	70–0	Green, Yellow and Red

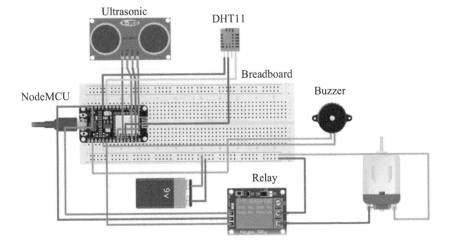

Figure 4.9 Configuration of sensor and NodeMCU diagram.

Table 4.2 Configuration between sensor and NodeMCU

Sensor	*Port*
Ultrasonic	D1,D2
DHT11	D4
Buzzer	D8
Relay	D7

The relay has been used to add open and close gates (turn on/off) for the fan motor, which is connected to a separate power line to provide the required power. Table 4.2 shows the list of connected sensors with NodeMCU.

4.4.2 System flowchart

The procedure of completing the IoT application at the transmitter is depicted in in Figure 4.10. When the baby starts moving, the system will

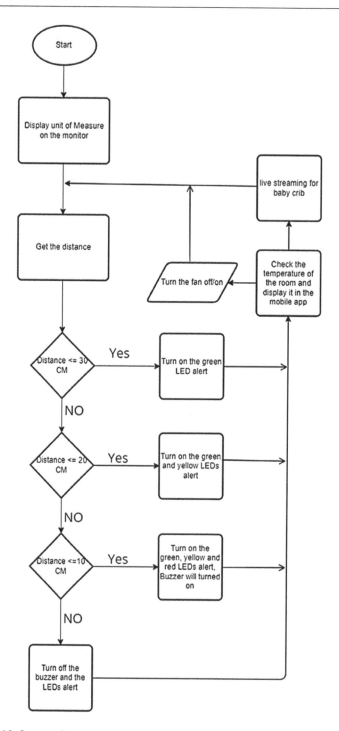

Figure 4.10 System flowchart.

display the measurement unit on the *Blynk* mobile app's monitor. The distance will be measured next under the following conditions, which are detailed in the attached Appendix:

```
IF Distance <=30
Then Turn on the Green LED Alert
ELSE IF Distance <=20
Then Turn on the Green and Yellow LEDs Alert
ELSE IF Distance <=10
Then Turn on the Green, Yellow and Red LEDs Alert
Buzzer will Turn On
ELSE
Then Turn off the Buzzer and LEDs Alert
```

Finally, the system will check the temperature of the room and display it in the *Blynk* mobile application, where it will be possible to turn the fan either ON or OFF while also allowing live streaming for the baby crib.

4.4.3 Design of receiver

The *Blynk* mobile application is used as a receiver to display the results of the measurements from the ultrasonic sensor and DHT11 sensor. In addition, it provides a live streaming, which allow the parents to monitor the baby. The system design of IoT implementation at the receiver side (*Blynk* App) is illustrated in Figure 4.11.

4.5 RESULT AND DISCUSSION

The system has been tested in two environments, namely, simulator environment and real environment. The first test was attempted to study the system in a simulator environment built by the team. Later, the same process was performed to test the system with a real situation where a baby was used to evaluate the response rate. The data collection of both studies was collected and analyzed. The following sections illustrate the detail of these experiments.

4.5.1 Simulation environment experiment

The simulation design contains a cartoon box, which serves as the room of the house. Inside the box, there is the crib, which contain the doll and an

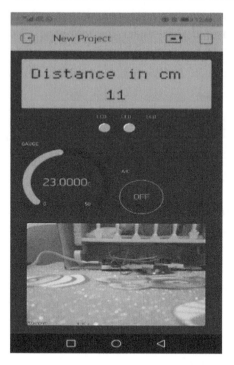

Figure 4.11 Blynk mobile application.

extended holder above the crib is used to hold the required sensor (ultra-sonic sensor). The experiment contains the following three main stages:

Stage 1: Manual caxlculation of the distance between the bottom and the edge of the crib. Then, the ultrasonic sensor is mounted in the extended holder fitted on the crib as referred to in Figure 4.12.

Stage 2: Connect the sensors (ultrasonic and DHT11) with the NodeMCU module. The proposed system can be placed anywhere surrounding the crib as shown in Figure 4.13.

The preliminary results obtained from experiment are presented in Table 4.3 wherein the distance calculation is taken from the top of crib to the doll.

Stage 3: Display the data in "*Blynk*" application.

The data acquired during the test will be sent and presented on the *Blynk* program as a result. The information supplied in the application is shown in Figures 4.14, 4.15, and 4.16, respectively. The distance between the infant and the head circumference was displayed on the screen. The free version of the application has limited features and accuracy; hence, the paid edition of the application was utilized to expand the capabilities of application.

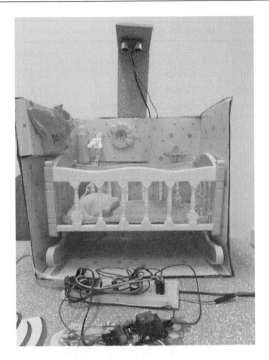

Figure 4.12 Simulator design.

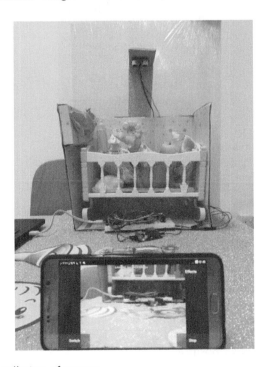

Figure 4.13 Installation of system.

Table 4.3 The results in the simulated environment

Distance	Color	Temperature
29 cm	Green	22.8°C
11 cm	Green, Yellow	22.8°C
10 cm	Green, Yellow and Red	23°C

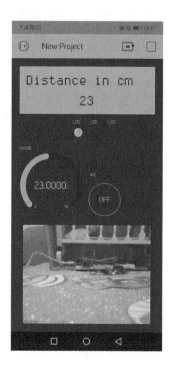

Figure 4.14 Safe situation.

4.5.2 Real environment design

The real design contains a crib made of wood house, and inside, there is an extended holder above the crib to install the ultrasonic sensor, which is shown in Figure 4.17.

This experiment followed the same three stages as described in the preceding section (section A). The baby was asked to lie down for a short period of time before being asked to stand. When the baby tries to reach the crib's edges while standing, the device begins to alert the parents. Figures 4.18 and 4.19 depict the baby's position.

Figure 4.15 Warning situation thus take care.

Figure 4.16 The baby is trying to escape from the crib (danger situation).

Figure 4.17 Design of a real environment.

Figure 4.18 Baby is sleeping.

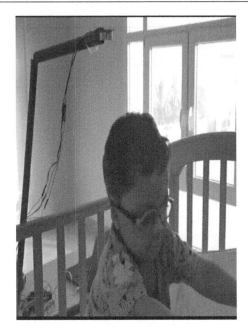

Figure 4.19 Baby is trying to escape from the crib.

Table 4.4 The results in a real environment

Distance	Color	Temperature
98 cm	Green	24°C
72 cm	Green, Yellow	24.1°C
42 cm	Green, Yellow and Red	24°C

The results obtained from experiment of each sensor are demonstrated in Table 4.4.

4.6 CONCLUSION AND FUTURE WORK

Parenting is considered a hard work, especially if the child is in the age where he or she is not aware about the sense of danger. The team has utilized the IOT technology to produce a useful device. The proposed system provides a promising result when it tested in a real environment. The response of the sensors is recorded instantly, which leads to believe that the system will be a vast help to the parent to keep track of their baby, while the baby is in his comfort zone (Crib). This work can be extended with a small modification to be employed to monitor elderly people.

NOTES

1 *Blynk* mobile application is a platform with iOS and Android apps to control Arduino.
2 Accessed dated on 15/04/2022 from https://multiverseken.in/2021/09/21/internet-of-things-cont/

REFERENCES

1 Wipulasundara, S. D., 2017, May. A novel concept for remotely monitoring babies. In *2017 Moratuwa Engineering Research Conference (MERCon)* (pp. 299–303). IEEE.
2 Cooper, B., Tagen, J., and MONDEVICES Inc., 2018. Subject motion monitoring, temperature monitoring, data gathering and analytics system and method. U.S. Patent 10,123,739.
3 Matsuoka, Y., Patel, S., Dixon, M., Greene, W., and Google LLC, 2019. Infant monitoring system with observation-based system control and feedback loops. U.S. Patent Application 15/859,654.
4 Singh, A. K., 2018. Monitor of respiratory movement and caretaking system in baby cradle. *International Journal of Advance Research, Ideas and Innovations in Technology* 4 (2018): 664–670.
5 Natividad, J. G., and Mendez, J. M., 2018, March. Flood monitoring and early warning system using ultrasonic sensor. In *IOP Conference Series: Materials Science and Engineering* (Vol. 325, No. 1, p. 012020). IOP Publishing.
6 Bhasha, P., Pavan Kumar, T., Baseer, K. K., and Jyothsna, V., 2021. An IoT-based BLYNK server application for infant monitoring alert system to detect crying and wetness of a baby. In *International Conference on Intelligent and Smart Computing in Data Analytics* (pp. 55–65). Springer, Singapore.
7 Jabbar, W. A., Shang, H. K., Hamid, S. N., Almohammedi, A. A., Ramli, R. M., and Ali, M. A., 2019. IoT-BBMS: Internet of things-based baby monitoring system for smart cradle. *IEEE Access*, 7, pp. 93791–93805.
8 Ishak, D. N. F. M., Jamil, M. M. A., and Ambar, R., 2017, August. Arduino based infant monitoring system. In *IOP Conference Series: Materials Science and Engineering* (Vol. 226, No. 1, p. 012095). IOP Publishing.
9 Goyal, M., and Kumar, D., 2013. Automatic E-baby cradle swing based on baby cry. *International Journal of Computers and Applications*, 71(21), pp. 39–43.
10 Dizdarević, J., Carpio, F., Jukan, A., and Masip-Bruin, X., 2019. A survey of communication protocols for internet of things and related challenges of fog and cloud computing integration. *ACM Computing Surveys (CSUR)*, 51(6), pp. 1–29.
11 Madakam, S., Lake, V., Lake, V., and Lake, V., 2015. Internet of Things (IoT): A literature review. *Journal of Computer and Communications*, 3(5), p. 164.
12 Corona, B., Nakano, M., and Pérez, H., 2004, Adaptive watermarking algorithm for binary image watermarks. In *International Atlantic Web Intelligence Conference*, Springer, pp. 207–215.
13 Reddy, A. A., and Chatterji, B. N., 2005, A new wavelet based logo-watermarking scheme. *Pattern Recognition Letters*, 26, pp. 1019–1027.

14 Kundur, D., and Hatzinakos, D., 2004, Towards robust logo watermarking using multiresolution image fusion. *IEEE Transcations on Multimedia*, 6, pp. 185–197.

15 Huang, P. S., Chiang, C. S., Chang, C. P., and Tu, T. M., 2005, Robust spatial watermarking technique for colour images via direct saturation adjustment. *IEE Proceedings-Vision, Image and Signal Processing*, 152, pp. 561–574.

16 Eggers, J., Su, J., and Girod, B., 2000, Robustness of a blind image watermarking scheme. In *Proceedings 2000 International Conference on Image Processing (Cat. No. 00CH37101)*, Vancouver.

17 Barni, M., Bartolini, F., and Piva, A., 2002, Multichannel watermarking of color images. *IEEE Transaction on Circuits and Systems of Video Technology* 12(3), pp. 142–156.

18 Gonzalez, F., and Hernandez, J., 1999, A tutorial on digital watermarking. In *Proceedings IEEE 33rd Annual 1999 International Carnahan Conference on Security Technology (Cat. No. 99CH36303)*, Spain.

19 Kunder, D., Multi-resolution Digital Watermarking Algorithms and Implications for Multimedia Signals, Ph.D. thesis, university of Toronto, Canada, 2001.

20 Mehul, R., 2003, Discrete wavelet transform based multiple watermarking scheme. In *Proceedings of the 2003 IEEE TENCON* (pp. 935–938).

21 Doshi, H. S., Shah, M. S., and Shaikh, U. S. A. (2017). Internet of things (Iot): Integration of blynk for domestic usability. *VJER-Vishwakarma Journal of Engineering Research*, 1(4), pp. 149–157.

APPENDIX: SYSTEM CONFIGURATIONS

```
#define BLYNK_PRINT Serial

#include "DHT.h"

#include <ESP8266WiFi.h>
#include <BlynkSimpleEsp8266.h>

#define BLYNK_PRINT Serial
#include <SPI.h>
#include <SimpleTimer.h>
#include <DHT.h>

#define DHT11_PIN 2
#define TRIGGERPIN D1
#define ECHOPIN D2

// You should get Auth Token in the Blynk App.
// Go to the Project Settings (nut icon).
char auth[] = "c1b38a983f93492eb0528fe203d7a238";

// Your WiFi credentials.
// Set password to "" for open networks.
char ssid[] = "HUAWEI nova 3e";
char pass[] = "123oman9";
```

```
#define DHTPIN 2
#define DHTTYPE DHT11//DHT 11

DHT dht(DHTPIN, DHTTYPE);
SimpleTimer timer;

void sendSensor()
{
 float h = dht.readHumidity();
 float t = dht.readTemperature(); // or dht.
readTemperature(true) for Fahrenheit

 if (isnan(h) || isnan(t)) {
  Serial.println("Failed to read from DHT sensor!");
  return;
 }
 // You can send any value at any time.
 // Please don't send more that 10 values per second.
 Blynk.virtualWrite(V7, h);//humditly
 Blynk.virtualWrite(V8, t);//temp

}

WidgetLCD lcd(V5);
//WidgetLCD lcd2(V6);

void setup()
{
 //Debug console
 Serial.begin(9600);
pinMode(TRIGGERPIN, OUTPUT);
 pinMode(D8, OUTPUT);

 pinMode(ECHOPIN, INPUT);
 Blynk.begin(auth, ssid, pass);

dht.begin();

  timer.setInterval(1000L, sendSensor);

 //You can also specify server:
 //Blynk.begin(auth, ssid, pass, "blynk-cloud.com", 8442);
 //Blynk.begin(auth, ssid, pass, IPAddress(192,168,1,100),
8442);

 lcd.clear(); //Use it to clear the LCD Widget
 //lcd2.clear(); //Use it to clear the LCD Widget
 lcd.print(0, 0, "Distance in cm"); //use: (position X:
0-15, position Y: 0-1, "Message you want to print")
 //lcd2.print(0, 0, "TEMP IN C");
 //Please use timed events when LCD printintg in void loop
to avoid sending too many commands
 //It will cause a FLOOD Error, and connection will be
dropped
}
```

```
void loop()

{
 lcd.clear();
//lcd2.clear();

 lcd.print(0, 0, "Distance in cm"); //use: (position X:
0-15, position Y: 0-1, "Message you want to print")
// lcd2.print(0, 0, "TEMP IN C"); // use: (position X: 0-15,
position Y: 0-1, "Message you want to print")

 long duration, distance;
 digitalWrite(TRIGGERPIN, LOW);
 delayMicroseconds(3);

 digitalWrite(TRIGGERPIN, HIGH);
 delayMicroseconds(12);

 digitalWrite(TRIGGERPIN, LOW);
 duration = pulseIn(ECHOPIN, HIGH);
 distance = (duration/2) / 29.1;

 if (distance <= 30) {
  Blynk.virtualWrite(V2, 255);
}
 else {

 Blynk.virtualWrite(V2, 0);
 }
 if (distance <= 20) {
Blynk.virtualWrite(V3, 255);

}
 else {

  Blynk.virtualWrite(V3, 0);
 }

 if (distance <= 10) {
  Blynk.virtualWrite(V4, 255);

}
 else {
  Blynk.virtualWrite(V4, 0);

 }

if (distance <= 10) {
   digitalWrite(D8, HIGH);
    delay(2000);
```

```
    digitalWrite(D8, LOW);
}

 Serial.print(distance);
 Serial.println("Cm");
 lcd.print(7, 1, distance);
   // lcd2.print(7, 1, t);

Blynk.run(); // Initiates Blynk
 timer.run(); // Initiates SimpleTimer

 Blynk.virtualWrite(V5, distance);

 Blynk.run();

 delay(3500);
}
```

Chapter 5

Cloud security still an unsolved puzzle

A complete overview

Shaik Khaja Mohiddin
Lincoln University College, Malaysia

Mohammed Ali Hussain
KLEF (Deemed to be University), Vaddeswaram, India

CONTENTS

5.1   Introduction 89
5.2   Need for layered security 90
5.3   Attacks and vulnerabilities 93
5.4   Usage of blockchain in cloud 93
        5.4.1   Consensus algorithm 93
5.5   Limitation of cloud computing 95
5.6   Comparative study of machine learning for cloud security 95
5.7   Conclusion 99
References 100

5.1 INTRODUCTION

Controlling user access to cloud security resources can be difficult. With hundreds of people accessing systems from across the world and using a variety of devices, planning and thinking about how to handle this can be a daunting task. Having multiple levels of security makes it easier for hackers of all stripes to exploit. Using Figure 5.1, you can see how a broken chain, or a weak link, can cause havoc at any level. We are increasingly living in a distributed world where numerous gadgets are vying for quick and safe access to data. There are a variety of computer services that can be delivered via the internet on a demand basis through the use of cloud computing. When we utilize a service, we are often only charged for what we really use. IT is a rapidly expanding field, and meeting the service needs of industry is a difficult task. When on-premises resources are not enough, it is necessary to take use of the appealing features offered by cloud service providers. Virtualization, software as a service, and cloud computing's infrastructure are all examples of typical cloud computing services (IaaS). However, no single cloud can

Figure 5.1 Weakest link will break and causing trouble.

meet the needs of every customer, as they are all unique. By enabling the establishment of cloud/fog technologies that are completely decentralized, smart contracts or blockchain have had the capacity to change the current shape of cloud marketplaces. Decentralized cloud alternatives that are completely integrated and allow large suppliers to comply with all these kinds of standards are also being recommended by many. All throughout the world, huge corporations are renting out virtual servers for their websites. Users and employees are located in one region of the world, but the systems they access are located elsewhere. There are "moving targets" to protect since servers can be relocated from one data center to another depending on the time of day or increased demand in a different part of the world [1]. The rapid expansion of smart industry [2] in the first half of the 21st century is in synchronization, and as of the latest data, it is close to a $50 billion business. Embedded systems-based industries, where data-driven decision-making is combined with emotional intelligence and sentiment analysis, are now possible because of the rapid rise of communication and information and technology [2, 3]. IoT plays a key role in establishing a long-term link between physical industrial surroundings [4, 5] and the digital realm of computing systems. A new system known as the Cyber-Physical System (CPS) is created as a result of the correct augmentation, causing a significant shift in industrial advancement. When IoT is incorporated into a wide range of industries and sectors such as food and beverage production and distribution as well as transportation and utilities, productivity improves across the board [6, 7]. At the same time, machine effort reduces the physical labor requirement, resulting in higher-quality output.

5.2 NEED FOR LAYERED SECURITY

The device layer is the most vulnerable one. From the user, as indicated, layers of security to examine, we travel through each point where we must consider security. The primary interface device is usually the user layer. To gain access to a cloud system, most people rely on a laptop, tablet, or smartphone. Chrome, Internet Explorer, Opera, Firefox, and Safari are the most commonly used web browsers over most devices. It is possible that each phone vendor has a different browser that does not meet security requirements of your organization. It is possible that a browser that functions well on one phone may have security vulnerabilities on another. A careful programmer must not just program for what the system should do, but also for what the system was not meant to accomplish. The application layer follows. The server operating system is the third layer. Only a very small percentage of the world's coders are capable of building operating systems. To keep this layer of the system healthy, we rely on operating system vendors. Finally, we will take a look at the physical infrastructure and components of the network. Starting with both the user and working backwards to the network, all layers of security should be taken into account, as shown in Figure 5.2. The SNMP is a widely adopted standard for establishing communication between various pieces of hardware and software (Table 5.1).

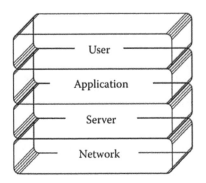

Figure 5.2 Layers of security.

Table 5.1 A brief description of security layers

Layer	Explanation
Application	Software engineers can choose from a wide variety of programming languages for creating cloud-based applications. Due to their ability to deal with computer hardware and high-speed processing, lower-complexity programming languages like C are favored by the majority of programmers. Higher-level languages like Ruby and Java by become more popular in software development because of the rise in processor power over the last decade. Programming for the cloud typically involves the usage of frameworks like Microsoft.NET, Oracle and Adobe AIR, Database. The fundamental code for cloud apps can also be created using web-based languages such as Adobe Flash, Flex, and HTML/AJAX.
Hosting Infrastructure Hardware and Networking	It is critical to protect the hardware that powers your infrastructure. In order to keep off undesirable visitors and hackers, physical security of company systems is essential. A person with physical access might remove power cords, network cords, put in thumb drives, re-boot servers to an USB key, or steal the entire physical server if necessary. Locked doors on racks of servers and security methods to track but only allow authorized workers inside the computer room are common

(Continued)

Table 5.1 (Continued) A brief description of security layers

Layer	Explanation
Hosting Infrastructure Hardware and Networking	features of many hosting providers. The vast majority of data center facilities are also monitored by video cameras throughout the clock. In addition to safeguarding the server hardware, it is also necessary to safeguard the network hardware. Non-authorized staff should not have access to routers, switches, and patch cord management solutions. The most popular method of protecting network hardware is to keep it in a protected computer room or phone cabinet. Installing devices that are capable of capturing data can be done if an intruder has physical access to your network. Physical safety is only the beginning. The second aspect of network security is ensuring that only trustworthy devices can access the network. Network cards' MAC addresses and apps work together to make this possible. All ports of an active management switch are assigned MAC addresses, which prevents other devices from connecting to the switch and entering the network. This can be done on-site at the network's physical location, enabling remote access to its cloud services.
Server	The majority of the Internet is powered by Linux and its various varieties, as well as Microsoft's Windows server. Host operating system selection is often dictated by the app development platform selected by the Programmers, project manager, and administrator of the project. Server operating systems have a number of essential elements that should be taken into account while developing applications. It is possible that the price of software and web hosting will be a problem. There are numerous hosting alternatives available for the second most prominent operating systems. It is important to ask a number of important questions before choosing on a server service provider, such as who has access to the servers and the hardware that runs it. In addition, it is vital that you perform routine server maintenance. Ask who is responsible for updating the software on your server platform, as security upgrades are critical. Additionally, hardware maintenance is performed to ensure the system's long and healthy lifespan. It is possible that a disc drive will fail and have to be repaired. Concerns about power supplies are also warranted. There are a number of server remote monitoring that can alert you to issues with your server, in addition to regular maintenance. These include everything from doing a disc space check to making heavy use of memory. Many of the modern servers can also monitor the actual temperature of the case. Network traffic above normal levels can cause a few of the server monitoring to display an error.
User Interface	There are various reasons why web browsers are so prevalent in today's user interfaces. A simple explanation is that most people have it, regardless of which platform they are using. Anything from smartphones and tablets to laptops and desktops has access to a web browser. They are available on all of the major operating systems, including Linux, Windows, Chrome, and Apple. There are even a few web browsers available that are available for all major operating systems. Two of the most popular browsers are Firefox and Chrome [8].

5.3 ATTACKS AND VULNERABILITIES

CIA are the three pillars of computer security. The protection of confidential information entails keeping it hidden from those who do not have a right to see it. Confidentiality can be maintained through the use of three different methods. There is cryptography, which uses mathematical modifications to conceal plain text data. In the second place, there is security system, which specifies who has the access to which sections of the system or information. An authorized user can only perform certain activities on a chunk of data or a system module that they have been granted access to [9, 10, 11]. All layers of abstraction in cloud computing services can be vulnerable to attack. Vulnerabilities can occur at every level of abstraction in a cloud, as shown in Figure 5.3 and Table 5.2.

5.4 USAGE OF BLOCKCHAIN IN CLOUD

5.4.1 Consensus algorithm

Each blockchain network can come to an agreement through the establishment of a consensus algorithm. In a public (decentralized) blockchain network, computers connected must consent to validate transactions; there is no central authority in this model [17]. There are consensus mechanisms in place to ensure that all transactions go through without a hitch, but that the rules of the protocol are being adhered to. To put it another way, protocols are the basic regulations for utilizing the blockchain network, and this algorithm is the process by which they are adhered to [18]. In order for the blockchain network to function, it must adhere to a set of rules that specify how each participant and each portion of a network must function. As a result, the algorithm governs the system and the steps it needs to do in

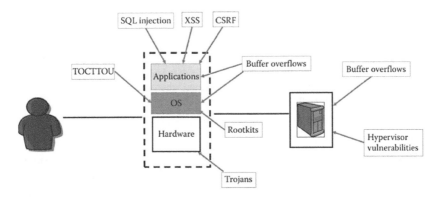

Figure 5.3 Cloud security vulnerabilities.

Table 5.2 Vulnerability layers

Vulnerability layer	Description
Application	An adversary can breach a system by exploiting vulnerabilities in a cloud application at the application level. If a user input is not properly sanitized, it is possible for an attack like SQL injection to occur in a web-based cloud service. For example, a SQL injection vulnerability can be exploited to allow an attacker to inject code into a powerful scripting engine that is then performed by a SQL query interpreter. Despite the fact that it has been studied since the mid-2000s, it is still frequently reported in vulnerability databases. Consider a typical situation in which a user interacts with a web server running a web application that saves its data in a database in order to get a sense of the danger this vulnerability poses to users. In most cases, the web application code and the database code reside on separate computers. For the most part, consumers can look for books by title, author, and publisher via a book retailer's web application. The application performs SQL queries to extract book details from a database containing the whole catalogue. Assume that a user wants to find all of Wiley's books. An engine on the web application side collects and processes these data, understanding them as user-supplied information. It then creates a SQL command using the application developer's scripts and user input, which is subsequently executed.
OS	Extensions and Malicious drivers can also be installed on operating systems. A major portion of modern kernel processing cores is made up of kernel extensions, particularly device drivers. It is possible to communicate with an ever-increasing number of different I/O devices without having to reboot the system or recompile. The problem is that they have the highest level of permissions and might be susceptible or malevolent, putting the system at risk. Modern operating systems have not embraced most of the ideas in the literature for detecting malicious extensions [12, 13, 14].
Hypervisor, Storage, Hardware, and Network	VM migration, snapshot, and rollback weaknesses in cloud computing's code can also be exploited [15]. These flaws can be exploited to undermine system integrity, expose sensitive data, or even cause a denial of service (DoS) attack. Public sources of virtual machine images may contain malware or code that is vulnerable or unpatched. Cloud computing has a number of weaknesses that are not present in the on-premises systems. It is possible that data reside in different nations, each with its own set of rules governing the ownership of data [16]. It is also possible that data leakage will occur if secondary storage is not adequately cleaned when the data are relocated or removed.

order to agree with the rules set by the protocol and provide the intended outcome. The consensus algorithm of a blockchain determines the legitimacy of blocks and transactions in a virtual financial transaction environment. PoS and PoW are consensus techniques in the Bitcoin protocol [19].

The PoW consensus algorithm was the first to be devised. There are numerous cryptocurrencies that use this technique, including Bitcoin. The proof-of-work algorithm is essential to the mining process. The more processing power is available, the more attempts can be made per second at solving the puzzles in PoW mining. Mining is defined by the sequence in which the blocks are arranged [20]. PoW mining necessitates the use of large industrial-scale machinery. Miners are compensated for finding and fixing cryptographic flaws and creating new blocks. When a block is closed and a new one is formed in PoW, virtual currency is made available and has a mining cap. In the event that this limit is reached, mining will cease and the network will collect fees. Due to the security of PoW against DDoS, these blockchain algorithms make it difficult for hackers to exploit the system, which necessitates a large amount of computing power and effort. It is therefore more likely that the miners that have a large computational capacity will solve the next mathematical challenge of the block. When the dispersed network of nodes gets consensus and believes that a mathematical issue provided is acceptable evidence for the effort invested in the process, miners can only confirm small transaction blocks and upload them to the blockchain [21].

5.5 LIMITATION OF CLOUD COMPUTING

Elastic infrastructure, economic, on-demand resources, and pay for whatever you need are all examples of cloud computing. However, there are a few hidden costs that must be taken into consideration before these benefits may be realized (Table 5.3):

5.6 COMPARATIVE STUDY OF MACHINE LEARNING FOR CLOUD SECURITY

As network usage has skyrocketed in recent years, IDS have sprung up to keep up with the increased demand. These systems are specifically designed to detect network irregularities and outbreaks. Various machine learning and data mining approaches are being used to improve the detection process of IDSs and eliminate the current issues. Various IDS and cutting-edge machine learning classifiers will be examined in this study in an effort to improve IDS performance. Using several machine learning approaches, the author develops a classifier-based model of an effective IDS that can determine whether a network is good or harmful. Logistic Regression, Naive Bayes, Stochastic Gradient Descent, K-Nearest Neighbours Decision Trees Random Forests, and Support Vector Machines have been used to measure

Table 5.3 Limitations of cloud computing

Parameter	Explanation
Data movement	Any data required for calculation must be transported to the remote data center, and the resulting output must be transported back. Most public cloud providers charge extra for input-output (I/O) transactions, which also increase latency compared to using local servers. Self-driving cars, for example, are being developed and feature a slew of sensors, including numerous cameras. On the one hand, a remote Cloud may not have enough time to conduct the IP algorithms for real-time decision-making when driving because of the dynamic nature of traffic. Self-driving cars, on the other hand, must be able to run a server-like computer on board. According to some estimates, a self-driving car may create up to 5 terabytes of data each day, which would necessitate a mobile data center to store and process on-board.
Perception of cloud security	Cloud data centers may not be any less secure than traditional on-premises data centers, despite the fact that they can be accessed by many more individuals. People believe that the Public Cloud is less secure since they can no longer control it. There are more actions that can be taken like encrypting one's data in the Cloud and any virtual machine running on a multi-tenanted server when keys are held separately, in the author's perspective.
Loss of control	To help email service providers like Google's Gmail make money, these users' e-mails are often reviewed by bots before appropriate adverts are displayed. This, however, raises the issue of who owns and has access to the email content itself. E-mail providers cannot refuse to hand out e-mails if a judge subpoenas them in a legal matter, for example. For confidential data, such as photos or business documents, a user should maintain the content on their own computer.
Uncertain Performance	Cloud computing companies profit by sharing the same hardware resources with a large number of customers. While individual virtual machines (VMs) are segregated in memory and run-on different server cores, data from each VM must pass through resource sharing such as a storage controller and networking card. This not only causes bottlenecks at inlets and outlets, but also entry and departure to shared servers, analogous to heavy traffic in a data center. This causes an unnoticed performance loss in a running VM. This issue has previously been described as a noisy neighbor, and it causes a delay in work completion.

the accuracy of the model. Several well-known datasets, including KDD 1999, NSL KDD, and the DARPA set, were incorporated into the final product. When tested against each of the attacks, the model yields an acceptable accuracy of over 80% (Tables 5.4–5.7).

Table 5.4 A brief comparison of cloud security using ML approaches

Purpose of work	Used methodology	Used dataset	Outcomes
Reduce the number of false negatives in order to determine how many clusters there are. [22]	Intrusion Detection was carried out using the K-means method and an unsupervised machine learning technique. The K-means clustering is used in conjunction with a signature-based technique in this model.	NSL-KDD	A higher efficiency rate can be achieved if the proper number of clusters is recognized; however, a decrease in efficiency can be achieved if the cluster number fluctuates. The system will work well if the number of clusters is as specified; otherwise, it will be overly complicated.
Based on machine learning, a new IDS has been presented. [27]	Attacks in the dataset were detected using a variety of classifiers and feature selection methods.	KDD99	Using a combination of classifiers and selection procedures, we were able to attain extremely high accuracy. This study could be expanded to include the development of a system that can quickly identify an assault in a large dataset.
An ensemble approach of the intrusion detection system is used to calculate and reduce the false-positive rate, boosting classification accuracy. [21, 25, 26]	The Bagging technique and REP Tree are utilized to construct an intrusion detection system that is unique in its approach.	KDD 99	On the NSL-KDD dataset, the Bagging ML method can be stated to have the best classification accuracy. However, for the purposes of testing this strategy, just one set of data was used.
Methods such as discretized differential evolution (DDE) and C4.5 ML can be used to identify the optimal collection of attributes [24].	The suggested model incorporates Decision Trees and Differential Evolution techniques.	NSL-KDD Cup'99	There are 16 features that can be used to categorize associations using the suggested method. An accuracy rate of 88.73% was achieved while detecting unique attacks. In order to overcome this limitation, the generalization of traits had to be eliminated from future work. In addition, live networks can be searched for connections.

(Continued)

Table 5.4 (Continued) A brief comparison of cloud security using ML approaches

Purpose of work	Used methodology	Used dataset	Outcomes
The most important objective is to prevent an attack from occurring in the first place by appropriately identifying and reducing potential dangers. The goal is to detect and fix any systemic problems while also speeding up the learning process through the development of a high-speed algorithm. [23]	The dataset is analyzed by a factor called the NOF as part of an outlier detection technique. This intrusion detection process relies on a large number of data points.	KDD	The high-speed model was introduced because of difficulties such as excessive training time, low accuracy checking, and attack classification. All anomaly data present in the network system may be detected by the proposed IDS model, which has a higher performance speed. This concept is superior than the rest of ML.
Intrusion detection is improved by using a decision tree and rule-based algorithms to identify attacks in the system more quickly. [20]	Many well-known classifiers like REP Tree and JRip algorithm are also utilized in this study.	CICIDS 2017	It is possible to identify both regular and irregular attacks with low false alarm rates and high detection rates. Using this strategy, the dataset was able to be accurately analyze

Table 5.5 All of the classifiers constructed in NSL KDD dataset gave a high accuracy rate

	Cross-validation folds				
	2	5	10	30	50
DoS Attack	0.995	0.996	0.9974	0.9968	0.9971
Probe Attack	0.9908	0.992	0.9907	0.9916	0.9909
U-to-R Attack	0.995	0.996	0.9965	0.997	0.9964
R-to-L Attack	0.981	0.988	0.984	0.983	0.9853

Table 5.6 The accuracy of various state-of-the-art classifiers in the NSL-KDD dataset

Classifiers	Attacks			
	DOS (%)	Probe (%)	U2R (%)	R2L (%)
Logistic Regression	95	92	92	93
Naive Bayes	93	93	91	92
Stochastic Gradient Descent	92	89	91	90
k-Nearest Neighbor	91	92	92	90
Decision Tree	92	91	90	91
Random Forest Classifier	93	90	88	92
Support Vector Machine	93	93	92	91

Table 5.7 In the KDD Cup'99 dataset, state-of-the-art classifiers generated high accuracy results

Classifiers	Attacks			
	DOS (%)	Probe (%)	U2R (%)	R2L (%)
Logistic Regression	94	94	92	92
Naive Bayes	94	93	91	93
Stochastic Gradient Descent	92	92	91	92
k-Nearest Neighbor	89	91	88	91
Decision Tree	92	90	91	92
Random Forest Classifier	93	93	92	91
Support Vector Machine	93	91	92	91

5.7 CONCLUSION

Cloud computing service providers generate money by renting out the same gear to multiple users at a time. When a large amount of data is handled in the digital world, security and privacy are the primary concerns. Cloud computing and the blockchain platform promote openness while reducing assaults. This claim is supported by simulation, which shows that the proposed strategy increases security while decreasing privacy invasions. Cloud storage and processing have centralized access controls. Decentralized access control is now possible since we have integrated blockchain with the cloud. In spite of the fact that their VMs are segregated in memory and executing on various server cores, data from each VM must transit through shared resources like a memory controller and a networking card. Traffic jam-like bottlenecks are created in a data center, as well as at the exit points to the shared servers, as a result of this. This causes a sudden decrease in the running VM's performance. This issue, which has been described as a bothersome neighbor, causes a delay in getting things done. If the data are stored on a Cloud, jurisdictional boundaries may be crossed, which raises liability concerns if the data leak. This is especially true if the data pertains to someone's private life, such as shopping habits or medical records. Because both good actors and bad actors in cyberspace are employing ML approaches to circumvent security measures, the competition between them is heating up. The comparison tables clearly show that the NSL-KDD dataset outperforms the other two datasets in terms of performance. In comparison to the KDD Cup'99 datasets, the NSL-KDD dataset has less redundancy, which could account for this. This, like any other project, has its own set of constraints. In the experiment, the number of attacks might be further investigated. It is clear from this table that logistic regression classifiers have the greatest result, but this comes at a cost: overhead. The most significant aspect of this approach is that it is basic and easy to comprehend.

REFERENCES

1. Alcácer, V., Cruz-Machado, V., Scanning the industry 4.0: A literature review on technologies for manufacturing systems. *Engineering Science and Technology, an International Journal*, 22(3), 899–919, 2019.
2. Al-Wswasi, M., Ivanov, A., Makatsoris, H., A survey on smart automated computer-aided process planning (ACAPP) techniques. *International Journal of Advanced Manufacturing Technology*, 97, 809–832, 2018.
3. Tan, Y., Yang, W., Yoshida, K., Takakuwa, S., Application of IoT-aided simulation to manufacturing systems in cyber-physical system. *Machines*, 7(2), 1–13, 2019.
4. Boyes, H., Hallaq, B., Cunningham, J., Watson, T., The industrial internet of things (IIoT): An analysis framework. *Computers in Industry*, 101, 1–12, 2018.
5. Saqlain, M., Piao, M., Shim, Y., Lee, J.Y., Framework of an IoT-based industrial data management for smart manufacturing. *Journal of Sensor and Actuator Networks*, 8(25), 1–21, 2019.
6. Xu, H., Yu, W., Griffith, D., Golmie, N., A survey on industrial internet of things: A cyberphysical systems perspective. *IEEE Access*, 6, 78238–8259, 2018.
7. Kavitha, B.C., Vallikannu, R., IoT based intelligent industry monitoring system. In *6th International Conference on Signal Processing and Integrated Networks*, Noida, India, 7–8 March 2019.
8. Desktop Browser Market Share, Net Market share SM Copyright © 2006–2015, Net Applications.com 65 Enterprise, Aliso Viejo, CA, 92656, Available at https://www.netmarketshare.com/browser-market share.aspx
9. Bishop, M., *Computer Security: Art and Science*, Addison Wesley, 2003.
10. Stallings, W., Brown, L., *Computer Security Principles and Practice*, Pearson, 2012.
11. Goodrich, M., Tamassia, R., *Introduction to Computer Security*, Pearson, 2010.
12. Srivastava, A., Giffin, J., Efficient monitoring of untrusted kernel-mode execution. In *Network and Distributed System Security Symposium (NDSS)*, 2011.

13. Xiong, X., Tian, D., Liu, P., Practical protection of kernel integrity. In *Network and Distributed System Security Symposium (NDSS)*, 2011.
14. Oliveira, D., Wetzel, N., Bucci, M., Sullivan, D., Jin, Y., Hardware-software collaboration for secure coexistence with kernel extensions. *ACM Applied Computing Review Journal*, 14(3), 22–35, 2014.
15. Hashizume, K., Rosado, D.G., Fernández-Medina, E., Fernandez, E.B., An analysis of security issues for cloud computing. *Journal of Internet Services and Applications*, 4, 5, 2013.
16. Ertaul, L., Singhal, S., Gökay, S., Security challenges in cloud computing. In *Proceedings of the International Conference on Security and Management (SAM)* (pp. 36–42), 2010.
17. Mingxiao, D., Xiaofeng, M., Zhe, Z., Xiangwei, W., Qijun, C., A review on consensus algorithm of blockchain. In *2017 IEEE International Conference on Systems, Man, and Cybernetics (SMC)* (pp. 2567–2572). IEEE, Banff, Canada, 2017, October.
18. Nguyen, G.T., Kim, K., A survey about consensus algorithms used in blockchain. *Journal of Information Processing Systems*, 14(1), 2018.
19. Bach, L.M., Mihaljevic, B., Zagar, M., Comparative analysis of blockchain consensus algorithms. In *2018 41st International Convention on Information and Communication Technology, Electronics and Microelectronics (MIPRO)* (pp. 1545–1550). IEEE, Opatija, Croatia, 2018, May.
20. Baliga, A., Understanding blockchain consensus models. *Persistent*, 2017(4), 1–14, 2017.
21. Corchado, J.M., Blockchain technology: a review of the current challenges of cryptocurrency. In *Blockchain and applications: International Congress* (Vol. 1010, p. 153). Springer, Switzerland, 2019, June.
22. Gaikwad, D.P., Thool, R.C., Intrusion detection system using bagging ensemble method of machine learning, in: *2015 International Conference on Computing Communication Control and Automation* (pp. 291–295). IEEE, 2015, February.
23. Duque, S., Bin Omar, M.N., Using data mining algorithms for developing a model for intrusion detection system (IDS). *Procedia Computer Science*, 61, 46–51, 2015.
24. Jabez, J., Muthukumar, B., Intrusion detection system (IDS): anomaly detection using outlier detection approach. *Proceedings Computer Science*, 48, 338–346, 2015.
25. Popoola, E., Adewumi, A.O., Efficient feature selection technique for network intrusion detection system using discrete differential evolution and decision. *International Journal of Network Security*, 19(5), 660–669, 2017.
26. Biswas, S.K., Intrusion detection using machine learning: A comparison study. *International Journal of Pure and Applied Mathematics*, 118(19), 101–114, 2018.
27. Chandre, P.R., Mahalle, P.N., Shinde, G.R., Machine learning based novel approach for intrusion detection and prevention system: A tool based verification. In *2018 IEEE Global Conference on Wireless Computing and Networking (GCWCN)*, 2018.

Chapter 6

A layered architecture for delay tolerant networks and routing mechanism

Mohammed Ali Hussain
KLEF (Deemed to be University), Vaddeswaram, India

Arshad Ahmad Khan Mohammad
GITAM Deemed to be University, India

Thirupathi Regula
University of Technology and Applied Sciences, Muscat Al-Khuwair, Sultanate of Oman

CONTENTS

6.1 Introduction 103
6.2 A delay tolerant message-based overlay architecture 104
    6.2.1 Regions and border gateways 104
    6.2.2 Path selection and scheduling 104
6.3 Architecture of delay tolerant networks 105
    6.3.1 Layer communication 107
    6.3.2 Internal arrangement of border gateways 108
6.4 Conclusion 111
6.5 Future work 111
References 111

6.1 INTRODUCTION

Delay tolerant networking is an architecture of computer that seeks to address the technical issues in non-homogeneous networks that may lack continuous network connectivity [2]. Examples of such networks are those operating in mobile or extreme terrestrial environments or planned networks in space. The term tolerant in networking is the time needed to wait until the node gets connected with the waiting one. Disruption may occur because of the limits of wireless [10] radio range, sparsest of mobile nodes, energy resources, attack, and noise.

DOI: 10.1201/9781003355946-6

6.2 A DELAY TOLERANT MESSAGE-BASED OVERLAY ARCHITECTURE

The architecture of delay tolerant network is based on an abstraction of message switching. Message advancements are forwarded in the network [2]. The routers that handle them are known as gateways of delay tolerant network (DTN). As in normal architecture, DTN attempts to work under different organization structures and provide a store-and-forward door work between them when a hub speaks with at least two non-homogeneous organizations. For instance, inside the Internet, the overlay may work over transmission control protocol (TCP)/Internet protocol (IP); for profound space joints, it might give an entryway administration to CFDP [5], and in further lenient sensor/actuator networks, it might give an interconnection a few yet-to-be-normalized sensor transport convention, every one of which contains their own of these systems' administration conditions sorted convention stacks and naming semantics created for their proposed application territory. By extraordinary DTN entryways situated at their correspondence hubs, it is conceivable to accomplish interoperability.

6.2.1 Regions and border gateways

The DTN architecture includes the concepts of regions and DTN gateways, as illustrated in Figure 6.1. In this example, three regions are shown (network 1, network 2, and network 3). All regions include a DTN gateways resident on each system. Network-1 includes a low earth-orbiting satellite link that also provides periodic connectivity. Dissimilar network protocols use interconnection points for communication among irregular networks, where those points are produced from region boundaries. If the nodes are able to communicate with each other without using gateways, then those are present in the same network. DTN uses a few types of dissimilar networks if it maintains single layered architecture [3]. The gateway suggests a point, by which data need to use in order to gain entry into a network. This gateway serves as a basis for transmission and control.

6.2.2 Path selection and scheduling

In the DTN architecture, it is assumed that there may be nonavailability of end-to-end route [4]. Rather, routes are used to move messages from their starting point toward their destinations based on time divisions or in a time slot manner. Communications are parameterized by their start and end times, capacity, latency, endpoints, and direction. To send the message, it is required to measure the predictability of a communication point that can be used as a hop point. The predictability depends on the availability. The measure of predictability in a communication point depends on its direction. A wireless [11] connection may be the absolute prediction from the point of

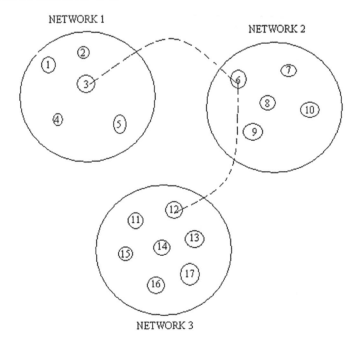

Figure 6.1 Node arrangement of delay tolerant network.

view of source while being completely unpredicted from the point of view of destination. The particular attributes of path selection and message scheduling are expected to depend on routing algorithms [6]. In this single-layered architecture [12], a few complex issues have been recognized: assurance of the presence and consistency of contacts, acquiring information on the condition of forthcoming messages given suspicions of high postponement, and the issue of proficiently allotting messages to contacts and deciding their transmission request. While basic heuristics for these issues can be executed without inordinate issues, each issue speaks to a noteworthy test and stays as future work.

A straightforward programming formulation of the (romanticized) directing/planning issue with contacts has recently been depicted in.

6.3 ARCHITECTURE OF DELAY TOLERANT NETWORKS

A layered architecture of delay tolerant network is shown in Figure 6.2; it contains hierarchies of layers, where each layer is composed of several nodes. Each layer is known as a network. The nodes of the network are composed of nodes with nearest possibility for communication. The communication channels of the layer are composed by using a number of successful attempts of the nearby node using non-gateway mechanism [5, 13].

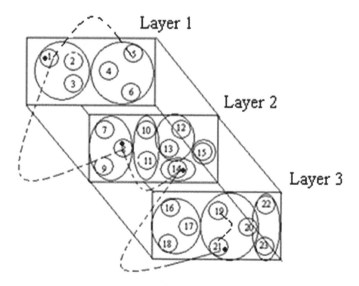

Figure 6.2 Layered architecture of delay tolerant network.

In this study, gateway indicates the border nodes that are used for communication, and gateway node contains a table that represents the nearest possible other node information. A combination of gateway information is maintained at every layer of the network. A network needs to maintain at least one gateway node because it is required to maintain connectivity among other networks. To detect the border gateways, the following algorithm will be effective.

Algorithm to detect border gateways:

```
Function total_network(1 to n)
For network 1 to n
Count nodes
Count degree for each node
Hoptime:=estimated packet return time
If Forwardtime:=0
Not a bordernode
else
Node[i]=forwardtime+hoptime

Node_detect(1 to m)
Foreverybordernode
Find the network
Connect networks
```

The abovementioned algorithm defines the number of border nodes and the network they belong to. First, the number of nodes is passed. Then, by using the hoptime and the forward time, a node is decided as the border gateway or a normal node. To find out hoptime, the following algorithm is used

Algorithm to find border gateways:

```
Function node(1 to m)
Send the empty packet with return address
Calculate the time to return
To find out the forward time the following algorithm is
used
Function node(1 to m)
Calculate the total nodes nearby
Send packet to each node
If node in same network
Count the neighbors
Else
Count as non neighbor
If total count nodes equals to sum of the neighbor
nodes
Than not a border
Else count the border node gives the number
```

6.3.1 Layer communication

Layer is a logical separation of nodes. The set of nodes whose communication is direct are grouped under a name called layer. Layered mechanism is performed by using the abovementioned algorithms. To make the layer communication, border gateways are used. Border gateways have the property known as any node communication. It is designed in a way that all nodes are reachable nodes for the border node. It can be communicated with any node present in the layer. It maintains all sort of information regarding every node present in the layer and also maintains the shortest path to communicate with every node. Each layer may contain more than one border gateway. The calculated number of border gateways are maintained in the layer table, which contains information about the nearest nodes and the nearest layered border nodes, which are calculated as shown in the algorithm. To communicate with the other layer node, first, the source node sends the address value to the layer it belongs to where the layer searches for the destination it is available in the current layer or not. If not, then the layer communicates with the table to find out the border nodes; from those nodes, the nearest possible node value is calculated that is present at another layer.

The border node, which is forwarding the message, must be able to follow store and forward mechanism strictly. Without this mechanism, it is not possible to achieve communication among different layers. The mentioned DTN in Figure 6.2 represents a layered mechanism.

It is assumed that by calculating the hoptime and forward time, nodes are separated to form the layers. In that example, the node5 communicates with node19; first, node5 approaches the border node present in the layer where node1 is the border gateway. Border gateway collects the information from the source node and reads the destination address; if the destination is one of the nodes of current layer, it communicates with the destination directly and passes the information. If it is present in other layers, then the first border node communicates with the nearby layer through its border gateway. It passes the request to the border gateway of the layer. Where the layer searches for a destination address provided by the request layer, if it is found in the layer, then it forwards the message; otherwise, the nearest border gateway is calculated. If the current border gateway is the nearest border gateway, then it will communicate with the border gateway present in another layer; otherwise, the message is forwarded to the nearest neighbor of the current layer. In this way, a message is passed from source to destination of various layers. The communication mechanism is discussed in the following section.

6.3.2 Internal arrangement of border gateways

The internal architecture of the border gateway contains the following: A routing table of nodes, layer information table, and border gateway management table. Routing table consists of nodes of the layer and their communication paths; most of them are shortest paths. Layer information table maintains information about the other border gateway nodes of the layers and internal routing tables [7]. Border management table contains information regarding overall border gateways, through which it is possible to pass the information through layers.

1) *Routing table*: Routing table for this layered architecture is entirely different from the normal routing table of the network. This routing table consists of various calculated measures that specify nodal detection and their interconnection. Routing table in the layers is useful for that layer only and not used by the other layers (Figure 6.3).

This routing table [8] is used to find out the shortest paths in current network only. The following diagram indicates a network that consists of four nodes; it is assumed that each node of the network is connected to every other node present in the network. The route path depends on the nodes, which are indicated by using route table present in the network. In the first measure of the route table, it maintains information regarding the current

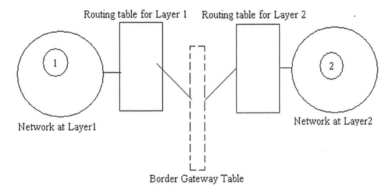

Figure 6.3 Communication establishment through different tables in network.

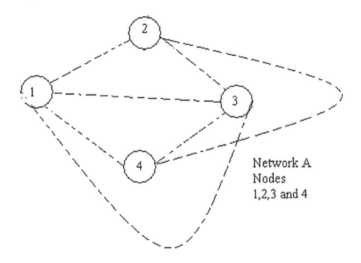

Figure 6.4 Example network for route table.

network nodes that are active. It is unpredictable to mention in a route table that at what time the nodes of a network are active, but by using the range approach, it can be predicted at what time network nodes will be active. Delay tolerant network does not give guarantee of the live nodes; rather, it suggests a mechanism that makes comfort to send the messages. The example given below shows a network of four nodes and their connected paths.

The below mentioned table format shows the route establishment by different nodes present in the network at Figure 6.4. Node has the possibility to communicate with every node in the network, so the hop path of the table contains all the live node values. This is assumed for all the nodes present in the network (Figure 6.5).

Nodes of the system	Hop path
1	2,3,4
2	1,3,4
3	1,2,4
4	1,2,3

Figure 6.5 Route table for network at Figure 6.4.

The hop path suggests possible nodes by which routing may be done [9]. This routing may not be able to produce the shortest path but possible to detect and generate path through live nodes.

2) *Layer information table*: This table contains the information regarding the layers, such as all the information like border gateways, number of nodes in the layer, shortest path among the nodes present in the layer, conversion factors, and other sort of information. Layer information table is formed from the network that forms the layer division. Layer division is done by always using the established path nodes. These nodes in the network are found by sending a blank packet to the adjacent node present in the network; if the packet returns to the source one, that is, the node that sends the packet, then the node is counted as a local node and considered as a node of layer. The formation of all kinds of these nodes forms a layer. The below mentioned figure shows the process by which a layer is formed (Figure 6.6).

The above structure shows that a blank message is sent to all the nodes present in the network where some nodes, after getting the messages, sending

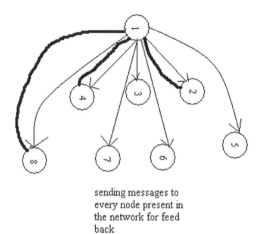

sending messages to
every node present in
the network for feed
back

Figure 6.6 Node message forwarding for layer formation.

Border Node	Layer	Comm. Possibility
1	2,3,4	2,3,4
2	1,2	1,2,3
3	1,5	1,2,3,4,5

Figure 6.7 Example layer table for network at Figure 6.4.

acknowledgment are treated as nearby nodes and are used to construct a layer.

3) *Gateway management table*: This table consists of information regarding all the border gateways that are present in the network according to their layer number. The use of this layer is to find out the number of nodes that acting as a border gateway and how to establish communication with other layers of the network (Figure 6.7).

6.4 CONCLUSION

With the advent of Delay Tolerant Network, it is possible to establish communication over networks that are nonhomogeneous and irregular. The single-layered architecture provides good communication. With the help of grouping of nodes into different layers, it is effective to establish communication in a quick and reliable manner.

6.5 FUTURE WORK

It may be useful if it is possible to establish intercommunication channels in between or among the layers, by which it is possible to add more number of nodes and more number of networks to the existing one.

REFERENCES

1 Geva, A. (1998), ScaleNet—Multiscale neural-network architecture for time series prediction. *IEEE Transactions on Neural Networks*, 9(5), 1471–1482.
2 Vemulakonda, R., and Kapu, N. (2012), *Probability Based Path Detection Routing in Delay Tolerant Networks*, IJARCSEE.
3 Hussain, M. A., Vemulakonda, R., Ahad, A., Satya Rajesh, K., and Umar, S. (2013), *Through Estimated Probability, Path Detection Routing in Delay Tolerant Networks; Advances in Engineering and Technology Series*. DOI:03. AETS.2013.2.24.
4 SrinivasaRao, Y., and Ali Hussain, M. (2019), Adaptive quality of service medium access control protocol for IEEE 802.11 based mobile Ad hoc network, *International Journal of Innovative Technology and Exploring Engineering*, 8(4), 430–433.

5   Ganesan, T., and Rajarajeswari, P. (2019), Genetic algorithm approach improved by 2D lifting scheme for sensor node placement in optimal position, in *Proceedings of the International Conference on Intelligent Sustainable Systems, ICISS 2019*, pp. 104–109.

6   Bhandari, R.R., and Raja Sekhar, K. (2019), Mobility aware clustering routing algorithm (MACRON) to improve lifetime of wireless sensor network, *International Journal of Recent Technology and Engineering*, 8(2), 76–85.

7   Satyanarayana, K.V.V., and Vijay Kumar, S. (2019), Adaptive framework combining sensors for data monitoring, *International Journal of Innovative Technology and Exploring Engineering*, 8(7), 1290–1293.

8   Dhage, M.R., and Vemuru, S. (2018), A effective cross layer multi-hop routing protocol for heterogeneous wireless sensor network. *Indonesian Journal of Electrical Engineering and Computer Science*, 10(2), 664–671.

9   Venkateswararaorao, M., and Srinivas, M. (2018), A multi factorization approach in wireless sensor network for efficient communication, *Journal of Advanced Research in Dynamical and Control Systems*, 10, 593–598.

10   Gummadi, A., and RaghavaRao, K. (2018), EECLA: Clustering and localization techniques to improve energy efficient routing in vehicle tracking using wireless sensor networks, *International Journal of Engineering and Technology (UAE)*, 7, 926–929.

11   Radhouene, M., Chhipa, M.K., Najjar, M., Robinson, S., and Suthar, B. (2017), Novel design of ring resonator based temperature sensor using photonics technology, *Photonic Sensors*, 7(4), 311–316.

12   Krishna, M.N.V., Harsha, N.S., Kasula, V.D.K., and Swain, G. (2017), Optimization of energy aware path routing protocol in wireless sensor networks, *International Journal of Electrical and Computer Engineering*, 7(3), 1268–1277.

13   Hussain, M. A., and Duraisamy, B. (2020), Minimizing the packets drop by system fault in wireless infrastructure less network due to buffer overflow and constrained energy, *International Journal of Advanced Science and Technology*, 29(5).

Chapter 7

A lightweight identity-based authentication scheme using elliptic curve cryptography for resource-constrained IoT devices

Yasin Genc and Erkan Afacan

Faculty of Engineering Gazi University, Maltepe/Ankara, Turkey

CONTENTS

7.1 Introduction 114
7.2 Related work 115
7.3 Definitions 116
    7.3.1 Internet of Things (IoT) 116
    7.3.2 Architecture of Internet of Things 119
        7.3.2.1 Perception layer 120
        7.3.2.2 Network layer 121
        7.3.2.3 Application layer 121
    7.3.3 Resource-constrained Internet of Things devices 121
    7.3.4 Elliptic curve cryptograph (ECC) 121
        7.3.4.1 Point addition 122
        7.3.4.2 Point subtraction 123
        7.3.4.3 Point doubling 124
        7.3.4.4 Scalar multiplication 124
        7.3.4.5 Elliptic curve discrete logarithm
                problem (ECDLP) 124
    7.3.5 Identity-based encryption (IBE) 124
7.4 Proposed scheme 125
    7.4.1 Set-up phase 126
    7.4.2 Things/device register phase 127
    7.4.3 Mutual authentication phase 127
    7.4.4 Message phase 128
7.5 Implementation of the proposed scheme 129
7.6 Security requirements 133
    7.6.1 Privacy 133
    7.6.2 Data integrity 133
    7.6.3 Mutual authentication 133
    7.6.4 Accessibility 134
    7.6.5 Non-repudiation 134
    7.6.6 Identity privacy 134

DOI: 10.1201/9781003355946-7

7.7   Security analysis.. 134
      7.7.1   Mutual authentication 134
      7.7.2   Privacy 135
      7.7.3   Data integrity... 135
      7.7.4   Identity privacy 135
      7.7.5   Non-repudiation 136
      7.7.6   Forward security 136
      7.7.7   Random oracle model security 136
7.8   Performance analysis 137
      7.8.1   Computation cost analysis 138
      7.8.2   Communication cost analysis............................. 139
7.9   Conclusion.. 139
References.. 140

7.1 INTRODUCTION

Today, Internet of Things (IoT) technology is increasing in popularity with its use in applications such as smart grids, sensors, robots, smart agriculture, smart cities, smart homes, smart transportation systems (ITS), and e-health [1–6]. IoT is a network of things that enables many things/devices to communicate with each other. Unlike a basic network structure consisting of computers, this network refers to the concept that many things such as smart phones, smart watches, sensors, medical devices, and vehicles come together. Although the IoT has many benefits, it also brings serious security problems [7]. IoT devices enable us to receive services by sharing our personal data with the applications we use throughout the day. However, this can pose a serious security issue. Personal data such as our personal behaviors, health measurements, the way we speak, and our composure in the face of events can be produced. The processing of these data without our consent can cause serious problems [8]. Theft of our personal data or the wrong results of the applications will cause serious damage.

Wireless communication technologies are the basic communication method in IoT [3]. However, this communication technology is inherently vulnerable to cyber-attacks. For this reason, it is of great importance to ensure confidentiality and data security. Access control, authentication, data integrity, and confidentiality are the main security problems in IoT [7, 8]. There are many methods to ensure security. The first thing that comes into mind is cryptography. Cryptography methods and authentication schemes are commonly used to avoid security problems [9]. However, IoT devices with constrained resources in features such as processing power, storage, and bandwidth cannot perform expensive mathematical operations [10]. The choice of cryptographic method and authentication scheme gains an important dimension due to these constrained resources features of IoT devices. However, these restrictions should not compromise security criteria.

The public key cryptography (PKC) method is widely used today. But this method is difficult to use in systems with constrained resources due to the need for public key infrastructure (PKI) and certificates. With the identity-based encryption (IBE) method, identity information is used as a public key. Thus, the need for PKI and certificates is eliminated [12]. Things/devices that are included in the IoT have unique identity (such as an IP address or Mac address) that are suitable for IBE. However, the pairing-based mathematical operations used in IBE are not suitable for resource-constrained devices due to their cost. It is more appropriate to use elliptic curve cryptography (ECC)-based mathematical operations instead of pairing-based. Thus, a lightweight method is obtained for resource-constrained IoT devices.

In this chapter, a lightweight identity-based authentication scheme using ECC for resource-constrained IoT devices has been proposed. Due to the constrained resources of IoT devices, lightweight encryption based on ECC and identity-based authentication has been used together. In the proposed scheme, things/devices can use anonymous identity. In this way, they can preserve their privacy by using their anonymous identity in communications where they want to remain anonymous. However, the system administrator is known to which device the anonymous IDs belongs. Thus, if it detects any malicious behavior, then the device will be punished or removed from the network. The security of the proposed scheme is proven by a random oracle model. Our scheme performs both mutual authentication and message signing together. Moreover, besides the general message, it can also send encrypted messages for confidential information. Thus, the security of confidential information is ensured. In addition, the concept of IoT, ECC, and IBE methods is explained, and computation and communication costs are compared with the existing schemes.

7.2 RELATED WORK

Many mutual authentication schemes for resource-constrained IoT devices have been proposed in the literature. These studies, which have different characteristics, basically try to minimize the lack of resource constraints. Authentication schemes developed to ensure security use different cryptographic methods. Different authentication schemes are used in IoT devices [13–23]. RFID is one of the most widely used among resource-constrained IoT devices. Therefore, many authentication schemes have been proposed. In RFID [26], tree-based and third-party authentication methods are used. Symmetric and asymmetric key schemes are suggested as cryptographic methods for secure communication in the IoT [8]. Authentication schemes are used in IoT; they can be classified as mutual, based on PKC, digital signature, and one-time password and zero knowledge proof [24, 42].

ECC-based authentication schemes are widely used for restricted devices due to the security they provide and the lower key size compared with RSA.

In this way, a scheme that can be used practically in resource-constrained IoT devices can be created while providing high security. Chen et al. [25] proposed an untraceable authentication scheme for RFID. However, this scheme has security flaws. Based on this vulnerability, Shen et al. [14] proposed an authentication scheme for use in RFID. This scheme has proposed an ECC-based secure scheme, taking into account the security vulnerabilities of the previous schemes. Islam et al. [27] proposed self-certified public key agreement scheme.

Lightweight encryption algorithms are a very suitable approach for resource-constrained devices. ECC is suitable for use in lightweight encryption algorithms with the features it provides. Pham et al. [23] proposed lightweight authentication scheme for IoT ecosystem. This scheme allows devices to hide their identities and mutual authentication. Satapathy et al. [15] proposed a lightweight authentication scheme for smart homes. It is designed for resource-constrained devices. Naeem et al. [17] noted scalability in the mutual authentication. They proposed a secure and scalable authentication scheme using ECC. Rostampour et al. [18] proposed authentication scheme using for IoT edge devices. It is convenient to use for resource-constrained IoT devices such as BLE sensor. Arshad et al. [28] proposed scheme using ECC for SIP. It has low computational cost and is secure. Fotouhi et al. [19] proposed a hash chain based lightweight two-factor authentication scheme. Salman et al. [29] proposed identity-based authentication scheme. This scheme is identity-based so it does not need PKI. Yasin et al. [12] proposed IBE scheme for IoT. Markmann et al. [22] proposed federated end-to-end authentication scheme. It is using IBE and ECC. Lohachab et al. [30] proposed inter-device authentication scheme using MQTT for IoT. Lara et al. [31] proposed lightweight authentication scheme for M2M in Industrial IoT. It is also suitable for use in resource-constrained devices. Alzahrani et al. [16] based their proposed device-to-device authentication schemes on ECC and this scheme provides communication without any third party.

7.3 DEFINITIONS

In this section, the basic concept is explained to better understand the proposed scheme. First, the concept of IoT is explained and information about resource-constrained IoT devices is given. Then, ECC and IBE methods are examined.

7.3.1 Internet of things (IoT)

Internet of Things is a huge network of heterogeneous interconnected things/devices. Historically regarded as the beginning of the IoT, the system was first developed to monitor the coffee machine by academics at Cambridge University in 1991. However, the concept of the IoT was first put forward by Kevin Ashton in 1999 [32]. Today, with the development of new technologies and the spread of IoT devices, it has become a network technology that has reached gigantic dimensions. The reason why it has become so widespread is that it has a field of use in many different disciplines. The fact that the number of identifiable IP addresses in today's IPv4 technology has become insufficient has accelerated the transition to IPv6 technology. The use of 2^{128} (approximately 3.4×10^{38}) IP addresses together with IPv6 technology has removed the restrictions in address definitions of IoT devices. The IoT includes basic components such as IoT devices, internet, data storage, and processing, especially the communication protocols used in the communication of things with each other. Technologies in the IoT ecosystem work in harmony with each other. In this ecosystem, sensors, data storage units, application services, microprocessors, and security services are used together with IoT devices [1, 2, 4]. In Figure 7.1, the general view of the IoT is given.

IoT affects many areas of human life. The fact that this effect is so great is undoubtedly that IoT applications make human life easier. Thanks to Industry 4.0 and developments in communication technologies, IoT applications have become widespread. In many regions of the world, different applications and projects are developed based on IoT. Among these areas, smart cities, industrial, construction sector, connected vehicles, smart energy management, health services, and smart agriculture applications are the trend [6]. Figure 7.2 shows the frequency of use of IoT applications and the percentage of usage and trend change in different regions of the world.

Figure 7.1 IoT overview.

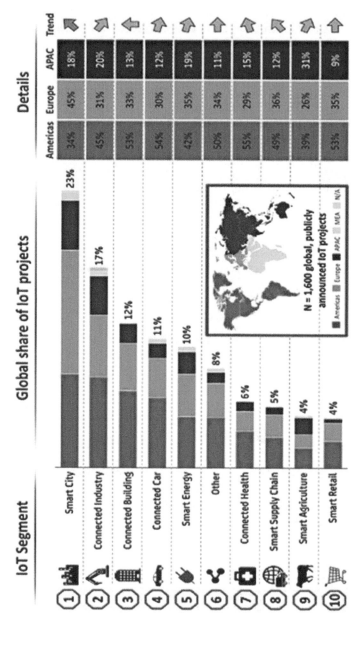

Figure 7.2 IoT applications [34].

Each application area brings with it many opportunities. Let us explain some of these applications. Smart cities offer applications to eliminate the problems that may arise as a result of the migration of people from villages to cities. Many applications such as garbage collection systems [1], parking systems, lighting systems, and traffic monitoring systems are used in smart cities. Thus, the increasing population in cities will be served much better with smart city applications.

In emergencies, the time required to save people's lives is very limited. People lose their lives in natural disasters such as earthquakes, floods, accidents, tsunamis, and avalanches. However, deaths can be minimized with the IoT applications to be developed. Sensors can be used quite effectively to report emergencies. For example, emergency situations such as gas leaks can be reported to people and the nearest emergency centers by sensors [1]. Another example is the forewarning system in case of an earthquake and the applications developed to find the most suitable way for emergency exit will save people's lives

Smart home applications are one of the most frequently used applications by end users, because comfort is indispensable for people in our homes where we live our daily lives. Many electronic devices in our homes are connected to each other to create home automation. We can control this automation as we want with smart phones. Intelligent cleaning robots, which were very rare until 10 years ago, have become an indispensable member of homes today. Thanks to IoT applications, we can remotely control the cleaning and ventilation processes we do at home. Thus, we have accomplished these works while we are at work.

IoT is widely used in agriculture. IoT applications are used in the process of agricultural products from production to consumption. In order to prevent damage to agricultural products, harmful insects, weather changes, and diseases can be detected and precautions can be taken. Thus, the harvest will be more efficient and will make a direct economic contribution.

IoT applications in the healthcare field are used to monitor the health status of patients. In emergencies, necessary interventions are carried out. With remote access to the health status of patients, the quality of care increases and costs decrease.

ITS is a rapidly developing field today. In this field, especially IoT devices are widely used. There is a very intense use of IoT in the areas of connected vehicles, VANET, MANET, and Internet of Vehicle (IoV). Similar to these application areas, IoT applications provide efficiency and comfort in many areas (Figure 7.3).

7.3.2 Architecture of Internet of Things

There are architectural structure recommendations in areas such as application requirements, network topology, communication protocols, business

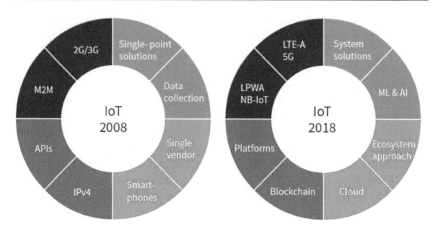

Figure 7.3 Change of related fields in IoT between 2008 and 2018 [35, 36].

Figure 7.4 Architecture of the IoT.

and service models by many organizations and working groups, including organizations such as ITU, IEEE, Cisco, and ETSI [2, 36]. In this subsection, the commonly used three-layer architecture is explained. Each layer has different tasks and technologies. In Figure 7.4, the architecture of the IoT is shown.

The layers in the IoT architecture are perception layer, network layer, and application layer. These layers are described in the following sections.

7.3.2.1 Perception layer

First, let us explain the perception layer, which is the lowest layer. In this layer, things/devices are defined. Then, it collects data around objects/devices through sensors. Technologies such as RFID, GPS, sensors, and WSN are used in the perception layer. RFID, on the one hand, is a non-contact identification system that transmits the environmental information of any thing/device by radiofrequency. WSN, on the other hand, are devices used to receive information such as physical environmental conditions and location of objects. GPS is a global positioning system and is used to obtain location information [2, 4]. Sensors are of great importance for the collection of data.

7.3.2.2 Network layer

The network layer is the place where the communication and connection of all things/devices in the IoT is carried out. It enables processing and transmission of data collected in the perception layer. Internet, Wi-Fi [7], Bluetooth, MQTT, and XMPP technologies are used in this layer.

7.3.2.3 Application layer

The application layer is at the top of the architecture and includes applications that serve the end user. It can be configured according to the same standard among the connected objects in lieu of the service provided. Applications such as smart grid, smart city, smart transportation, and e-health are included in this layer [7].

7.3.3 Resource-constrained Internet of Things devices

The concept of IoT device describes devices with communication, data storage, data processing, and perception capabilities with other devices. It consists of sensors and embedded systems that require wireless connectivity. There are IoT devices with different functions used in areas such as consumers and industry. The IoT device ecosystem includes many different objects/devices. Resource-constrained devices have an important place in these devices. Constrained IoT devices have low storage space, low bandwidth, limited processing capability, limited power supply, and small physical area [38].

Many widely used RFID and sensors are resource-constrained IoT devices. These things have small memory and low computing power. Therefore, the projects should be designed according to the limited resources, because these IoT devices are used almost everywhere today. It is not possible to achieve the desired full efficiency in projects realized without considering limited resources.

7.3.4 Elliptic curve cryptograph (ECC)

Elliptic curve cryptograph is a PKC method introduced in the mid-1980s. It is very popular today and is used in many applications. Compared to RSA, it provides the same level of security with a shorter key size [39]. Thus, it requires less memory size. In this method, mathematical operations are usu-ally carried out on finite fields [40].

Let $\mathbb{F}_p$ be a prime finite field, where p represents the prime number. Similarly, it can be defined in a binary field $\mathbb{F}_{2^m}$ and an extension field $\mathbb{F}_{p^n}$. The elliptic curve E over $\mathbb{F}_p$ is denoted by $E(\mathbb{F}_p)$ or $E/\mathbb{F}_p$. Weierstrass equation, which is elliptic curve E equation, is given in Equation (7.1),

$$E : y^2 = x^3 + A_1 x + A_2 \quad (\mathrm{mod}\, p) \tag{7.1}$$

where A_1, A_2 are integers less than prime number p. Equation (7.2) should be satisfied. If Equation (2) is not satisfied, the values of A_1 and A_2 are reselected.

$$4A_1{}^3 + 27A_2{}^2 \neq 0 \quad (\mathrm{mod}\, p) \tag{7.2}$$

Let us choose the values of A_1 and A_2 for the elliptic curve E on $\mathbb{F}_p$ as -1 and 0, respectively. The obtained elliptic curve $y^2 = x^3 - x$ equation is shown in Figure 7.5.

7.3.4.1 Point addition

Let us describe any two points $Q_1(x_1, y_1)$ and $Q_2(x_2, y_2)$ on the $E/\mathbb{F}_p$. The addition of two points is shown as below. This mathematical operation is called point addition in elliptic curves.

$$Q_3(x_3, y_3) = Q_1(x_1, y_1) + Q_2(x_2, y_2) \tag{7.3}$$

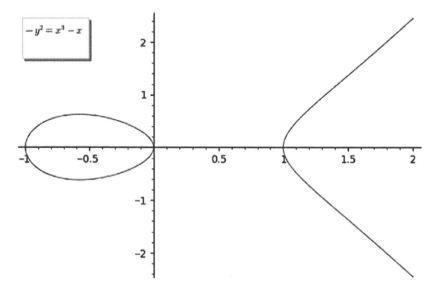

Figure 7.5 Elliptic curve $E(-1,0)$.

In the point addition operation shown in Equation (7.3), if $x_1 \neq x_2$, the following operations are performed.

$$x_3 = \delta^2 - x_1 - x_2 \tag{7.4}$$

$$y_3 = \delta(x_1 - x_3) - y_1 \tag{7.5}$$

$$\delta = \frac{y_2 - y_1}{x_2 - x_1} \tag{7.6}$$

Finally, $Q_3(x_3, y_3)$ is obtained. But if $x_1 = x_2$, then this case is defined as infinity point (O). In Figure 7.6, point addition on elliptic curve is shown.

7.3.4.2 Point subtraction

Let us describe any two points $Q_1(x_1, y_1)$ and $Q_2(x_2, y_2)$ on the $E/\mathbb{F}_p$. The negative of any point on the elliptic curve is described as shown below. Then, the point addition operation is performed.

$$-Q_1(x_1, y_1) = Q_1(x_1, -y_1) \tag{7.7}$$

$$Q_3(x_3, y_3) = Q_2(x_2, y_2) + Q_1(x_1, -y_1) \tag{7.8}$$

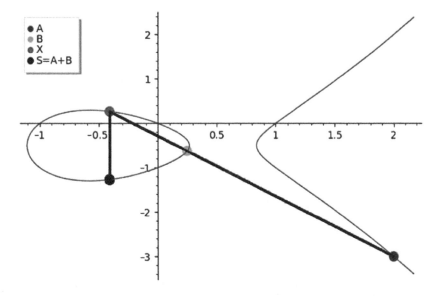

Figure 7.6 Point addition on elliptic curve.

7.3.4.3 Point doubling

Let us describe any two points $Q_1(x_1, y_1)$ and $Q_2(x_2, y_2)$ on the $E/\mathbb{F}_p$. If $Q_1(x_1, y_1)$ and $Q_2(x_2, y_2)$ are equal, point doubling is performed as follows.

$$Q_3(x_3, y_3) = Q_1(x_1, y_1) + Q_2(x_2, y_2) \tag{7.9}$$

where $Q_1(x_1, y_1) = Q_2(x_2, y_2)$ and $Q_3(x_3, y_3) = Q_1(x_1, y_1) + Q_1(x_1, y_1) = 2Q_1(x_1, y_1)$. x_3 and y_3 are found as below.

$$x_3 = \delta^2 - 2x_1 \tag{7.10}$$

$$y_3 = \delta(x_1 - x_3) - y_1 \tag{7.11}$$

$$\delta = \frac{3x_1^2 + A_1}{2y_1} \tag{7.12}$$

7.3.4.4 Scalar multiplication

Let us describe any points $Q_1(x_1, y_1)$ on the $E/\mathbb{F}_p$. For scalar multiplication operation, point addition and point doubling operations are performed. The scalar multiplication $13Q_1$ is calculated as shown in Equation (7.13).

$$13Q_1 = 2(2(Q_1 + Q_1)) + 2(Q_1 + Q_1) + Q_1 \tag{7.13}$$

7.3.4.5 Elliptic curve discrete logarithm problem (ECDLP)

Let us describe any points Q_1 on the $E/\mathbb{F}_p$. Suppose the degree of point Q_1 is q. Let us pick a random number $k \in Z_q^*$. Q_2 is obtained by the operation in Equation (7.14). Even if one knows the points Q_1 and Q_2, it is quite difficult to calculate the value of k. The security of ECC is built on ECDLP [43].

$$Q_2 = k.Q_1 \tag{7.14}$$

7.3.5 Identity-based encryption (IBE)

The identity-based encryption idea was put forward by Shamir in 1984 [44]. The main purpose of this idea: instead of generating the public key for users, select a public key from information belonging to itself such as e-mail, ID number. Thus, there is no need for PKI and certificates. Users can utilize information they cannot deny as a public key. However, IBE was not used in any application for a certain period of time. In 2001, Boneh and Franklin presented the first significant viable solution for the IBE. A scheme based on Weil pairing is proposed that can be used for practical applications.

With this development, the use of IBE has become increasingly common in the following years and today. However, the cost of pairing mathematical operations is seen as an important problem. Therefore, proposals for pairing-free IBE using elliptic curves are becoming common.

7.4 PROPOSED SCHEME

The proposed method consists of four phases. For secure communication of things/devices, they must first establish a common protocol. In the network structure, there is the server, as the central authority (CA) server and the things/devices need to be communicated. The reason for the need of a CA is to generate a public key parameter, create an anonymous identity, detect insecure things/devices, and ensure their punishment. Before things/devices communicate, they initiate sessions with each other by key exchange and mutual authentication. A general representation of the proposed scheme is given in Figure 7.7. This figure is a representation of the communication between the two devices and the CA server. First, the devices register to the CA server with their real IDs. Then, the devices authenticate with each other with the system parameters sent to the devices by the CA. The notation and description used in the scheme are given in Table 7.1. The implementation phases of the proposed method are described in detail below.

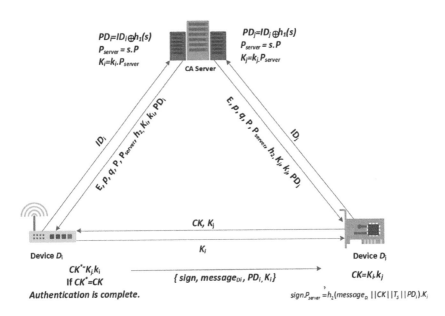

Figure 7.7 The proposed scheme.

Table 7.1 Notation and description of the proposed scheme

Notation	Description
CA	Central authority
D_i, D_j	i[st] and j[st] device
G	Elliptic curve addition group
P_{server}	Public key of CA
$\mathbb{F}_p$	Finite field
CK	Common Key
sign	Signature of device D_i
Enc, Dec	Encryption and Decryption
$message_{D_i}$	Message sent by the device D_i
$\|, \oplus$	Concatenation and XOR operation

7.4.1 Set-up phase

In this section, system parameters are created by the CA. These parameters are given to the things/devices registered with CA. Thus, any device that cannot register with the CA cannot log in into the system. This also allows checking whether registered devices are secure. The steps of this phase are as follows.

1. The CA chooses A_1, A_2 and p values for the elliptic curve $E(A_1, A_2)$ over $\mathbb{F}_p$. $A_1, A_2 \in \mathbb{F}_p$ and p is a prime number large enough. Then, it is checked whether A_1 and A_2 values satisfy the Equation (7.15), and if not, A_1 and A_2 values are selected again.

$$4A_1^3 + 27A_2^2 \neq 0 \pmod{p} \tag{7.15}$$

2. The base point P of the selected elliptic curve $E(A_1, A_2)$ is chosen and its order q is determined.
3. Two secure one-way hash functions $h_1 : \{0,1\}^* \to Z_q^*$ and $h_2 : \{0,1\}^* \to Z_q^*$ are chosen.
4. The CA chooses a random private key $s \in Z_q^*$ and calculates its public key as Equation (7.16).

$$P_{server} = s.P \tag{7.16}$$

After all steps are done, the CA creates the public parameters $\{E, p, q, P, P_{server}, h_1, h_2\}$ of the system.

7.4.2 Things/device register phase

In this section, the devices that want to be included in the communication network are registered into the system by the CA. Devices only report their unique identity to the CA. This unique identity can be IP address, MAC address, or IMEI number. The connection between pseudo-identity and real identity of devices is known only to the CA. If there is any problem with the device, it will be detected and penalized by the CA. The steps of this phase are as follows.

1. The real identity of the device is unique to itself and is expressed by ID_i, where i is the registration order of the device. The device gives the real identity ID_i to the CA and registers in the system.
2. The CA calculates the pseudo-identity PD_i of the device D_i as in Equation (7.17).

$$PD_i = ID_i \oplus h_1(s) \tag{7.17}$$

3. The CA selects a random private key $k_i \in Z_q^*$ for device D_i and calculates its public key K_i as Equation (7.18).

$$K_i = s.k_i.P = k_i.P_{server} \tag{7.18}$$

4. The CA transmits the system parameters $\{E, p, q, P, P_{server}, h_2\}$, the public key K_i, device private key k_i, and the pseudo identity PD_i to the device in a secure way and is stored on the device. The CA does not share $\{h_1\}$, it just uses it to generate pseudo-id. This step is performed for each registered device.

7.4.3 Mutual authentication phase

In this section, mutual authentication is performed between the devices registered in the system. Mutual authentication is needed before secure communication between devices can start. After mutual authentication between devices, the session is started. The session duration is for a certain period and the session is terminated at the end of the period. The common key CK is determined by mutual authentication and CK is used by the devices during the session. Mutual authentication between device D_i and device D_j is performed as follows.

1. Device D_i sends the public key K_i to device D_j.
2. Device D_j calculates the common key CK using K_i as shown in Equation (7.19).

$$CK = K_i.k_j \tag{7.19}$$

3. Device D_j sends the calculated common key CK and public key K_j to device D_i.
4. Device D_i performs the operation in Equation (7.20) and checks whether Equation (7.21) is satisfied. If provided, mutual authentication is carried out. Otherwise, mutual authentication is denied.

$$CK^* = K_j.k_i \qquad (7.20)$$

$$CK^* \overset{?}{=} CK \qquad (7.21)$$

7.4.4 Message phase

Devices that want to communicate with each other must first have completed the mutual authentication phase. A session is opened with the common key CK on the devices and communication begins. The session duration depends on a certain time and this time is indicated by T_s. When the device D_i will send a general message, it signs the message with a digital signature. However, the secret message is encrypted and signed with a digital signature and sent to the other device. The steps of this phase are as follows.

1. Device D_i creates the signature $sign$ of its message as follows. $message_{D_i}, CK, T_s, PD_i$ define device D_i's message, the common key, the session duration, and device D_i's pseudo-id, respectively.

$$\chi = h_2(message_{D_i} \| CK \| T_s \| PD_i) \qquad (7.22)$$

$$sign = \chi k_i \qquad (7.23)$$

2. Device D_i sends parameters $\{sign, message_{D_i}, PD_i, K_i\}$ to device D_j.
3. First, device D_j calculates Equation (7.24) to check the reliability of the message. The common key CK and T_s information is available in device D_j.

$$sign.P_{server} \overset{?}{=} h_2(message_{D_i} \| CK \| T_s \| PD_i).k_i.P_{server} \qquad (7.24)$$

4. If the following equality is satisfied, the signature and message are verified.

$$sign.P_{server} \overset{?}{=} h_2(message_{D_i} \| CK \| T_s \| PD_i).K_i \qquad (7.25)$$

Any device may want to make encrypted messaging with the other device with which it communicates as a result of mutual authentication. In this case, the device D_i encrypts the message and sends to the device D_j. Encryption and decryption of the message by the devices is described as follows.

1. Device D_i encrypts the message using the common key CK and the session duration T_S information as follows.

$$Enc\left(message_{D_i}\right) = message_{D_i} \oplus h_2(CK\|T_S) \tag{7.26}$$

2. Device D_i sends the encrypted message to the receiving device D_j.
3. Device D_j decrypts the encrypted message using the common key CK and the session duration information T_S. The decryption process is performed as follows.

$$Dec\left(message_{D_i}\right) = Enc\left(message_{D_i}\right) \oplus h_2(CK\|T_S) \tag{7.27}$$

$$Dec\left(message_{D_i}\right) = message_{D_i} \tag{7.28}$$

The proof of Equation (7.27) is performed as follows.

Let us assume that device D_j perform XOR operation with $h_2(CK\|T_S)$, which is calculated on both sides of encrypted message in Equation (7.26).

$$Enc\left(message_{D_i}\right) \oplus h_2(CK\|T_S) = message_{D_i} \oplus h_2(CK\|T_S) \oplus h_2(CK\|T_S) \tag{7.29}$$

from here, Equation (7.30) is obtained.

$$message_{D_i} = Enc\left(message_{D_i}\right) \oplus h_2(CK\|T_S) \tag{7.30}$$

Thus, D_j decrypts the encrypted message using the common key CK and the session duration T_S.

7.5 IMPLEMENTATION OF THE PROPOSED SCHEME

In this section, the proposed scheme is implemented with the elliptic curve P-384 proposed by NIST [33]. The parameters of elliptic curve NIST P-384 are given in Table 7.2. C++ is used as the programming language. The implementation steps from the proposed model are given below.

The CA chooses a random private key $s \in Z_q^*$ and computes its public key $P_{server} = s.P$ as shown in Equation (7.16).

$s = 35553997510151970283539678241129177709416977708861$
$38710989922471512651927536981803105622023720958617 53$
$407232435722809.$

Table 7.2 NIST P-384 parameters

Parameter	Value
p	0xFFFFFFFFFFFFFFFFFFFFFFFFFFFFFFFFFFFFFFFFFFFFFFFF FFFFFFFFF FFEFFFFFFFFF0000000000000000FFFFFFFF
A_1	0XFFFFFFFFFFFFFFFFFFFFFFFFFFFFFFFFFFFFFFFFFFFFFFFFFFFF FFFF FFFF FFFEFFFFFFFFF0000000000000000FFFFFFFC
A_2	0XB3312FA7E23EE7E4988E056BE3F82D19181D9C6EFE81411203140 88F5013875AC656398D8A2ED19D2A85C8EDD3EC2AEF
q	0XFFFFFFFFFFFFFFFFFFFFFFFFFFFFFFFFFFFFFFFFFFFFFFFFC763 4D81F4372DDF581A0DB248B0A77AECEC196ACCC52973
P_x	0XAA87CA22BE8B05378EB1C71EF320AD746E1D3B628BA79B9859F 741E0 82542A385502F25DBF55296C3A545E3872760AB7
P_y	0X3617DE4A96262C6F5D9E98BF9292DC29F8F41DBD289A147CE 9D A3113B5F0B8C00A60B1CE1D7E819D7A431D7C90EA0E5F

$$P = (P_x, P_y) = (2624703509579968926862315674456698189185292349110921338781561590092551885473805008902238805397571978665087247673208783257109614890299855467512895201081792878530488613155947092059024805031998844192244386437603929473330780865116278 71).$$

$$P_{server} = s.P = (1099289233907372626856869605780793963205582728676742425911961723735237832584210465275237541176365991180523499238321311129824186990228316791567730447563089086882758585552441747498712728219568431890894211758471533518232428699454443397 3).$$

Later, devices are registered by CA with unique identification numbers. Device D_i, unique identification number ID_i can be defined as follows.

$$ID_i = 43288676645690930856546209006289020914386478049211843158885821066 00.$$

The CA calculates the pseudo-identity PD_i of the device D_i as in Equation (7.17). h_1, SHA-512 has been chosen as the secure hash function.

$$h_1(s) = 10347011365501292394880242733042526965886625173957420579134138980672906317841341655726315384388702681516347635692410590403437038060776886074840755122730525.$$

Later, XOR operation is performed between the unique identification number ID_i of device D_i and $h_1(s)$, then, the pseudo identity PD_i is calculated.

$$PD_i = ID_i \oplus h_1(s) = 10347011365501292394880242733042526965886625173957420579134138980672906317841341655726311075385027185996728762743371195265096056856518286820804893313231861.$$

The CA selects a random private key $k_i \in Z_q^*$ for device D_i and calculates its public key K_i as shown in Equation (7.18).

$$k_i = 88723408485254541831878710526666622763930602421772456862240679706179803374574351785855630252731738789865120627765528.$$

$$K_i = s.k_i.P = k_i P_{server} = (34813058727721490664722074182888774919476405416131886615269499423711177316910498664772616932546446529527162253241612, 12752737750319075099926124670475119621356533406298679022807626501203015594035942978737786863090477642659205120493522).$$

Device D_j calculates the common key CK using K_i and k_j as below.

$$k_j = 1592663661496516190919297956048880424865451140189926715344230991524693348129329248253403825355523439882208666766 3892.$$

$$CK = K_i.k_j = (11113890850659441642848613940374104625562409655016751841343376167400891415445207806062514155010520425575903901780 20, 28491916164484516837834444970878689654774128718621521947894434437548593322314171127403298124310305942632025566860972).$$

Device D_j sends the calculated the common key CK and public key K_j to device D_i.

$$K_j = s.k_j.P = k_j P_{server} = (22511925843599866673160579840115879017047281433269191091069933403954775758276122807856031277889596868257597566485733, 14427941529065148084675432589060763496676852347284656628921012380993354413956798465972773417883283661184938157385009).$$

Device D_j calculates the common key CK^* using K_j and k_i as below.

$$CK^* = K_j.k_i = (111138908506594416428486139403741046255624096550167518413433761674008914154452078060625141550105290425575903901780202,28491916164484516837834444970878686547741287186215219478944344375485933223141711274032981243103059426320255668609722)$$

Finally, it is checked whether the common key CK^* and CK are equal. Since equality is ensured, mutual authentication is provided.

$$CK^* = CK \qquad (7.31)$$

If both devices want to send a message after performing the mutual authentication phase, device D_i first performs the following calculation. Here, the message is "sensor1: air temperature: 35 C, sensor2: humidity: 4%" and the session duration Ts is "25.04.2022" and other information is calculated above. All information concatenation operation ‖ after that, the hashing process is performed in Equation (7.32).

$$\chi = h_2(message_{D_i}\|CK\|T_S\|PD_i) \qquad (7.32)$$

$$\chi = 594758590110566659830522483933936052172348323881939438098230358926349779776360639502727141295175103358298562186986122569577204693586847795506530058751976411.$$

Then, the device D_i calculates its signature as in Equation (7.33).

$$sign = \chi k_i \qquad (7.33)$$

$$sign = \chi k_i = 52769009340493872557283714878810188523993230265101307868169523382256064836888468602222115973958081902295709377212766119967945953962809071703654261101548539706832705744607398329835442582122008792097156786650430014861882018802350468574280296799453375770614826701215770448.$$

Device D_i sends parameters $\{sign, message_{D_i}, PD_i, K_i\}$ to device D_j.

Device D_j scalar multiplies the signature by P_{server} and calculates the right side of the equation below. Finally, it checks whether the equality is satisfied.

$$sign.P_{server} \overset{?}{=} h_2(message_{D_i}\|CK\|T_S\|PD_i).K_j \qquad (7.34)$$

$$sign.P_{server} = (25019627254636104064663814544872181620$$
$$58993184040993893894171608014909754692711474281978$$
$$65238070977790938682213512, 48553768135259083797717$$
$$396337666045062756393601070302657013669992831834597$$
$$15026724086778552962906202333973110303\,62).$$

$$h_1(message_{D_i} \| CK \| T_S \| PD_i).K_j = (25019627254636104064663\,83145$$
$$448721816205899318404099389389417160801490975469271$$
$$14742819786523807097779093868221350\,12, 48553768135259$$
$$083797713963376660450627563936010703026570136699928 3$$
$$183459715026724086778552962906202333973110303 62.$$

Finally, $sign.P_{server} = h_2(message_{D_i} \| CK \| T_S \| PD_i).K_j$ is provided. Thus, the signature and message are verified.

7.6 SECURITY REQUIREMENTS

There are important security requirements to protect the IoT ecosystem and its devices against cyber-attacks. These requirements are defined in the following sections.

7.6.1 Privacy

Privacy is an important security feature in IoT, which may not be mandatory in some scenarios where data are publicly available [41]. Personal and confidential data should not be disclosed or read by unauthorized malicious third parties. A large amount of data are used in IoT applications to collect our personal information. For example, a smartwatch, heart rate, and blood pressure can collect my health data. Against such security problems, encryption or authorization algorithms between devices are used.

7.6.2 Data integrity

It is as important as the confidentiality of the data used in IoT applications that the data are not changed by malicious third parties. Malicious changes to the data will prevent IoT applications from working correctly and will have negative consequences as a result. Any change to be made on the data coming to the vital devices used in the hospital will cause the patient to die.

7.6.3 Mutual authentication

Authentication is an important step in checking the reliability of the device when connecting different devices with each other such as devices in the

IoT ecosystem and a central authority. It can be authorized by a structure being included in the network. Thus, devices perform authentication while communicating with each other. If an unauthorized device wants to communicate with other devices, it will not be able to perform the authentication step.

7.6.4 Accessibility

IoT devices should be accessible when needed. The different types of hardware used in IoT devices, communication protocols, accessibility in case of adverse situations, and service quality are important issues.

7.6.5 Non-repudiation

IoT devices are responsible for the actions they take and the data they send. In order to establish a secure system, devices must not deny the data they have sent. To achieve this, digital signatures are widely used. Devices sign the message or data they send with their own digital signature. Thus, in case of any problems afterwards, he cannot deny the action he has taken because the signature belongs only to him.

Ensuring the security requirements is carried out by using encryption and authentication algorithms. An important issue is that since IoT devices are resource-constrained devices, they may be insufficient when performing mathematical operations. Therefore, the selection of the encryption and authorization algorithm to be selected should be done carefully.

7.6.6 Identity privacy

It may be necessary to not know who the identity used during messaging belongs to. In these cases, anonymity is ensured using pseudo-identity. Knowing the real identity of the device will make it vulnerable to cyber-attack.

7.7 SECURITY ANALYSIS

Many important security problems can exist in the IoT. In this section, it is checked whether the proposed scheme meets the requirements that we define as security requirements. We also test the security of the proposed scheme under the random oracle model (ROM) as the formal security analysis.

7.7.1 Mutual authentication

In the proposed scheme, mutual authentication is carried out with the identities of the devices. When any device wants to communicate with another device, authentication is done with the common key CK. If the device cannot generate the common key CK, mutual authentication will not occur. The private key k_i, k_j of the devices and the public key K_j, K_i of the other devices are used to generate the common key CK. Equation (7.35) shows the generation of the common key CK.

$$CK = K_j.k_i = K_i.k_j \tag{7.35}$$

7.7.2 Privacy

If the data transmitted by the devices are confidential, the message is encrypted. However, since this process involves a cost, encrypting all messages will cause an unnecessary use of resource-constrained IoT devices. In the proposed model, general messages are transmitted only with digital signature and mutual authorization, and the message receiver only checks the authenticity of the message. If it is going to send a secret message, it encrypts the message and sends it to the other device. The receiving device decrypts the message with the common key CK, and the session duration T_s information. Encryption of a message is shown in Equation (7.36).

$$Enc(message) = message \oplus h_2(CK\|T_S) \tag{7.36}$$

7.7.3 Data integrity

Data integrity means that the message sent by the device reaches the receiving device without any modification by third parties. Digital signatures are an ideal way to protect data integrity. In the proposed model, the digital signature will not be verified if the sent message is changed. When the signature is created, the message must be authenticated with the common key CK, session duration T_S, and pseudo-identity PD_i. If the message changes, the signature will not be verified. The generation of the digital signature is given in Equation (7.37).

$$sign = h_2(message_{D_i}\|CK\|T_S\|PD_i).k_i \tag{7.37}$$

7.7.4 Identity privacy

Identity privacy prevents the device from being detected by other devices. In the proposed model, devices are given pseudo-identification by the CA at the registration phase. Thus, the real identity of the devices is hidden. However, when the device causing a security issue is detected, it is detected by the CA and removed from the network. The pseudo-identity PD_i generation using the real identity ID_j of the device and the hash value $h_1(s)$ of the CA's private key s is shown in Equation (7.38).

$$PD_i = ID_j \oplus h_1(s) \tag{7.38}$$

7.7.5 Non-repudiation

The device is responsible for the message it sends. The fact that the device uses pseudo-called identity does not mean that it cannot be held responsible for the messages it sends. The device cannot deny that the message does not belong to it, since they use its digital signature in the messages they sign. When a message like the one below is signed, the device cannot claim that the message does not belong to itself, since it also uses the pseudo-identity PD_i and common key CK.

$$sign = h_2(message_{D_i} \| CK \| T_S \| PD_i).k_i \qquad (7.39)$$

7.7.6 Forward security

Malicious third parties can replace the device based on the information they have obtained from the devices and can send and receive messages like a member of the system. In the proposed model, the session duration is within a certain period and mutual authorization is performed again with the common key. Estimating the s and k values used to generate the device's public key is very difficult due to ECLDP. Therefore, forward security is provided.

$$K_i = s.k_i.P = k_i P_{server} \qquad (7.40)$$

7.7.7 Random oracle model security

The formal security analysis of the proposed model is carried out under the (ROM). Adversary Λ and CA challenge each other in the ROM. CA organizes a game to test the security of the system. Let us first claim that the proposed model is security and then prove it. This analysis phase starts with the setup and ends with the $h1$-oracle and sign-oracle steps.

Theorem: Assuming the proposed model is security under ROM thanks to ECDLP. Let us prove this theory below.

Setup: First, the CA picks a random number of $s \in Z_q^*$ and sets its public key $P_{server} = s.P$. Then, it creates the system parameters $\{E, p, q, P, P_{server}, h_2\}$. Finally, it sends the system parameters to Λ.

h_2-**Oracle**: Initially, the CA maintains a list called a L_{h1} to record queries and answers. The list L_{h1} is arranged in a format as $(\chi, message, CK, T_S, PD_i)$. After Λ receives the system parameters sent to it, the challenge game starts and first performs the $\{message, CK, T_S, PD_i\}$ query. It then sends the query result to the CA. The CA checks if the result is in the L_{h1}. If the query result is in the L_{h1}, χ is sent to Λ. Otherwise, CA picks a random number $\chi \in Z_q^*$ and updates the parameters $(\chi, message, CK, T_S, PD_i)$ in the L_{h1}. Finally, it sends χ to Λ.

Sign-Oracle: CA picks the values $sign, \chi \in Z_q^*$ after the sign query performed by Λ. Then, the CA adds the parameters $(\chi, message, CK, T_S, PD_i)$ to

L_{h1}. It also transmits parameters $\{sign, \chi, message, PD_i, K_i\}$ to Λ. The Λ generates the parameters $\{sign, \chi, message, PD_i, K_i\}$, then CA checks if it satisfies in Equation (7.41).

$$sign.P_{server} \overset{?}{=} \chi K_i \tag{7.41}$$

If not, C ends the game and is proven security. However, if equality is achieved, which is undesirable, then according to the forgery lemma, Λ can generate a valid new message $\{sign^*, \chi^*, message, PD_i, K_i\}$. In this case, the following equations are obtained. Equation (7.43) is quite difficult to solve because of ECDLP.

$$sign^*.P_{server} = \chi^* K_i \tag{7.42}$$

$$sign^*.P_{server} = \chi^*.k_i.P_{server} \tag{7.43}$$

7.8 PERFORMANCE ANALYSIS

The proposed scheme is compared with different schemes to perform performance analysis. The parameters to be compared are computational cost and communication cost. These two parameters are very important in constrained IoT devices. The proposed model can perform both messaging and mutual authentication phases. In this respect, it differs from the models in the literature. In addition, another different aspect is that it is capable of sending both general messages and encrypted messages. The comparison is made as follows: First, the calculation costs of the authentication schemes are compared with the studies based on the mutual authentication scheme. Second, the costs of these phases were compared in studies based on signature generation and verification.

The execution time of the mathematical operations performed first with elliptic curves cryptography is given in Table 7.3. In addition, the execution

Table 7.3 Execute time and descriptions of mathematical operations

Operation	Execute time (ms)	Description
Teccm	0.4127	Point multiplication on ECC
Tecca	0.0032	Point addition on ECC
Th	0.0002	Hash function
Ti	0.1561	Inversion on modulation
Tm	Negligible	Multiplication on modulation
$\oplus$	Negligible	XOR operation
$\parallel$	Negligible	Concatenation operation

time is given for other mathematical operations. In order to compute the execution time of these mathematical operations, a computer with Intel (R) Core (TM) i7-7500U CPU processor and Ubuntu operating system are used. At the same time, C++ GMP [11] is used as a cryptography library. Mathematical operations are repeated 50 times and the average execution time is taken.

7.8.1 Computation cost analysis

Let us compare the proposed scheme with to the models in which mutual authentication is performed. In the proposed scheme, the device D_j computes the common key CK using its private key k_j. Thus, performing one point multiplication $Teccm$ operation. The device D_i performs the same process during the common key verification phase. As a result, the authentication computation cost is calculated as $2Teccm$. Similarly, it is calculated in [16], [27], [45], [46]. The computation costs for authentication of the models are summarized in Table 7.4.

As seen in Table 7.4, the proposed scheme in the Authentication phase is quite good compared with the existing schemes.

Let us compare the signature generation and verification phases during messaging, which is another feature of the proposed model, with similar models. In the proposed model, one hash function and multiplication on modulation operation is required for signing the message, and multiplication operation can be neglected. As a result, the signature generation cost is calculated as $1Th$. Similarly, it is calculated in [47–49]. The computation costs for signature generation of the models are shown in Table 7.5. In the message verification phase, two-point multiplication and one hash function are performed. As a result, the signature verification cost is calculated as $2Teccm + Th$. Similarly, it is calculated in [47–49]. The computation costs for signature verification of the schemes are shown in Table 7.5. Signature generation, signature verification, and millisecond are denoted as SG, SV, and ms, respectively. As seen in Table 7.5, the proposed scheme in the SG phase is quite good compared with the existing schemes. However, it gives good results in the SV phase, except in [48].

Table 7.4 Comparison of authentication computation cost

Scheme	Authentication computation cost	Execute time (ms)
[16]	$8Teccm + 2Tecca + 6Th$	3.3092
[27]	$6Teccm + 6Th$	2.4774
[45]	$8Teccm + 2Tecca + 9Th$	3.3098
[46]	$7\ Teccm + 8\ Th$	2.8905
The Proposed Scheme	$2\ Teccm$	0.8254

Table 7.5 Comparison of SG and SV computation cost

Scheme	SG (ms)	SV (ms)
[47]	$Teccm + Th = 0.4129$	$3Teccm + 2Tecca + 2Th = 1.2449$
[48]	$Teccm + Th = 0.4129$	$Teccm + Ti + Th = 0.569$
[49]	$2Teccm + Th = 0.8256$	$2Teccm + Tecca + 2Th = 0.829$
The Proposed Scheme	$Th = 0.0002$	$2Teccm + Th = 0.8256$

Table 7.6 Comparison of communication cost

Model	Communication cost (bytes)
[47]	108
[48]	108
[49]	164
The Proposed Scheme	80

7.8.2 Communication cost analysis

For the calculation of the communication cost, let us first determine the size of the elements used in bytes. Let us assume that the elements in Z_q^* are 20 bytes, the elliptic curve addition group G is 40 bytes, and the size of the real ID of the device and timestamp Ts are 4 bytes. In the proposed scheme, when the device signs the D_i, message sends the $\{sign, message_{D_i}, PD_i, K_i\}$ parameters to the D_j. This parameter is not included in the calculation since $message_{D_i}$ is in all schemes. The total communication cost, $K_i \in G$ and $sign, PD_i \in Z_q^*$ sent to device D_j is 40 + 2 * 20 = 80 bytes. Similarly, it is calculated in [47, 48, 49]. The communication costs of the schemes are shown in Table 7.6. As seen in Table 7.6, the proposed scheme gives good results compared with the existing schemes in terms of communication cost.

7.9 CONCLUSION

In this chapter, a lightweight identity-based authentication scheme for resource-constrained IoT devices is proposed. It uses ECC. IoT devices appear in every aspect of our lives. These devices, which are so common, are important in security. Because throughout the day, our personal data are collected by these devices and transferred to other devices or applications. The security of the devices to which the data are sent becomes an important problem in this part. Authentication of the devices to which the data are sent is the first step to ensure security. Thus, authenticated devices can securely exchange data. In the proposed model, digital signature is used for message security and integrity as well as mutual authentication. Moreover, if the messages are confidential, they can be sent after encryption by the device. The proposed scheme includes many applications with these features. Another important issue is that IoT devices are insufficient in terms of many resources such as low memory, low bandwidth, and low power. This criterion appears as an obstacle to the security related designs of IoT devices. In this chapter, a design is made considering these limitations. Afterwards, comparisons are made according to the existing schemes. The computation cost in the mutual authentication phase is quite good compared with the existing schemes. In the signature generation phase, it showed the same positive performance and gave better results than the existing schemes. In the signature verification phase, only [48] gives better results than our proposed. Finally, the communication cost is compared and the proposed method give good results compared with the existing schemes. Because of these features, it has the features of an efficient lightweight authentication scheme. We also tested our scheme, which gives good results in terms of performance, in terms of security. It has successfully passed random oracle model security analysis and other security tests. In order to make the proposed model more understandable, it is implemented with the program language and the results are verified. Thus, we propose a secure and efficient scheme that can be used in resource-constrained IoT devices.

REFERENCES

1 Balaji, S., Karan Nathani, and R. Santhakumar. "IoT technology, applications and challenges: a contemporary survey," *Wireless Personal Communications*, vol. 108.1, pp. 363–388, 2019.

2 Gupta, Brij B., and Megha Quamara. "An overview of Internet of Things (IoT): Architectural aspects, challenges, and protocols," *Concurrency and Computation: Practice and Experience*, vol. 32.21, p. e4946, 2020.

3 Chettri, Lalit, and Rabindranath Bera. "A comprehensive survey on Internet of Things (IoT) toward 5G wireless systems," *IEEE Internet of Things Journal*, vol. 7.1, pp. 16–32, 2019.

4 Kashani, Mostafa Haghi, et al. "A systematic review of IoT in healthcare: Applications, techniques, and trends," *Journal of Network and Computer Applications*, vol. 192, p. 103164, 2021.

5 Čolaković, Alem, and Mesud Hadžialić. "Internet of Things (IoT): A review of enabling technologies, challenges, and open research issues," *Computer Networks*, vol. 144, pp. 17–39, 2018.

6 Elijah, Olakunle, et al. "An overview of Internet of Things (IoT) and data analytics in agriculture: Benefits and challenges," *IEEE Internet of Things Journal*, vol. 5.5, pp. 3758–3773, 2018.

7 Hassan, Wan Haslina. "Current research on Internet of Things (IoT) security: A survey," *Computer Networks*, vol. 148, pp. 283–294, 2019.

8 Nguyen, Kim Thuat, Maryline Laurent, and Nouha Oualha. "Survey on secure communication protocols for the Internet of Things," *Ad Hoc Networks*, vol. 32, pp. 17–31, 2015.

9   El-Hajj, Mohammed, et al. "A survey of internet of things (IoT) authentication schemes," *Sensors*, vol. 19.5, p. 1141, 2019.

10 Ye, Ning, et al. "An efficient authentication and access control scheme for perception layer of internet of things," Applied Mathematics & Information Sciences, vol. 8, 2014. DOI: 10.12785/amis/080416.

11 GMP Library, Access Link: https://gmplib.org/

12 Genç, Yasin, and Erkan Afacan. "Identity-based encryption in the internet of things." In *2021 29th Signal Processing and Communications Applications Conference (SIU)*. IEEE, 2021.

13 Alizai, Zahoor Ahmed, Noquia Fatima Tareen, and Iqra Jadoon. "Improved IoT device authentication scheme using device capability and digital signatures." In *2018 International Conference on Applied and Engineering Mathematics (ICAEM)*. IEEE, 2018.

14 Shen, Han, et al. "Efficient RFID authentication using elliptic curve cryptography for the internet of things." *Wireless Personal Communications*, vol. 96.4, pp. 5253–5266, 2017.

15 Satapathy, Utkalika, et al. "An ECC based lightweight authentication protocol for mobile phone in smart home." In *2018 IEEE 13th International Conference on Industrial and Information Systems (ICIIS)*. IEEE, 2018.

16 Alzahrani, Bander A., et al. "An anonymous device to device authentication protocol using ECC and self-certified public keys usable in Internet of Things based autonomous devices," *Electronics*, vol. 9.3, p. 520, 2020.

17 Naeem, Muhammad, et al. "A scalable and secure RFID mutual authentication protocol using ECC for Internet of Things," *International Journal of Communication Systems*, vol. 33.13, p. e3906, 2020.

18 Rostampour, Samad, et al. "ECCbAP: A secure ECC-based authentication protocol for IoT edge devices," *Pervasive and Mobile Computing*, vol. 67, p. 101194, 2020.

19 Fotouhi, Mahdi, et al. "A lightweight and secure two-factor authentication scheme for wireless body area networks in health-care IoT," *Computer Networks*, vol. 177, p. 107333, 2020.

20 Benssalah, Mustapha, Izza Sarah, and Karim Drouiche. "An efficient RFID authentication scheme based on elliptic curve cryptography for Internet of Things," *Wireless Personal Communications*, vol. 117.3, pp. 2513–2539, 2021.

21 Gabsi, Souhir, et al. "Novel ECC-Based RFID Mutual Authentication Protocol for Emerging IoT Applications." *IEEE Access*, vol. 9, pp. 130895–130913, 2021.

22 Markmann, Tobias, Thomas C. Schmidt, and Matthias Wählisch. "Federated end-to-end authentication for the constrained internet of things using IBC and ECC." *ACM SIGCOMM Computer Communication Review*, vol. 45.4, pp. 603–604, 2015.

23 Pham, Chau DM, and Tran Khanh Dang. "A lightweight authentication protocol for D2D-enabled IoT systems with privacy." *Pervasive and Mobile Computing*, vol. 74, p. 101399, 2021.

24 Agrawal, Shubham, and Priyanka Ahlawat. "A survey on the authentication techniques in internet of things." In *2020 IEEE International Students' Conference on Electrical, Electronics and Computer Science (SCEECS)*. IEEE, 2020.

25 Chen, Yalin, and Jue-Sam Chou. "ECC-based untraceable authentication for large-scale active-tag RFID systems." *Electronic Commerce Research*, vol. 15.1, pp. 97–120, 2015.

26 Mbarek, Bacem, Mouzhi Ge, and Tomáš Pitner. "An efficient mutual authentication scheme for internet of things." *Internet of Things*, vol. 9, 2020, 100160.

27 Islam, S. K., and G. P. Biswas. "Design of two-party authenticated key agreement protocol based on ECC and self-certified public keys." *Wireless Personal Communications*, vol. 82.4, pp. 2727–2750, 2015.

28 Arshad, Hamed, and Morteza Nikooghadam. "An efficient and secure authentication and key agreement scheme for session initiation protocol using ECC." *Multimedia Tools and Applications*, vol. 75.1, pp. 181–197, 2016.

29 Salman, Ola, et al. "Identity-based authentication scheme for the Internet of Things." In *2016 IEEE Symposium on Computers and Communication (ISCC)*. IEEE, 2016.

30 Lohachab, Ankur. "ECC based inter-device authentication and authorization scheme using MQTT for IoT networks." *Journal of Information Security and Applications*, vol. 46, pp. 1–12, 2019.

31 Lara, Evangelina, et al. "Lightweight authentication protocol for M2M communications of resource-constrained devices in industrial Internet of Things." *Sensors*, vol. 20.2, 501, 2020.

32 Neisse, Ricardo, et al. "Dynamic context-aware scalable and trust-based IoT security, privacy framework." In *Chapter in Internet of Things Applications-From Research and Innovation to Market Deployment*, IERC Cluster Book, 2014.

33 Chen, Lily, et al. *Recommendations for Discrete Logarithm-Based Cryptography: Elliptic Curve Domain Parameters*. No. NIST Special Publication (SP) 800-186 (Draft). National Institute of Standards and Technology, 2019.

34 The Top 10 IoT Segments in 2018- based on 1600 real IoT projects. Access Link: https://iot-analytics.com/top-10-iot-segments-2018-real-iot-projects/.

35 IoT trend watch 2018. Access Link: https://cdn.ihs.com/www/pdf/IoT-Trend-Watch-eBook.pdf.

36 Itu, T. "Series y: global information infrastructure, internet protocol aspects and next-generation networks." Rec. ITU-T Y 2720, 2009.

37 Hammi, Badis, et al. "A lightweight ECC-based authentication scheme for Internet of Things (IoT)." *IEEE Systems Journal*, vol. 14.3 pp. 3440–3450, 2020.

38 Thakor, Vishal A., Mohammad Abdur Razzaque, and Muhammad RA Khandaker. "Lightweight cryptography algorithms for resource-constrained IoT devices: A review, comparison and research opportunities." *IEEE Access*, vol. 9, pp. 28177–28193, 2021.

39 Genç, Yasin, and Erkan Afacan. "Design and implementation of an efficient elliptic curve digital signature algorithm (ECDSA)." In *2021 IEEE International IOT, Electronics and Mechatronics Conference (IEMTRONICS)*. IEEE, 2021.

40 Genç, Yasin, and Erkan Afacan. "Implementation of new message encryption using elliptic curve cryptography over finite fields." In *2021 International Congress of Advanced Technology and Engineering (ICOTEN)*. IEEE, 2021.

41 Panchiwala, Shivani, and Manan Shah. "A comprehensive study on critical security issues and challenges of the IoT world." *Journal of Data, Information and Management*, vol. 2.4, pp. 257–278, 2020.

42 Pointcheval, David, and Jacques Stern. "Security arguments for digital signatures and blind signatures." *Journal of Cryptology*, vol. 13.3, pp. 361–396, 2000.

43 D. Hankerson, A. Menezes, and S. Vanstone, *Guide to Elliptic Curve Cryptography*. Springer-Verlag, 2004.

44 Shamir, Adi. "Identity-based cryptosystems and signature schemes." In *Advances in Cryptography*, vol. 196, 1984. Springer, Berlin, Heidelberg.

45 Jiang, Qi, Jianfeng Ma, and Youliang Tian. "Cryptanalysis of smart-card-based password authenticated key agreement protocol for session initiation protocol of Zhang et al." *International Journal of Communication Systems*, vol. 28, pp. 1340–1351, 2015.

46 Zhang, Liping, Shanyu Tang, and Zhihua Cai. "Cryptanalysis and improvement of password-authenticated key agreement for session initiation protocol using smart cards." *Security and Communication Networks*, vol. 7.12, pp. 2405–2411, 2014.

47 Cao, Xuefei, et al. "IMBAS: Identity-based multi-user broadcast authentication in wireless sensor networks." *Computer Communications*, vol. 31.4, pp. 659–667, 2008.

48 Kasyoka, Philemon, Michael Kimwele, and Shem Mbandu Angolo. "Multi-user broadcast authentication scheme for wireless sensor network based on elliptic curve cryptography." *Engineering Reports*, vol. 2.7, pp. e12176, 2020.

49 Bashirpour, Hamed, et al. "An improved digital signature protocol to multi-user broadcast authentication based on elliptic curve cryptography in wireless sensor networks (WSNs)." *Mathematical and Computational Applications*, vol. 23.2, 17, 2018.

Chapter 8

Protocol stack in wireless sensor networks for IoT-based applications

R. Dhanalakshmi, Akash Ambashankar and Ganesh Chandrasekhar
KCG College of Technology Chennai, Chennai, India

Arunkumar Sivaraman
School of Computer Science and Engineering Vellore Institute of Technology (VIT), Chennai, India

Mujahid Tabassum
Noroff University College (Noroff Accelerate), Kristiansand, Norway

CONTENTS

8.1 Introduction...146
8.2 Communication protocols 148
   8.2.1 Zigbee..148
   8.2.2 Open source IPv6 automation network (OSIAN)..............148
   8.2.3 DASH7 148
   8.2.4 Bluetooth low energy (Bluetooth LE) 148
   8.2.5 Amazon sidewalk..149
   8.2.6 Design issues in communication protocol..........................149
8.3 Medium access control protocols..149
   8.3.1 Self-organizing medium access control for sensornets
      (SMACS)..149
   8.3.2 Bluetooth 150
   8.3.3 Low energy adaptive clustering hierarchy (LEACH)..........150
   8.3.4 Berkeley media access control (B-MAC)............................150
   8.3.5 Sensor media access control (S-MAC) 151
   8.3.6 Design issues in MAC protocols..151
8.4 Routing protocols 152
   8.4.1 Regular ad hoc network routing approaches......................152
      8.4.1.1 Proactive routing 152
      8.4.1.2 Reactive routing...152
      8.4.1.3 Hybrid routing...152
   8.4.2 Wireless sensor network routing protocol approaches........153
      8.4.2.1 Flat network system..153
      8.4.2.2 Clustering system...153

DOI: 10.1201/9781003355946-8

        8.4.2.3 Data-based protocols 153
        8.4.2.4 Location-based protocols 154
    8.4.3 Wireless sensor network routing techniques 154
        8.4.3.1 Flooding 154
        8.4.3.2 Gossiping... 155
        8.4.3.3 Sensor protocols for information via
                negotiation (SPIN) 155
        8.4.3.4 Low energy adaptive clustering hierarchy 157
        8.4.3.5 Design issues in routing protocols 158
8.5 Transmission control protocols 159
    8.5.1 Traditional transmission control protocols........................ 159
        8.5.1.1 User datagram protocol 159
        8.5.1.2 Transmission control protocol 159
    8.5.2 Wireless sensor network transmission control protocols 160
        8.5.2.1 Congestion detection and avoidance 160
        8.5.2.2 Event-to-sink reliable transport.......................... 161
        8.5.2.3 Reliable multi-segment transport 161
        8.5.2.4 Pump slowly, fetch quickly.............................. 161
        8.5.2.5 GARUDA.. 162
        8.5.2.6 Ad hoc transport protocol 162
    8.5.3 Design issues in transmission control protocols................. 163
8.6 IoT applications of wireless sensor networks 163
8.7 Conclusion.. 164
References 165

8.1 INTRODUCTION

Wireless sensor networks are a key Internet of Things (IoT) concept. They are a collection of sensors that can communicate and collaborate to accomplish a common task. They are used to detect and record changes in their surroundings. These IoT sensors can communicate and exchange information within a small range, and collectively, they deposit information into a central database.

The sensors used in wireless sensor networks are autonomous and are capable of detecting changes in the physical quantities of their environment such as wind, humidity, pressure, and temperature. They commonly find applications in threat detection and environment monitoring.

The network is made up of nodes, with a single node containing one or more sensors [1]. Each node is then connected to the central database. The data gathered by each node are sent to the database and the connected nodes. The nodes may be arranged in any topology, without any particular order or sequence of placement. Each wireless node has a fixed range of communication and can communicate with all entities of the network within that range.

Based on the method of communication, wireless sensor networks can be classified as follows [1]:

1. **Single-Hop Communication**: A type of communication wherein the nodes that desire to communicate are within each other's range, and therefore, a single-hop is enough for the communication to occur.
2. **Multi-Hop Communication**: A type of communication wherein the nodes that desire to communicate are not within each other's range, and therefore, multiple hops are required for the communication to occur. In multi-hop communication, each node also acts as an intermediate node between a source and a destination node.

An IoT wireless sensor network is made up of many components, and each component has a distinct role. A typical wireless sensor network is made up of the following components [2],

1. **Hardware Components**: The major hardware component is a sensor to detect the changes in its environment. It records these changes and sends them to the other IoT sensors, as well as the central database. A sensor is connected to a node, which may be connected to other sensors.
2. **Wireless Interface**: A network interface controller, which connects to a radio-based computer network rather than a wire-based computer network.
3. **Protocol Stack**: Implementation of the networking protocol suite. The suite is the definition of the communication protocols, and the stack is the software implementation of the protocol.
4. **Operating Systems**: System software that controls computer hardware, software assets, and provides basic services for computer programs.
5. **Database**: A database is a collection of organized data, accessed and stored through a computer system.

IoT wireless sensor networks are made up of many nodes, which communicate with each other and the central database. This communication involves data and controls messages. There may exist many paths between the two nodes that desire to communicate with each other, but not all of them may be equally reliable and efficient. Moreover, factors such as path loss, Doppler shift, and fading also affect the quality of transmission through a particular path. Thus, a path must be selected only after taking all these factors into account.

Many protocols are required for the working of a wireless sensor network. These protocols can be divided into the following categories [1]:

1. Communication protocols
2. Media access control protocols

3. Routing protocols
4. Transmission control protocols

Each category of the mentioned protocol stack has a distinct purpose and is imperative in the operation of a wireless sensor network. These categories are discussed in detail in the remainder of this chapter.

8.2 COMMUNICATION PROTOCOLS

A communication protocol is a set of rules that are defined to enable communication between the members of a network. Communications protocols are essential in any wireless network; thus, they are essential in wireless sensor networks as well. Some communication protocols used in wireless sensor networks are discussed below [2].

8.2.1 Zigbee

Zigbee is an implementation of the IEEE 802.15.4 standard, which defines high-level communication protocols that are used to create personal area networks (PAN). It is ideal for wireless networks, which require a small range connection. Zigbee was designed to be a more economical wireless solution for small range requirements [3]. It is commonly used in home automation, local WI-Fi, and other such low-range applications. The low cost, high battery life, and low power consumption make Zigbee an ideal technology to be used in IoT Wireless Sensor Networks.

8.2.2 Open source IPv6 automation network (OSIAN)

OSIAN is a free and open-source version of the IPv6 Network Protocol, which has been specifically redesigned for wireless sensor networks [3]. Its design makes it suitable for IoT networks with nodes of small memory sizes.

8.2.3 DASH7

DASH7 is an open-source protocol based on the ISO/IEC 18000-7 standard that has been designed for wireless sensor networks. It exhibits a long battery life along with a range of up to 2 KM and data transfer speeds of about 167 Kbits/s, which makes it ideal for wireless sensor networks.

8.2.4 Bluetooth low energy (Bluetooth LE)

Bluetooth low energy is a technology used to create wireless PANs that can be used in IoT applications. Despite the name, it has nothing to do with the traditional Bluetooth technology [4]. The main aim of Bluetooth LE is to provide a similar communication range to Bluetooth while reducing power consumption and cost. This makes it feasible for use in wireless sensor networks.

8.2.5 Amazon sidewalk

Amazon Sidewalk is a communication protocol designed and developed by Amazon that uses Bluetooth LE for short-range communications. Thus, it can provide communication at a lower bandwidth usage. The distinct feature of Amazon Sidewalk is that it combines various wireless physical layer protocols and makes them available in a single application layer known as the "Sidewalk Application Layer" [4]. This technology is currently being used to facilitate communication between Amazon Echo IoT devices.

8.2.6 Design issues in communication protocol

When selecting a communication protocol for IoT wireless sensor networks, some of the major factors to look out for are [4] as follows:

- **Cost Factor**: Since an IoT wireless sensor network uses many nodes, there is a lot of exchange of messages between these nodes. Thus, the cost of a single communication between these nodes must be very less.
- **Energy Consumption**: The energy consumed by a node for each communication must be minimized to prevent the overuse of resources.
- **Battery Life**: Each node in an IoT wireless sensor network is wireless and works on battery power. Thus, the communication protocol being used must ensure that the nodes are not required to use a lot of battery power.

8.3 MEDIUM ACCESS CONTROL PROTOCOLS

MAC protocols are used to control each node's access to the communication channel. MAC protocols transfer data in the form of frames from one hop to another [4]. The following MAC protocols [10] are used in Wireless Sensor Networks,

8.3.1 Self-organizing medium access control for sensornets (SMACS)

SMACS uses a protocol known as medium access control to enable the formation of random network topologies without the need to establish global synchronization among the network nodes. A unique characteristic of SMACS is the use of a hybrid method called TDMA/FH also known as non-synchronous scheduled communication, which activates links to be created and a network is scheduled concurrently without the need for expensive overheads information of global integration or time synchronization [5].

8.3.2 Bluetooth

A technology in which compact TDMA protocol is used as the main media access control is known as Bluetooth. It was created to replace cables and infrared links of all devices, which they have succeeded. A combination of devices accessing a shared channel is known as Piconets. A combination of piconets can form an ad hoc network known as Scatternets. Bluetooth is implemented in IoT wireless sensor network to shorten energy consumption [6]. It is used in the following four operational modes:

- **Active mode:** When an IoT node is in the active state, it listens for incoming packets. Upon receiving a data packet, it checks its address. If the packet does not contain the receiving node's address, the packet is simply discarded.
- **Sniff mode:** When an IoT node is in a sniff mode, it listens for incoming data packets only at a particular date and time. The main goal of this mode is to reduce the workload and activity period of the receiving node.
- **Hold mode:** When an IoT node is in a hold mode, it is awaiting another process to be completed. It is inactive for a fixed period and awaits further instruction.
- **Park mode:** When an IoT node is in a park mode, it is awaiting another process to invoke this node. It is inactive for an indefinite time and awaits invoking instruction.

8.3.3 Low energy adaptive clustering hierarchy (LEACH)

LEACH is a method of hierarchical structure that groups nodes into meaningful clusters. Every node gets the head of the cluster in turns [8]. To achieve communication, it uses TDMA between nodes with the head of the cluster. The head transmits the message received to other nodes in the cluster by using the TDMA scheduling method to prevent collision of the messages. Using this scheduled time, each node knows when to be active; this lets us achieve low power consumption and makes the nodes be in a synchronized manner [8].

8.3.4 Berkeley media access control (B-MAC)

Wireless sensor network uses lower power carrier sense MAC protocol. Instead of using traditional methods for organizing networks and clusters, B-MAC uses small Versions of protocols from MAC. It uses CCA (clear channel assessment) and back-offs from packets for adjudication of the channel, acknowledgement from the link layer, and optimize power consumption to low. To achieve less power conditions, it employs a unique scheme for sampling to cut off the duty cycle and eliminate blank sensing [8].

- Whenever an IoT node is active, it listens for activity. If an activity is detected, the node activates its radio components and is active till the data are received [8].
- When receiving is done, the IoT node goes into sleep mode, and if no data are received, then it goes into the sleep mode [7].

B-MAC allows on-the-go rearrangement and duplex interfaces are supplied to achieve better performance like throughput, latency, or power conservation for the system services.

8.3.5 Sensor media access control (S-MAC)

MAC uses the S-MAC protocol to explicitly decrease energy consumption caused when nodes colloids, inactive nodes, overhead controls, and tunneling nodes. The main goal of this is to utilize energy efficiently by achieving high stability and scalability [9]. S-MAC uses some protocol to ensure reduction in performance per-hop fairness along with characteristics with latency and S-MAC uses various other techniques to achieve this.

- **Periodic Listen and Sleep Operations**: This is performed by ensuring a low duty cycle for nodes. During the periodic process, each node enters a sleep phase in which the components are inactive. [9]. The nodes go active when it senses traffic on the message-passing network.
- **Schedule Selection and Coordination**: All corresponding nodes share the sleep and active mode details, so that they all listen and sleep at the same time. To perform this, they have a scheduled exchange time slot for each node to synchronize [10]. Every node maintains a table for the scheduled time for exchanging information with each other.

8.3.6 Design issues in MAC protocols

The various design issues in MAC protocols are [11]:

- The bandwidth efficiency of MAC
- Synchronizations in the channels
- Hidden and exposed terminal problems in the nodes
- Error-prone shared broadcast channel
- Mobility of nodes

8.4 ROUTING PROTOCOLS

Routing is the process of identifying a suitable path, among other paths, that can be used to establish a connection from one node to another. In IoT wireless sensor networks, routing introduces a new challenge in the form of balancing productivity and efficiency [12]. While conserving battery life and staying on standby when not in use, each node must also be able to quickly respond to any connections and not contribute to latency or delay of the network.

8.4.1 Regular ad hoc network routing approaches

Many routing protocols exist for general-purpose routing. They can be categorized into the following approaches [12].

8.4.1.1 Proactive routing

Proactive routing, also known as table-based routing, is a routing approach that proactively ensures that every node has the most updated routing table. This ensures that every node knows the best path to another node. Proactive routing is achieved by periodically sending updated routing information to all neighbors of each node. Proactive routing can happen in either a peer-to-peer manner or a hierarchical manner [13]. While hierarchical proactive routing may be used for wireless sensor networks with slight overhead, peer-to-peer proactive routing is extremely inefficient in a wireless sensor network.

8.4.1.2 Reactive routing

Reactive routing, also known as dynamic routing, is a method of routing where routing occurs dynamically. No explicit global routing table is maintained. Instead, each node needs to dynamically calculate the best path to a particular node. This is done using a route discovery message. The route discovery message is flooded to all neighbors of a particular node. Upon receiving a route discovery message, each neighbor will send a response message. The neighbor whose response reaches first is determined as the best path [13]. While this method of routing is bandwidth-efficient, it certainly reduces responsiveness and increases the delay of the network. This makes it less suitable for use in IoT wireless sensor networks.

8.4.1.3 Hybrid routing

Hybrid routing is a combination of reactive and proactive routing approaches. In a sense, it takes the best of both routing approaches. In this approach, the network is broken down into smaller clusters. Reactive routing is used among clusters, while Proactive routing is used within each cluster [13]. The major drawback of this approach is the cost incurred in the maintenance of the clusters.

Thus, it is evident that these regular IoT routing techniques are not suitable for Wireless Sensor Networks because they do not provide the power and energy efficiency required. Hence, there are certain approaches to routing that are specific to Wireless Sensor Networks.

8.4.2 Wireless sensor network routing protocol approaches

Many routing protocols have been designed for wireless sensor networks, which incorporate the required constraints. These protocols are categorized into the following approaches [13].

8.4.2.1 Flat network system

In a flat network system, all nodes are considered peers. This IoT architecture proves to be beneficial in wireless sensor networks, as the cost of maintenance of the network is low. Moreover, this type of network offers good fault tolerance, as multiple paths exist between the nodes. Some examples of flat network system protocols are as follows:

1. Flooding
2. Gossiping

8.4.2.2 Clustering system

In the clustering system, the nodes are organized into groups or clusters, with one node selected either at random or based on some predetermined parameter, to be the representative of the cluster [14]. This system offers greater stability and scalability, which are both essential for wireless sensor networks.

Some examples of clustering system protocols are as follows:

1. Low Energy Adaptive Clustering Hierarchy (LEACH)
2. Threshold-sensitive Energy-efficient Sensor Network Protocol (TEEN)

8.4.2.3 Data-based protocols

In the data-based approach, routing is done based on some attributes possessed by each node. Thus, the routing process does not involve every node.

It only involves the nodes relevant to the attribute. Every node has one or more attributes, depending on the data it can provide. The node whose attributes match those desired is considered the best path [15].

Some examples of Data Based routing protocols are as follows:

1. Sensor Protocols for Information via Negotiation (SPIN)
2. Gradient-Based Routing (GBR)
3. Directed Diffusion

8.4.2.4 Location-based protocols

The location-based approach is a specific case of the data-based approach, wherein the node is selected only based on its relative location. This method is useful when the location of the node has significant importance in the context of the data collected. This method is efficient, as only the relevant nodes are contacted by the requesting node, which conserves the bandwidth of the network [14]. Some examples of location-based routing are as follows:

1. Minimum Energy Communication Network (MECN)
2. Small Minimum Energy Communication Network (SMECN)
3. Geographic Adaptive fidelity

8.4.3 Wireless sensor network routing techniques

There are many techniques for routing in wireless sensor networks, the most significant techniques [15] are described in the following sections.

8.4.3.1 Flooding

Flooding is an IoT technique wherein when a node receives any data, it forwards it to all its neighbors. This way, messages are flooded throughout the network until the message is delivered to the intended receiver. Flooding is very useful in wireless networks for path discovery and information dissemination purposes. The main advantages of this method are that it is simple and does not require an expensive topology. But due to its simplicity, flooding has certain issues [16] as well.

- **Excessive Duplication**: Flooding causes an excessive duplication of data packets in the network. This can cause wastage of bandwidth and increase the delay and latency of the network. To prevent excessive duplication, a field, known as the hop count field, stores the diameter of the network as a maximum value. For each hop the packet makes, the hop count is decremented by one. Once the hop count reaches 0, this packet is discarded.

This technique is effective, as the path length from one node to another should not exceed the diameter. Thus, the hop count should not become 0. If it does, then this path is not the shortest path from the source to the destination. Once that has been determined, the packet can be discarded.

- **Traffic Implosion**: Traffic implosion is an issue in flooding wherein the same data packet is sent to a node from multiple sources.
- **Geographical Overlapping**: Geographical overlapping is another issue in flooding where two nodes that received data from similar nodes are sending similar data to the same node.
- **Resource Blindness**: One of the major issues of flooding is its resource blindness characteristic. The simplicity of the algorithm fails to account for the load that is applied to each individual sensor. Flooding causes overuse of resources at each sensor, which is not ideal in a wireless sensor network. Although the issue of excessive duplication was handled using the hop count field, the other issues of flooding could not be handled so easily [16]. Thus, a new technique was created, which dealt with these issues, and it was named Gossiping.

8.4.3.2 Gossiping

Gossiping is an IoT technique that improves upon flooding and aims to overcome the issues of traffic implosion, geographical overlapping, and resource blindness that occur in flooding while retaining the advantages of flooding. While in flooding the data packet is broadcast to all neighbors indiscriminately, in gossiping, the data packet is sent to only one randomly selected neighbor. Upon receiving a packet, the neighbor sends it to one of its neighbors selected randomly [17]. This process is repeated until (a) the packet reaches the intended destination, and (b) the hop count field decreases to zero.

Gossiping can avoid the issues experienced in flooding by limiting the number of packets sent by a node. But by doing that, the latency of the network sharply increases, as only one path is being covered at a time.

8.4.3.3 Sensor protocols for information via negotiation (SPIN)

The SPIN protocols are a group of IoT protocols that aim to perform routing using the concepts of negotiation and data naming. These protocols can efficiently circulate the data collected at individual nodes to those who require the data. While flooding and gossiping may be easy to implement, their simplicity comes at the cost of large overheads in the form of increased latency or overuse of bandwidth. This in turn reduces the overall lifetime of a wireless sensor network. Thus, these protocols are not feasible for use in wireless sensor networks. To tackle the issues faced by flooding and gossiping, the SPIN protocols take on a new approach to data dissemination. They make use of the principles of data naming and negotiation to efficiently disseminate the data throughout the network [18]. Moreover, to further reduce the load on each node, SPIN protocols make use of resource adaptation, which allows them to gauge the level of remaining resources. If the resources are running low, then certain activities are cut off. This greatly boosts the efficiency and lifetime of each sensor and, thus the entire network. To optimally carry out the negotiation process, SPIN protocols make use of three messages.

- **ADV – Advertisement Message**: When a node has new data that it needs to share with the other nodes, it uses the ADV message. The ADV message contains some meta-information about the new data that has been collected. This is advertised to the remaining nodes of the network. Since the meta-information is only a description of the actual data, it is easy to transport even across a large network.
- **REQ – Request Message**: The ADV message is sent to all nodes in the network. If a node requires the advertised data, it sends a REQ message to the advertising node, requesting the advertised data. The REQ message contains the meta-information from the ADV message, to denote the data that is being requested.
- **DATA – Data Message**: The DATA message contains the actual data that is being sent by the source node. Upon receiving a REQ message from a node requesting a particular data, the source node sends the requested data using the DATA message. The DATA message is quite large, as it contains the unabstracted data collected by the node. Thus, instead of sending this large data to every node, it is now only being sent to the nodes, which want the data, greatly conserving the bandwidth and lifetime of the system.

The SPIN group of protocols is made up of the following four variants [18],

- **SPIN-PP**: SPIN-PP is the simplest of the SPIN protocols. It is designed for point-to-point communication. SPIN-PP follows a three-way handshake in the following steps:
  1. The Source Node sends advertisement of data.
  2. The Interested Node sends a request for advertised data.
  3. The Source Node sends the requested data to the Interested Node.
- **SPIN-EC**: SPIN-EC is a modified version of SPIN-PP, which comes with an additional threshold-based resource awareness feature. When the resource levels of a node come down close to the threshold, the node ceases to participate in too many activities, conserving its lifetime. A node only engages in an activity if it knows that it can

complete all stages of the activity, without resource levels going below the threshold.

- **SPIN-BC**: While both SPIN-PP and SPIN-EC are designed for P2P communication, SPIN-BC is designed for broadcast networks. In broadcast networks, a common channel is used for communication; therefore, any message sent to one node is heard by all the other nodes as well. In SPIN-BC, if a node is interested in advertised data, it waits before sending a REQ message. If another node sends a REQ message instead, the node cancels its REQ message, as the DATA message will be sent on a common channel. Thus, redundant REQ messages can be eliminated in this manner.

- **SPIN-RL**: SPIN-RL is an enhanced version of the SPIN-BC broadcast network protocol, which aims to eradicate any loss of data that may occur due to errors. It does so by repeatedly broadcasting the ADV and REQ messages. After sending a DATA message, SPIN-RL nodes wait for a period before responding to a request for the same data to further improve the reliability of the network. The SPIN protocols have proven in simulations that they can successfully overcome the defects of flooding and gossiping and are much more energy-efficient. SPIN protocols do have a drawback wherein if an intermediate node is unable to complete the transfer of a message, it simply drops it, thereby not ensuring complete coverage of the network.

8.4.3.4 Low energy adaptive clustering hierarchy

The LEACH protocol is an IoT routing protocol that is designed to maximize the lifetime while minimizing the energy usage of the network. Using data aggregation, it can optimally send only the required messages. This protocol breaks the network down into logical clusters, where each cluster is appointed a cluster head. Based on a TDMA scheme, a cluster head assigns each of its cluster members a time slot to transmit its data. The cluster head gathers the incoming data and saves it into a buffer. Then, the cluster head removes the redundant data. The collected data are then transmitted to the central database. The activities of LEACH are classified into the following two phases [11]:

- **Setup Phase**: The setup phase involves two activities.
  - **Cluster head selection**: The first step of the setup phase is cluster head selection. Since the role of cluster head consumes a lot of energy, it is rotated among all the nodes so that no single node needs to bear the burden for a long time. To determine which node becomes the cluster head, a random number between 0 and 1 is generated and compared with the threshold T(n). If the generated number is lower than the threshold T(n), then the node becomes the cluster

head. The threshold value T(n) for a particular node n is calculated by the following function [4],

$$
T(n) = \begin{cases} 0 & if\, n \notin G \\ \dfrac{P}{1 - P\left(r\,\mathrm{mod}\left(\dfrac{1}{P}\right)\right)} & \forall n \in G \end{cases}
$$

Where, P = a predetermined number of nodes, n = the particular node, G = the nodes not cluster head in last 1/P rounds, r = current round

Thus, in the last 1/P rounds, the nodes which assumed the role of cluster head will not take the role again, thereby evenly spreading the burden of being a cluster head.

- **Cluster formation**: Once the cluster heads have been selected, they advertise this to the other nodes. The other nodes then select a cluster to join and inform their respective cluster head. After the cluster formation, each cluster head assigns a time slot to each of its cluster members using a TDMA-based scheme. Each cluster head also selects a CDMA code and passes it on to every cluster member.
- **Steady-state Phase**: Once the setup phase is complete, the nodes begin collecting data from their environment. Periodically, each cluster head gathers these data from their cluster members. The cluster head then proceeds to remove redundant data and sends the data to the central database. Although LEACH has an excellent rating for energy conservation, it does have a few drawbacks:
  - For LEACH to work, every node needs to be able to reach the central database in a single hop, which may not always be possible.
  - The duration of the steady state affects the energy conservation of the network. If the steady-state period is short, more energy is used up over time. But if the steady-state period is long, it causes a greater load on the cluster heads.

8.4.3.5 Design issues in routing protocols

IoT Wireless Sensor Networks have certain characteristics that cause existing routing protocols to be inefficient. These characteristics must be considered while designing new protocols for Wireless Sensor Networks to facilitate an efficient and productive network.

One such characteristic is the ad hoc nature of wireless sensor networks. The nodes in wireless sensor networks are generally not arranged in any specific order. Another characteristic is the limited resources available at each node, which is detrimental to the intensity of work that can be done by each node [19]. Moreover, the natural data collected by the sensors vary from network to network, depending on the use case. Therefore, it becomes more difficult to create a generalized solution that will work for all types of data.

8.5 TRANSMISSION CONTROL PROTOCOLS

Transmission control protocols are a staple in any IoT architecture. They provide a method to process the communication of data packets. In transmission control protocols, the outgoing contents are disassembled into smaller fragments or datagrams at the source and reassembled into the original message at the destination. Transmission control protocols are of two types, namely, connection-oriented protocols and connectionless protocols. Connection-oriented protocols make use of a setup phase to establish a connection between two nodes and a teardown phase to terminate the connection. Connectionless protocols require no such phases to establish or terminate a connection between the two nodes [19]. They directly send the data to the receiver. But they do not provide the reliability of connection-oriented protocols.

8.5.1 Traditional transmission control protocols

8.5.1.1 User datagram protocol

User datagram protocol (UDP) is a connectionless, unreliable, transmission control protocol (TCP). It does not have a mechanism for providing acknowledgments, as it does not assign a serial number to the data packets. Moreover, in case of loss of data packets, UDP does not have a recovery mechanism to make up for the lost packets. UDP does not provide flow or congestion control either. Since there are no serial numbers for the datagrams, ordered delivery of packets is essential in UDP. The main advantage of UDP is the lack of overheads required to transfer data from source to destination. No major costs are incurred during transfer and the energy used by each node is minimal [20].

8.5.1.2 Transmission control protocol

Transmission control protocol is a reliable, connection-oriented transmission control protocol. It is made up of the following three phases [20]:

- **Connection Establishment**: In this phase, a connection is set up between the source and the destination nodes. This happens through a three-way handshake. The source node sends an SYN message, requesting to connect with the destination node. The destination node may respond with an SYN/ACK message. To this, the source node responds with an ACK message and moves on to the Data Transmission phase.
- **Data Transmission**: In this phase, TCP provides orderly and reliable transmission of messages between the source and destination nodes. Here, ACK is used to retrieve messages lost in transit. This is achieved with the help of serial numbers in the header of the datagram.
- **Termination**: After the data transfer is complete, the connection is terminated. Termination requires an extensive teardown of the connection

that was established in the first step. TCP offers many features such as Flow Control and Error Control. Every packet has serial numbers, so ordered delivery of packets is not required. Moreover, TCP supports the acknowledgments mechanism. Therefore, lost packets that are not acknowledged can be retransmitted.

But with all these features, TCP also has certain drawbacks [29]. It requires very costly Connection Establishment and Termination phases. Moreover, acknowledgments also cause a significant load on the communication channel. Overall, TCP incurs a large overhead, which is not feasible in IoT Wireless Sensor Networks.

Thus, we can see that the traditional Transmission Control Protocols do not satisfy the constraints required in IoT Wireless Sensor Networks. Therefore, newer protocols are required that consider the unique characteristics of Wireless Sensor Networks to provide efficient transportation between nodes. The following are the protocols designed specifically for these characteristics.

8.5.2 Wireless sensor network transmission control protocols

Wireless sensor network transmission control protocols are designed specifically for use by the IoT wireless sensor network. They can be categorized [10] as follows:

- **Upstream Protocols**: Protocols, where data travel from the sensors to the central database, are known as Upstream Protocols.

  Examples: CODA, ESRT, RMST.

- **Downstream**: Protocols, where data travel from the central database to the sensor nodes, are known as Downstream Protocols.

  Examples: PDFQ, GARUDA

8.5.2.1 Congestion detection and avoidance

Congestion detection and avoidance (CODA) is a congestion control mechanism that has three components: congestion detection, open-loop hop-to-hop backpressure, and closed-loop end-to-end backpressure. CODA monitors the load and buffering in the channels to detect congestion. When the load reaches the threshold value, it means that the congestion has occurred and the node that detects congestion informs incoming nodes that congestion has occurred using Open-loop hop-to-hop backpressure [20]. So, the incoming message reduces their transmission rate using the AIMD method.

CODA regulates other nodes using closed-loop end-to-end backpressure by sending an ACK to each node requesting them to reduce their transmission rate, and if the congestion is cleared, it would send out ACK stating that it is okay to return to the origin's transmission rate. One disadvantage of CODA is that it increases the ACK message passing time in a unidirectional way when the congestion is heavy and this message could even be lost and the response time is heavy.

8.5.2.2 Event-to-sink reliable transport

Event-to-sink reliable transport (ESRT) is a function that allows congestion control and reliability. This method periodically creates a graph with the number of successfully received messages versus the time interval. Using this figure, ESRT deduces a transmission rate for the node. ESRT sends out this value to other nodes informing the transmission rate of the node and uses an end-to-end concept to provide reliability by adjusting the transmission rate of the node. The advantage of ESRT is the conservation of energy by providing the transmission rate. The disadvantage of ESRT is that it sends out the same transmission rate to all nodes, which causes an irregular rate at each node.

8.5.2.3 Reliable multi-segment transport

Reliable multi-segment transport (RMST) is an upstream transmission control protocol that has been designed on top of the directed diffusion protocol to enable reliable transportation of data packets across the network. It works in cache and non-cache modes [3]. In cache mode, intermediate nodes maintain the cache of every packet that they transmit so that it may be recovered in the event of packet loss. In non-cache mode, only the source maintains a cache of the transmitted packets [21]. If the receiver detects packet loss, it issues a NACK. If any of the intermediate nodes have cached the missing packet, they forward the cached version of the missing packet. In non-cache mode, the NACK is forwarded to the source and the source resends the missing packet from its cache. While RMST handles packet loss well, it does not have a proper congestion control mechanism. Moreover, resource utilization of RMST is high.

8.5.2.4 Pump slowly, fetch quickly

Pump slowly, fetch quickly (PSFQ) is a downstream transmission control protocol that transfers data from the central database down to the sensor nodes. It is made up of the following three activities [1].

- **Pumping**: The process where the data are broadcast from the central database to its neighbors is known as pumping. In PSFQ, pumping is done at a slow rate.

- **Fetching**: When a node detects packet loss, it attempts to fetch the missing packet from its neighbors. Fetching is done at a high speed.
- **Reporting**: Once all the data have been pumped out by the source, it requests a status report from the nodes, through which it can assess the quality of transmission and retransmit data if required.

Pumping is set as a slow process to facilitate enough time for fetching to take place when loss of data packet occurs. Although this enables PSFQ to have high reliability, due to the slow pump, the entire network faces an increased delay.

8.5.2.5 GARUDA

GARUDA is a downstream transmission protocol. Based on integer I, the nodes are classified into two types [28]:

- **Core**: The nodes which are 3i hops from the central database are called Core Nodes. Only these nodes maintain a cache of data that they transfer.
- **Non-Core**: The nodes which are not core nodes automatically become non-core nodes. Each non-core node selects the nearest core node and gets attached to it.

If a core node experiences data loss, it issues a NACK message to the other core nodes. Since the other core nodes cache all the data they receive, they will be able to transfer any lost packets to the other nodes. If a non-core node experiences data loss, it contacts its core node. Since core nodes cache all data that they receive, the core node will be able to retransmit the lost packet. In this manner, GARUDA can recover lost packets and effectively prevent packet loss downstream. GARUDA does not have any mechanism for Congestion Control.

8.5.2.6 Ad hoc transport protocol

Ad hoc transport protocol (ATP) works using the concept of end-to-end feedback of network assistance and receiver control algorithm. ACK is used to retrieve lost messages. In this method, an intermediate does compute a collection of distributed messages in the queue and transmission delay known as D [27]. An end-to-end rate is achieved by taking the value 1/D. This value is calculated for all nodes in transit, and if the value reaches the maximum threshold, it is piggybacked to all other nodes. The destination node calculates the required transmission rate and updates the source node so that the sender can pass messages at a rate that the destination node can accept, which increases reliability. APT uses SACK (selective ACKs) to detect lost messages in transit and it decouples reliability from congestion control to provide better throughput.

8.5.3 Design issues in transmission control protocols

The design issues that should be considered in a transmission control protocol for IoT wireless sensor networks are listed as follows [22]:

- **Energy Consumption**: Energy consumption should be at a minimum in wireless sensor networks, as each node only has a limited level of resources. Moreover, the workload should be distributed across all nodes and not be concentrated on a particular node.
- **Lost Packet Recovery**: Connections between nodes in wireless sensor networks are vulnerable to environmental effects and unpredictable. Therefore, packet loss during transmission is very likely. Thus, transmission control protocols should have a mechanism to recover lost packets.
- **Congestion Control**: Wireless sensor networks can include hundreds of nodes, all of which share a common communication network. Therefore, congestion is a likely situation and transmission control protocols must have a congestion control mechanism.

8.6 IoT APPLICATIONS OF WIRELESS SENSOR NETWORKS

Since wireless sensor networks are made up of multiple wirelessly connected sensors, which can communicate with each other, they have many IoT applications in areas such as home automation, intrusion detection, and medical purposes.

- **Military Applications**: Wireless sensor networks are built to be an extremely secure, impenetrable network that can be used to gather intelligence [23]. These admission-critical sensor networks are advantageous in IoT military applications, which are sensitive and mission-critical. In the military, wireless sensor networks can be used for communication purposes, intelligence gathering, threat detection, and targeting systems.
- **Home Automation**: The sensors used in wireless sensor networks are usually quite small in size and can be embedded into everyday objects. This paves way for the use of wireless sensor networks in home automation and other pervasive computing applications [24, 25]. Currently, Amazon Echo is the most common application of

wireless sensor network in home automation. The Amazon Echo is a small speaker-like device that can be placed all around the home. The sensors of Echo can detect human speech and are used to provide many functionalities such as controlling other devices wirelessly [26, 27].

- **Environmental Monitoring**: Using their ability of widespread detection and data collection, wireless sensor networks can be used to monitor changes in environmental conditions such as weather, humidity, and wind speed. Such data are useful for weather reporting and weather forecasts [28]. Moreover, this type of environmental data can also be collected over a certain period and be used to create datasets that can aid further research into the effects of the environment in various scenarios.

- **Intrusion Detection**: Wireless sensor networks are designed to be robust and secure while providing quick and timely responses to any events [29]. Moreover, the size of each sensor is quite small and can easily be hidden. These qualities make wireless sensor networks ideal for use in intrusion detection systems. If any of the sensors detect an intruder, an alarm can be raised and the authorities can be notified immediately.

- **Medical Applications**: Wireless sensor networks provide accurate data and can be made extremely sensitive to detect even small changes [28, 29]. They can be used for patient monitoring and other investigatory and diagnostic purposes.

8.7 CONCLUSION

In this chapter, we covered wireless sensor networks and the various protocols required to enable their functionality. We saw that the IoT protocols for wireless sensor networks can be categorized into Communication, Medium Access Control, Routing, and Transmission Control Protocols, with each protocol serving a distinct purpose in the working of wireless sensor networks. Moreover, the various protocols were discussed in detail, highlighting the working, advantages, limitations, and applications of each protocol. This led to an increased understanding of wireless sensor networks and the concepts involved in designing these protocols.

Finally, we went over the possible IoT-based applications for wireless sensor networks, which illustrate the role of each category of protocols in the overall working of wireless sensor network. On the one hand, the various nuances of wireless sensor networks make it difficult to design suitable protocols. But on the other hand, it is these very nuances that make them ideal for use in many mission-critical applications of the military and medical domains.

REFERENCES

1 Chegini, H., Naha, R.K., Mahanti, A., & Thulasiraman, P., "Process automation in an IoT–fog–cloud ecosystem: A survey and taxonomy," *IoT*, vol. 2, no. 1, pp. 92–118, 2021.

2 Dhanalakshmi, R., & Chellappan, C., "Fraud and Identity Theft Issues," in *Strategic and Practical Approaches for Information Security Governance: Technologies and Applied Solutions* (pp. 245–260). IGI Global, 2012.

3 Stann, F., & Heidemann, J., "RMST: Reliable data transport in sensor networks," in *Proceedings of the 1st IEEE International Workshop on Sensor Network Protocols and Applications (SNPA'03)*, Anchorage, AK, May 2003.

4 Rajesh, S.A., Sivaraman, A.K., & Lakshmi, M., "A routing optimization algorithm via fuzzy logic towards security in wireless ad-hoc networks," in *2014 International Conference on Circuits, Power and Computing Technologies [ICCPCT-2014]* (pp. 1321–1323). Kumaracoil, India, 2014.

5 Lee, I., & Lee, K., "The Internet of Things (IoT): Applications, investments, and challenges for enterprises," *Business Horizons*, vol. 58, no. 4, pp. 431–440, 2015.

6 Luo, J., Chen, Y., Wu, M., & Yang, Y., "A survey of routing protocols for underwater wireless sensor networks," *IEEE Communications Surveys & Tutorials*, vol. 23, no. 1, pp. 137–160, 2021.

7 Gayathri, R., Vincent, R., Rajesh, M., Sivaraman, A.K., & Muralidhar, A., "Web-acl based dos mitigation solution for cloud," *Advances in Mathematics: Scientific Journal*, vol. 9, no. 7, pp. 5105–5113, 2020.

8 Handy, M., Haase, M., & Timmermann, D., "Low energy adaptive clustering hierarchy with deterministic cluster head selection," in *IEEE MWCN*, Stockholm, Sweden, September 2002.

9 Nath, K., Dhanalakshmi, R., Vijayakumar, V., Aremu, B., Kumar Reddy, K.H., & Gao, X.Z., "Uncovering hidden community structures in evolving networks based on neighborhood similarity," *Journal of Intelligent & Fuzzy Systems*, vol. 39, no. 6, pp. 8315–8324, 2020.

10 Rashid, B., & Rehmani, M.H., "Applications of wireless sensor networks for urban areas: A survey," *Journal of Network and Computer Applications*, vol. 60, pp. 192–219, 2016.

11 Dhanalakshmi, R., & Chellappan, C., "Detection and Recognition of File Masquerading for E-mail and Data Security," in *Recent Trends in Network Security and Applications* (pp. 253–262). Springer Berlin Heidelberg, 2010.

12 Cloudin, S., & Mohankumar, P., "Adaptive mobility-based intelligent decision-making system for driver behavior prediction with motion nanosensor in VANET," *International Journal of Heavy Vehicle Systems*, vol. 253, no. 4, pp. 391–405, 2018.

13 Gayathri, R., Magesh, A., Karmel, A., Vincent, R., & Sivaraman, A.K., "Low cost automatic irrigation system with intelligent performance tracking," *Journal of Green Engineering*, vol. 10, no. 12, pp. 13224–13233, 2020.

14 Shabbir, N., & Hassan, S.R., "Routing Protocols for Wireless Sensor Networks (WSNs)," in *Wireless Sensor Networks-Insights and Innovations*. Intechopen, New Zealand, 2007.

15 Kothandaraman, D., Balasundaram, A., Dhanalakshmi, R., Sivaraman, A.K., Ashokkumar, S., Vincent, R., & Rajesh, M., "Energy and bandwidth based link stability routing algorithm for IoT," *Computers, Materials & Continua*, vol. 70, no. 2, pp. 3875–3890, 2021.

16 Sowmya, K.V., Teju, V., & Pavan Kumar, T., "An extensive survey on IOT protocols and applications," in *International Conference on Intelligent and Smart Computing in Data Analytics* (pp. 131–138). Springer, Singapore, 2021.

17 Swetha, S., Suprajah, S., Vaishnavi Kanna, S., & Dhanalakshmi, R., "An intelligent monitor system for home appliances using IoT," in *2017 International Conference on Technical Advancements in Computers and Communications (ICTACC)* (pp. 106–108). IEEE, 2017.

18 Tournier, J., Lesueur, F., Le Mouël, F., Guyon, L., & Ben-Hassine, H., "A survey of IoT protocols and their security issues through the lens of a generic IoT stack," *Internet of Things*, vol. 16, p. 100264, 2021.

19 Md, A.Q., Agrawal, D., Mehta, M., Sivaraman, A.K., & Tee, K.F., "Time optimization of unmanned aerial vehicles using an augmented path," *Future Internet*, vol. 13, no. 12, 308, 2021.

20 Heinzelman, W., Chandrakasan, A., & Balakrishnan, H., "Energy-efficient communication protocol for wireless microsensor networks," in *Proceedings of the 33rd Hawaii International Conference on System Sciences (HICSS'00)*, Maui, HI, January 2000.

21 Dhanalakshmi, R., Anand, J., Sivaraman, A.K., & Rani, S., "IoT-Based Water Quality Monitoring System Using Cloud for Agriculture Use," in *Cloud and Fog Computing Platforms for Internet of Things* (vol. 28, no. 3, pp. 1–14). CRC Press, 2022.

22 Tseng, Y.-C., Hsu, C.-S., & Hsieh, T.-Y., "Power-saving protocols for IEEE 802.11-based multi-hop ad hoc networks," in *Proceedings of the 21st Annual Joint Conference of the IEEE Computer and Communications Societies (InfoCom'02)*, New York (pp. 200–209), June 2002.

23 Rani, S., Kataria, A., Chauhan, M., Rattan, P., Kumar, R., & Sivaraman, A.K., "Security and privacy challenges in the deployment of cyber-physical systems in smart city applications: State-of-art work," in *International Conference on Innovative Technology for Sustainable Development (ICITSD), Materials Today: Proceedings* (pp. 103–112). Elsevier, Chennai, India, 2022.

24 Siva Rama Rao, A.V.S., & Dhana Lakshmi, R., "A survey on challenges in integrating big data," in Deiva Sundari, P., Dash, S., Das, S., Panigrahi, B. (Eds.) *Proceedings of 2nd International Conference on Intelligent Computing and Applications. Advances in Intelligent Systems and Computing* (vol. 467). Springer, Singapore, 2017.

25 Kothandaraman, D., Manickam, M., Balasundaram, A., Pradeep, D., Arulmurugan, A., Sivaraman, A.K., Rani, S., Dey, B., & Balakrishna, R., "Decentralized link failure prevention routing (dlfpr) algorithm for efficient internet of things," *Intelligent Automation & Soft Computing*, vol. 34, no.1, pp. 655–666, 2022.

26 Sarah, I., Soundarya, K., Dhanalakshmi, R., & Deenadayalan, T., "DYS-I-CAN: An aid for the dyslexic to improve the skills using mobile application," *2020 International Conference on System, Computation, Automation and Networking (ICSCAN)* (pp. 1–5), 2020.

27 Sharma, T., & Tabassum, M., "Enhanced algorithm to optimize QoS and security parameters in ad hoc networks," in *Design Methodologies and Tools for 5G Network Development and Application* (pp. 1–27). IGI Global, 2021.

28 Perumal, S., Tabassum, M., Narayana, G., Ponnan, S., Chakraborty, C., Mohanan, S., Basit, Z., & Quasim, M.T., "ANN based novel approach to detect node failure in wireless sensor network," *CMC-Comput Mater Contin (TechScience)*, vol. 69, no. 2, pp. 1447–1462, 2021.

29 Liang, C.B., Tabassum, M., Kashem, S.B.A., Zama, Z., Suresh, P., & Saravanakumar, U., "Smart Home Security System Based on Zigbee," in *Advances in Smart System Technologies* (pp. 827–836). Springer, Singapore, 2021.

Chapter 9

Secure communication in Internet of Things devices using steganography

Manjot Kaur Bhatia, C. Komalavalli and Chetna Laroiya

Jagan Institute of Management Studies, New Delhi, India

CONTENTS

9.1   Introduction...169
    9.1.1   Objectives of the paper..172
    9.1.2   Overview of the proposed model.......................................175
        9.1.2.1   Sender side..177
        9.1.2.2   Receiver side...178
    9.1.3   Proposed embedding and extraction algorithm 180
        9.1.3.1   Rivest Shamir Adleman algorithm.........................180
        9.1.3.2   Embedding algorithm 180
        9.1.3.3   Extraction algorithm...181
9.2   Analysis 183
9.3   Conclusion..187
References...187

9.1 INTRODUCTION

Developing trends in embedded technologies and the Internet have enabled objects surrounding us to be interconnected with each other. Internet of Things (IoT) is a platform through which devices are interconnected with the support of the internet, thus providing the link between the physical and digital world together. Seamless integration of users, devices, and applications distributed in different locations enable the communication between all of them with the support of IoT devices. A large number of personal devices such as laptops, mobiles, and smart watch are connecting to the internet for accessing different types of services. The enormous volume of data that are generated would be saved and processed for making the data understandable and useful. Data from different devices are transmitted over the network raising a potential threat to the privacy and security of the data. The success of IoT requires a merger of different communication infrastructures together so that the IoT devices can be connected to the traditional internet.

IoT has a wide range of applications such as medical care and supply chain management [1]. The adoption of IoT applications is facing several problems such as data privacy, data confidentiality, and data authenticity.

DOI: 10.1201/9781003355946-9

Secure communication of the data from the IoT devices to the client is playing a vital role. Increasing IoT devices, the large volume of data generated by these devices, and networks pose security challenges. Because we have less control over the communication system involving IoT devices and the system is distributed in nature, the system attracts intruders for hacking. Once compromised, they can take the control of the network and can perform malicious attacks and activities. They can take control over the data collected and transmitted by the device [1].

With the advent of medical care based on IoT systems, the transmission of medical records in the network becomes a part of day-to-day life. Therefore, it attracts the researchers' community for safeguarding that data of the medical domain from the intruders. Therefore, it is required to develop a systematic approach for secure communication of patient's diagnostic data and retains the integrity of the data.

Whenever two devices communicate with each other, sensitive data are transferred between the devices over the network. For enhancing the security over the network, encryption techniques are much needed in the system. Encryption helps to protect the data from intruders and other kinds of malicious attacks. Cryptography provides confidentiality, integrity, nonrepudiation, and authentication while transferring the data from one device to another.

There are many data security technologies and processes, namely, authentication, access control, backup, data masking, tokenization, cryptography, and steganography.

Cryptography [1, 2] ensures the privacy and integrity of data. Depending upon the application, it is required to keep communications secret over the open channels and to prove the authenticity of incoming data. Cryptography is the technique of encrypting and decrypting the data for sharing messages very securely between the applications. It transforms the simple text into the unintelligible form so that understanding the data for the users becomes very difficult [2]. The system comprises plain text, encryption, decryption algorithm, Ciphertext, and Keys. Encryption converts the text into ciphertext with the support of a key and decryption is the reverse process. Key is playing a major role in encrypting and decrypting the data.

Three most common encryption types of algorithms are as follows:

1) Symmetric Algorithm or Private Key, which uses a single key for both Encryption and Decryption.
2) Asymmetric or Public key Algorithm where one key for Encryption and another for Decryption is used.
3) Hash functions are also one of the techniques for securing the data.

Steganography [3, 4] is the other technique for secured communication. Steganography is used for hiding information. Image embedding in spatial and transform domain is the technique of steganography [4]. The messages

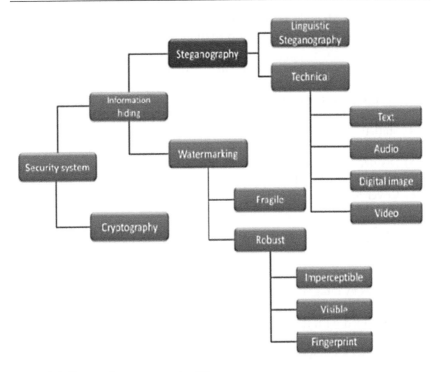

Figure 9.1 Types of steganography [5].

are directly embedded into the least significant bits. Steganography encompasses hiding information so that it seems that no information is hidden at all. In steganography, no one can have a clue of information hidden in the image. As shown in Figure 9.1, hiding a secret message within a cover medium such as image, video, text, and audio is known as steganography.

Image Steganography [4] uses two algorithms for embedding and extraction of messages. Messages embedded into the image will not be visible to the third party. The extraction involves extracting a message from the stego image. Both cryptography and steganography are designed for security purposes but are different in their functionality. Cryptography precludes unauthorized access from finding the content and steganography precludes the finding of the content.

Steganography [3] systems can be categorized by the type of media such as graphics, sound, text, and executable used for the covers and the techniques by which the covers can be modified. Although steganography can be achieved using many cover media, here, we are concerned with hiding a secret message in digital images.

1) Substitution system: This method replaces the unneeded bits of a cover with the support of bits from the secret message.

2) Transform domain techniques: The frequency domain is the base for this technique and hidden information is communicated through this domain.

3) Spread spectrum techniques: The stream of data to be transmitted are distributed into small pieces in a direct sequence spread spectrum. Each one of those pieces is allocated to a frequency channel of the spectrum

4) Statistical method: One bit of secure data is embedded into the digital carrier.

5) Distortion techniques: Changing the cover image to hide the information is applied in this technique.

6) Cover generation methods

9.1.1 Objectives of the paper

1. The paper aims to improve the security of communication between IoT devices by integrating both cryptography and stenography techniques.

2. Sensed data from the devices are encrypted first for security and embedded with the image with the help of steganography techniques for secure communication. Steganography enhances the security of data by hiding within the image.

3. Data are extracted from the image and decrypted with the help of the cryptography algorithm.

The rest of this paper is structured as follows: In Section II, theoretical background for the proposed framework is described, while in Section III, the proposed framework along with the proposed steganography technique is discussed in detail. In Section IV, the results achieved from the evaluation of the proposed work are given in detail. Finally, the conclusions drawn from the study are presented in Section V.

1. Literature review

Manju Khari et al. [1] proposed the elliptic Galois cryptography protocol and techniques applied to encrypt data from different data sources. They have discussed the Matrix XOR encoding steganography technique and optimization algorithm as well. Adaptive Firefly algorithm is used for the selection of cover blocks. Evaluation of various parameters and comparison of those parameters with the existing techniques are studied. They adopted this technique only for medical purposes. IOT data can be different.

Steganography [6, 7] played a very important role in communication. Authors [5] discussed the major points of steganography such as image quality and recoverability of the secrete data. In their model, data are compressed before embedding using Huffman Coding. They have used two control parameters P_Even/P_Odd for tracking the secret message and mapping of the bits, thus improving steganography.

Manogaran et al. [8] suggested a medical sensor device for monitoring human body clinical measurements such as respiratory rate, pressure, blood sugar, and temperature. They discussed the new architecture with the help of a big data knowledge system. A sensor monitors the vital parameters of the human body, and if there is any variation in the parameter, the message containing health information will be generated and informed to the doctor for further observation. The drawback of the system is that medical devices are necessary to attach to the human body and only can be applied for industrial applications.

Saleh et al. [9] discussed the new technique for secure communication by combining both cryptography and steganography and introduced a new algorithm. They modified the AES algorithm and introduced the AES_MPK algorithm for hiding the message. They have applied this technique only for text data, not for audio or video. Capacity is also a constraint for the proposed method.

Chervyakov et al. [10] proposed a new data storage scheme for reducing data redundancy and data loss, thus ensuring the speed of encoding and decoding. They considered parameters for managing workload and storage properties. The authors discussed that safety and reliability can be increased by an appropriate redundant residue number system. By selecting accurate RRNS, an increase in the speed of processing encrypted data can be achieved.

A. K. Bairagi et al. [11] also suggested three methods for the security and hiding of information in the deepest layer for enabling the communication over the IOT network, to avoid the attack of the network. Minimal possible distortion in the least significant bit is utilized for hiding the information in the deepest layer of the image and signs of the information can also be used. Imperceptibility and ability are improved with the help of this technique.

Authors [12] presented a secured hybrid model for the diagnostic data of medical images. Integration of diagnostic in medical images was discussed in their model. The proposed model is developed through integrating either 2-D discrete wavelet transform 1 level (2D-DWT-1L) or 2-D discrete wavelet transform 2 levels (2D-DWT-2L) steganography technique with the hybrid encryption scheme. This scheme is the combination of Advanced Encryption Standard, and Rivest, Shamir, and Adleman algorithms. They have evaluated results on both color and gray-scale images with different text sizes.

Secure communication with minimum time consumption, the authors from [13] purposed a technique called Jackknife regressive. In this technique, data are monitored by IOT devices and stored in the dataset. The proposed architecture trains the data into multiple layers and the data are analyzed in the first hidden layer with the help of the jackknife regression function. Encryption is performed in the next hidden layer and the data are sent to the cloud server. Decryption is achieved using the SS decryption algorithm and the data are kept in the database for added processing. This process enhances the security of communication.

Lo'ai Tawalbeh et al. [14] discussed IoT security, privacy issues, and challenges. The proposed cloud/edge supported IoT systems for ensuring security and privacy of the IOT network. Three-layer model was proposed, which also evaluated the performance. A lower layer represents IoT nodes, the middle layer represents the Raspberry Pi 4 hardware kit, and the top layer represents cloud-enabled IOT environment in AWS. The security protocols and critical supervision sessions were implemented between each of these layers to certify the privacy of the users' information. They have also included security certificates.

Information security and privacy is an important concern while transferring information through the IoT network. The Least Significant Bit (LSB) [15] insertion is the commonly used steganography method that replaces the least significant bit of cover image with the secret information bits. The LSB method takes advantage of the natural weakness of the Human Visual System (HVS) [16] in identifying the negligible difference between the colors. LSB replaces the selected bits of the cover image with the information bits.

Bhatia et al. [17] developed an information hiding method for secure communication over the internet. In the abovementioned method, the author selected the pixels corresponding to the positions of the 8-rooks on the chessboard and then information bits are embedded into the LSB of the selected bits. It enhances the security of the information by randomizing the pixel selection.

Bhatia et al. [18] developed an image steganography method using on spread spectrum approach. In the proposed method, the cover image is decomposed into RGB planes; information bits are modulated and spread into the three image planes. Finally, image planes are encrypted, combined as one stego image, and transferred at the receiver end.

Muttoo et al. [19] proposed secure data hiding technique using steganography. In this method, the author divided the cover image into 8*1 bytes blocks and expanded 8 pixels of each block into ASCII bits. The author selected bits corresponding to the positions of the 8-queen solution from each bit block and compared them with ASCII bits of characters in the message. Experimental results for the 8-queen method are discussed in the form of PSNR and embedding capacity.

Riccardo Bonetto et al. [20] discussed the security procedures for constrained IoT devices. They proposed a lightweight process and protection of IoT devices is achieved by providing encryption and authentication mechanisms. They introduced the solution that is based on offloading the computationally intensive tasks into trusted and unconstrained modes. The node is responsible for the calculation of session keys on behalf of constraint devices.

In this paper [21], the authors described a secure communication methodology against network flow attacks in IoT devices. They purposed an architecture called Recursive Internetworking Architecture (RINA) and developed a three-host system over a closed environment. This architecture is based on a single type of layer called Distributed IPC Facility and can be repeated depending on the requirement. It provides IPC services for the group of application processes that are configured with the same policy.

The development of IoT raised the security issues due to heterogeneity and asymmetric nature of communicating devices. Secure communication among the IoT devices is the objective this research.

2. Proposed model

Connectivity between smart devices and the cloud creates an internet boundary known as the IoT. A different form of data is transferred via IoT structure originating from many sensors. Like any other network, IoT platforms can provide dissemination of digitalized data, thereby increasing the chances of security attacks. It is important to address the issues related to the security and authentication of the IoT network. Among the security issues which could limit the use of IoT applications are data confidentiality and data privacy.

The combination of many smart gadgets, services, and interconnections creates room for privacy breaches. In this line, proposed is a reliable data transfer model for a secure IoT connection.

9.1.2 Overview of the proposed model

This paper proposes a model of communication between any two IoT devices over the cloud. This model implements two-layered security on the data under transmission. Different sensors transmit data over the cloud. The encryption algorithm at IoT devices encrypts the data received from sensors using RSA and then the encrypted message is hidden/embedded in the image. To make the message more secure after embedding, the proposed hiding algorithm (KNIGHT TOUR) is based on the selection of embedding bits using closed Knight tour and Queen Position on a 4×4 cross board (each character of the encrypted message in put in a successive 4×4 block of the image). The embedded image called stego image travels through the cloud and is received by other IoT devices. At the receiving end, the decrypted message is extracted from the stego image using anti-steganography [22]. Furthermore, the message is decrypted by RSA, and the data are retrieved by the receiving devices.

The following diagram 9.2 depicts the diagrammatic representation of the proposed architecture (Figure 9.2).

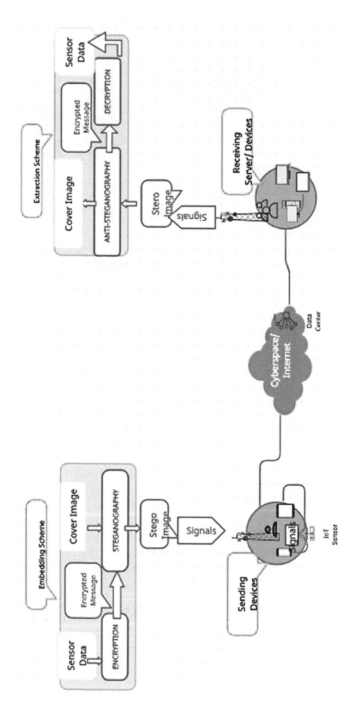

Figure 9.2 Block diagram.

9.1.2.1 Sender side

1. Sender position: Data message is captured here and is processed to ensure its privacy
   a. p and q are two prime numbers in the range 1–99.
   b. Message msg is encrypted using (n =p*q, e) as key, where gcd(l*e) =1 , l=p-1*q-1and encrypted message m is created
   c. Encrypted message m is converted to encrypted message bit m[i,1-7]
   d. Message bits m[i,1-7] is converted to stego image B [8] (Figures 9.3 and 9.4)
2. Internet (Cyberspace) – The network or storage space through which data travels between IOT devices and other devices, which is prone to security attacks.

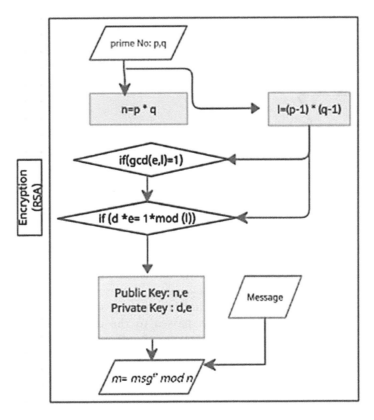

Figure 9.3 Encryption of message.

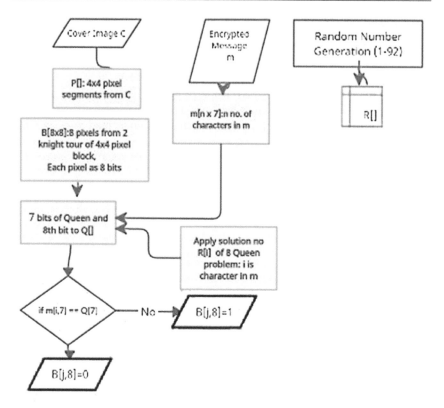

Figure 9.4 Insertion of the encrypted message (m) into a cover image.

3. Receiver position – Decodes the secret information from a stego-image.
   a. The extraction process is used for retrieving the bits m of encrypted message [i,1-7] from the stego image.
   b. m[i,1-7] is encrypted message bits where i is the number of characters in the encrypted message.
   c. m[i,1-7] is converted to character message m.
   d. Encrypted message m is passed to the decryption algorithm using receiver's private key (n=p*q,d) where d*e=1 mod (l), l=p-1 * q-1.

9.1.2.2 Receiver side (Figures 9.5 and 9.6)

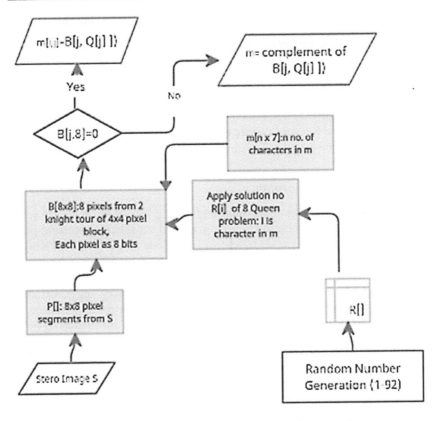

Figure 9.5 Extraction of encrypted message bits from the stego image.

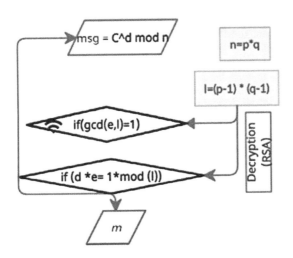

Figure 9.6 Decryption of message (m) to plain message.

9.1.3 Proposed embedding and extraction algorithm

9.1.3.1 Rivest Shamir Adleman algorithm

Rivest Shamir Adleman (RSA) is an asymmetric algorithm, which works on two different keys, that is, Public and Private keys. Public key is shared to everyone and private is kept private. The RSA algorithm is an asymmetric cryptography algorithm. Asymmetric implies that it requires two different keys, that is, **Public Key** and **Private Key**. As the name implies, the Public Key is given to everyone and the Private key is maintained as a secret.

9.1.3.2 Embedding algorithm

The proposed embedding algorithm divides the cover image into 4*4 pixel segments. In the algorithm, the stego key is used for selecting starting position of the knight in 4*4 pixel block, and solutions of all the closed Knight Tours starting from different positions in 4*4 chessboards are saved.

Then, 8-pixels corresponding to two closed knight tours in 4*4 image block is chosen. The selected 8 pixels are converted into 8-bit ASCII code generating an 8*8 bit matrix. The 7-bits corresponding to the positions of the queen in seven columns leaving the eighth column bit are saved in an array Q []. The message character is converted into a 7-bit ASCII code and saved in a two-dimensional array m [i,7]. Each value of array Q[j] is compared with the jth bit of ith message character m[i,j], where j varies from 1 to 7. If the bits are found to be the same, the eighth column bit of the corresponding row is marked as "0" otherwise as "1."

ALGO I: Embedding algorithm

Input: Cover Image, message m, Knight tour solutions, 8-queen's solution set Q
Output: Stego image S

1. Take cover image C
2. Convert the secret message into a 7-bit ASCII code.
3. Store the above-generated ASCII code in a two-dimensional array m(n,7), where n is the number of characters in the secret message
4. Divide Cover image C into 4 × 4 pixels segments.
5. Generate random numbers from 1 to 92 and store them in an array R[]
   For each message character: i=1 to n (n: no. of characters)

```
{ //1st loop
  Select 4*4 pixel segment i.e. P[i]
  The starting pixel position for two knight tours
  is already given (stored in a vector).
```

```
Apply two closed knight tour moves on the 4*4
pixels of the segment
Select eight pixels from two knight tours
positions
Convert the above-selected 8 pixel values from
byte to 8-bit ASCII code
resulting in 8*8 bit matrix, that is, B[8]
If i>=92
then
Apply 8-Queens solution no. R[i-91] to the 8*8
bit matrix
Else
Apply 8-Queens solution no. R[i] to the 8*8 bit
matrix
Choose the 7-bits corresponding to Queens
positions in 8*8
chessboard excluding the last column, store in
an array Q[7]

Take 7-bits of i^th message character, that is,
  m(i,7)
        For j=1 to 7
                { // 2^nd inner loop
                Compare j^th bit of i^th message
                character, that is, m[i,j] with
                Q[j]
                If m[i,j] matches Q[j]
                Mark the last column bit of the j^th
                row B[j,8]=0
                Else
                Mark the last column bit of the
                j^th row B[j,8]=1
                } //2^nd inner loop
    }// 1^st loop
```

9.1.3.3 Extraction algorithm

ALGO 2: *Extraction algorithm*

Input: Stego Image S, Knight tour, 8-queen's solution set Q
Output: Message m

1. Take stego image S
2. Convert the secret message into a 7-bit ASCII code.
3. Store the above-generated ASCII code in a two-dimensional array
   m(n,7), where nis the no. of characters in the secret message

4. Divide stego image S into 8×8 pixels segments.

5. Generate random numbers from 1-92 and store them in an array R[]
   For each message character: i=1 to n (n: no. of characters)

```
{ //1st loop
   Select 8*8 pixel segment, that is, P[i]
   Find out the starting pixel position of the
   knight tour from where the knight tour starts by
   applying soft dipole representation on the pixel
   values of that segment.
   Apply knight tour moves on the 64 pixels of the
   segment
   Select eight pixels from alternate positions
   Convert above selected 8 pixel values from
   byte to 8-bit ASCII code, resulting in 8*8 bit
   matrix, that is, B[8]
If i>=92
   then
   Apply 8-Queens solution no. R[i-91] to the 8*8
   bit matrix
   Else
   Apply 8-Queens solution no. R[i] to the 8*8 bit
   matrix
For j=1 to 7
     {//2nd loop
Save all the Queen's positions excluding last
column position in Q[j]
Extract bit corresponding to Queen's position in 8*8
   chessboard excluding the last column
       That is, B[j, Q[j] ]
         if B[j,8]=0
           then
              m[i,j]= B[j, Q[j] ]
           otherwise
              m[i,j]= complement of ( B[j, Q[j] ])

                } //2nd inner loop
   }// 1st loop
```

The proposed extraction algorithm divides the image into 4*4 pixels blocks. In the proposed algorithm, two closed Knight tours are applied to each image block. The knight to select the same pixels, as selected for message embedding in each 4*4 pixel block, uses the previously stored starting positions. The extraction algorithm selects 8 pixels visited by two closed knight tours in each 4*4 block and converts them to 8-bit ASCII code resulting in an 8*8 bit matrix. Extraction algorithm uses 8-Queen's solution on an 8*8 bit matrix, and 7 bits corresponding to queen's position are selected excluding last bit. If the last column bit corresponding to the queen's position is "1," then the bit is reversed at the queen's position and the reversed bit is saved. The extracted 7-bits give one message character. Each 4*4 pixel block hides a single character of a secret message.

9.2 ANALYSIS

The proposed secure communication model uses RSA algorithms to encrypt **m** number of messages that results in **m** encrypted messages. The **m** encrypted messages are further hidden into a cover image using the proposed embedding algorithm, generating a stego image. In our experiment, we used three different key lengths, that is, 512 bits, 1024 bits, and 2048 bits. The length of the encrypted message is 88, 172, and 344 characters long respectively, which in turn will generate 616, 1204, and 2408 bits to represent the message in ASCII code. In our experiments, we embedded various numbers of messages in different image formats like bmp, png, jpg to hide the secret message of different lengths (in bits). RSA guarantees confidentiality and authenticity over an insecure communication channel. The integer number n used in RSA is called "modulus," which defines the length of the RSA key. The security of RSA lies in the integer factorization method. It is said that if n = 1024 bits, it is not possible to factor it, but RSA 1024 bit (which is approximately 310 decimal digits) is not considered secured enough. Now it is reasonable to use RSA with 2048 bit or more if one needs long-term security (Table 9.1).

Tables 9.1, 9.3, and 9.5 show the number of encrypted messages embedded in a cover image generated with different encryption key sizes. The length of encrypted message changes with a change in key size.

Results in the form of PSNR (Peak-Signal-to-Noise ratio) are generated for LSB, 8-Rooks, 8-Queens, and proposed algorithm (Knight tour), as shown in Tables 9.2, 9.4, and 9.6. Comparison of results shows that the PSNR [Equation (9.1)] of the proposed algorithm is better than other techniques (Table 9.2).

$$\text{PSNR} = 10 * \log 10 \frac{255^2 * \text{M} * \text{N}}{\sum_{i=0}^{M-1} \sum_{j=0}^{N-1} \left(p_{i,j} - q_{i,j} \right)^2} \text{dB} \qquad (9.1)$$

Table 9.1 Message bits <4000

Key size	Encrypted message(bytes)	Encrypted message(bits)	No. of messages embedded	Total message bits embedded
512	88	616	6	616*6 = 3696
1024	172	1204	3	172*3 = 516
2048	344	2408	1	2408*1 = 2408

Table 9.2 PSNR with (message bits <4000).

Cover Image	LSB	8-rooks	8-queens	Knight tour
Lena.bmp	56.06	36	51.26	59.67
Pepper	56.05	41	51.34	58.54
Baboon	57.04	40	51.28	58.66
Flower	57.15	50	51.33	59.76
Jet	58.03	45	51.26	59.58
Mountain.png	58.12	38	51.24	59. 88

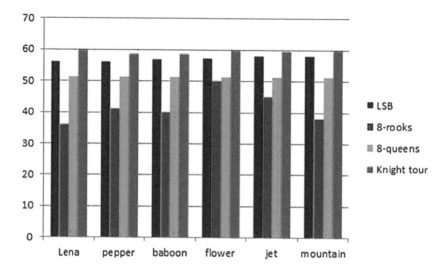

Figure 9.7 PSNR of different embedding methods shown in Table 9.2.

Table 9.3 Embedding message bits <14,000

Key size	Encrypted message(bytes)	Encrypted message(bits)	No. of messages
512	88	616	22
1024	172	1204	11
2048	344	2408	5

Various graphs in Figures 9.7, 9.8, and 9.9 have been put up to efficiently show the PSNR (Tables 9.2, 9.4, 9.6) comparison between the proposed work and the existing methods.

Table 9.6 PSNR comparison of different embedding methods with embedded message bits <42,000

Table 9.4 PSNR with (message bits <4000)

Cover Image	LSB	8-rooks	8-queens	Knight tour
Lena.bmp	55.012	33	50.26	58.13
Pepper	55.041	38	50.34	57.66
Baboon	56.03	37	50.28	57.45
Flower	56.004	48	50.3	58.77
Jet	57.016	44	50.26	58.56
Mountain.png	57.001	37	50.24	58.23

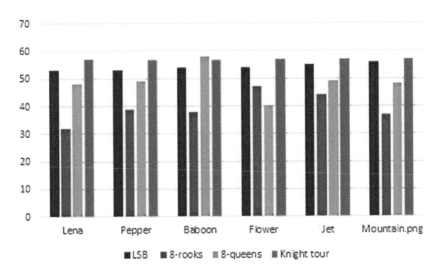

Figure 9.8 PSNR of different embedding methods shown in Table 9.4.

Table 9.5 Embedding message bits<42000

Key size	Encrypted message(bytes)	Encrypted message(bits)	No. of messages
512	88	616	68
1024	172	1204	34
2048	344	2408	17

Table 9.6 PSNR with (message bits <42,000)

Cover image	LSB	8-rooks	8-queens	Knight tour
Lena.bmp	53.01	32	48.06	57.03
Pepper	53.037	39	49.01	56.76
Baboon	54.008	38	58.02	56.58
Flower	54.024	47	40.02	57.03
Jet	55.043	44	49.07	57.03
Mountain.png	56.006	37	48.08	57.01

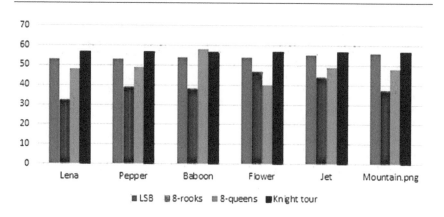

Figure 9.9 PSNR of different embedding methods shown in Table 9.6.

Table 9.7 Comparison of existing steganography tools

Tool	Interface	Cover image	Stego image	Message length	Encryption algorithms	MSE	PSNR
Open Stego.		14KB	149 KB	14 Kb	AES 128 AES 256	11158	76
Hide' N Send		11 KB	148 Kb	1 Kb	AES 256 Rc2 Rc4	11645	74
Rstego		14kb	129kb	1 Kb	AES 256	11375	76
Quick stego		IPR 442 Kb	IPR 6067 KB	4000 kb	No encryption	11459	75
SSuite Piscel		18 kb	196kb	14 Kb	No encryption	12415	72

9.3 CONCLUSION

In this paper, a secure communication method using steganography is proposed for IoT devices. The message hiding algorithm in the proposed model is using knight tour to choose pixels from image blocks, making the pixel selection more random. To enhance the security of the message, it is encrypted using the RSA encryption algorithm and converted into bits. Bits of the encrypted message are compared with the bits at the positions of 8-Queens in 8*8 chessboards. The proposed algorithm is highly secured for message hiding, as it is not substituting message bits with the bits of image pixels. PSNR is used to compare cover image and stego image. Experiments are conducted on various image formats to compare the PSNR of the proposed algorithm with some existing image steganography algorithms. As one image could carry more than one message, this model could be used for even asynchronous data transfer, as the source of the message could be accumulated at the source itself in every epoch.

REFERENCES

[1] Khari, M., Garg, A. K., Gandomi, A. H., Gupta, R., Patan, R., & Balusamy, B. (2020). Securing data in Internet of Things (IoT) using cryptography and steganography techniques. *IEEE Transactions on Systems*, 50(1), 73–80.

[2] Gura, N., Patel, A., Wander, A., Eberle, H., & Shantz, S. C. (2004). Comparing elliptic curve cryptography and RSA on 8-bit CPUs. In *Cambridge: Proceedings of the Sixth Workshop on Cryptographic Hardware and Embedded Systems* (pp. 119–132).

[3] Phad, V. S., Bhosale, R. S., & Panhalkar, A. R. (2012). A novel security scheme for secret data using cryptography and steganography. *International Journal Computer Network and Information Security*, 2, 36–42. doi:10.5815/ijcnis.2012.02.06

[4] Stolbikova, V. (2016). Can elliptic curve cryptography be trusted? A brief analysis of the security of a popular cryptosystem. *ISACA Journal*, 3, 1–5.

[5] Douglas, M., Bailey, K., Leeney, M., & Curran, K. (2018). An overview of steganography techniques applied to the protection of biometric data. *Multimedia Tools and Applications*, 77, 17333–17373.

[6] Hashim, M. M., Abdulrazzaq, A. A., Rahim, M., Shafry, M., & Taha, M. S. (2019). Improvement of image steganography scheme based on LSB value with two control random parameters and multi-level encryption. In *IOP Conference Series:Material Science & Engineering* (vol. 518, p. 052002). 10.1088/1757-899X/518/5/052002

[7] Sumathi, C. P., Santanam, T., & Umamaheswari, G. (2013). A study of various steganographic techniques. *International Journal of Computer Science & Engineering Survey (IJCSES)*, 4(6), 9–25.

[8] Manogaram, G., Thofa, C., Lopez, D., & Sundarasekar, R. (2017). Big data security intelligence for healthcare indistry 4.0. In *Cybersecirity for indistry 4.0* (pp. 103–126). Switxerland: Springer.

[9] Saleh, M. E., Aly, A. A., & Omara, F. A. (2016). Data security using cryptography and steganography technique. *International Journal of Advanced Computer Science and Applications*, 7, 390–397.

[10] Chervyakov, N. (2019). AR-RRNS: Configurable reliable distributed data storage systems for Internet of Things to ensure security. *Future Generation Computer Systems*, 92, 1080–1092.

[11] Bairagi, A. K., Khondoker, R., & Islam, R. (2016). An efficient steganographic approach for protecting communication in the Internet of Things (IoT) critical infrastructures. *Information Security Journal A Global Perspective*, 25, 197–212.

[12] Elhoseny, M., Ramírez-González, G., Abu-Elnasr, O. M., Shawkat, S. A., Arunkumar, N., & Farouk, A. (2018). Secure medical data transmission model for IoT-based healthcare systems. *IEEE Access*, 6, 20596–20608.

[13] Hashim, M. M., Rhaif, S. H., Abdulrazzaq, A. A., Ali, A. H., & Taha, M. S. (2020). Based on IoT healthcare application for medical data authentication: Towards a new secure framework using steganography. In *IOP Conference Series: Materials Science and Engineering* (vol. 881). Iraq: IOP Publishing Ltd.

[14] Tawalbeh, L., Muheidat, F., Tawalbeh, M., & Quwaider, M. (2020). IoT privacy and security: Challenges and solutions. *Applied Science*, 10. 10.3390/app10124102

[15] Daneshkhah, A., Aghaeinia, H., & Seyedi, S. H. (2011). A more secure steganography method in spatial domain. In *Second International Conference on Intelligent Systems, Modelling and Simulation*. 10.1109/ISMS.2011.39

[16] Chen, Y. Z., Han, Z., Li, S.-P., Lu, C.-H., & Yao, X.-H. (2010). An adaptive steganography algorithm based on block sensitivity vectors using HVS features. In *2010 3rd International Congress on Image and Signal Processing* (pp. 1151–1155). China: IEEE. 10.1109/CISP.2010.5646724

[17] Bhatia, M. (2017). 8-rooks solutions for image steganography technique. *International Journal of Next-Generation Computing*, 8, 127–139. 10.47164/ijngc.v8i2.314

[18] Bhatia, M., Muttoo, S. K., & Bhatia, M. (2015). An image steganography method using spread spectrum technique. In *Fourth International Conference on Soft Computing for Problem Solving, Advances in Intelligent Systems and Computing* (vol. 336). Springer. 10.1007/978-81-322-2220-0_18

[19] Muttoo, S. K., Kumar, V., & Bansal, A. (2012). Secure data hiding using eight queens solutions. *International Journal of Information Security and Privacy (IJISP)*, 6, 55–70.

[20] Bonetto, R., Bui, N., Lakkundi, V., Olivereau, A., Serbanati, A., & Rossi, M. (2012). Secure communication for smart IoT Objects: Protocol stacks, use cases and practical examples. In *2012 IEEE International Symposium on a World of Wireless, Mobile and Multimedia Networks (WoWMoM)* (pp. 1–7).

[21] Samyuel, N., & Shimray, B. A. (2021). Securing IoT device communication against network flow attacks with Recursive Internetworking Architecture (RINA). *ICT Express*, 7(1), 110–114.

[22] Altaay, A., Sahib, S. B., & Zamani, M. (2012). An introduction to image steganography techniques. In *International Conference on Advanced Computer Science Applications and Technologies* (pp. 122–126).

Chapter 10

Next-generation networks enabled technologies

Challenges and applications

Umesh Gupta, Deepika Pantola, Aditya Bhardwaj and Simar Preet Singh

Bennett University Greater Noida, Noida, India

CONTENTS

10.1 Introduction 191
10.2 Architecture of next-generation network 194
    10.2.1 Need for next-generation network 194
    10.2.2 Features of next-generation network 196
10.3 Next-generation network enabling technologies 196
    10.3.1 5G 197
    10.3.2 Edge intelligence 198
    10.3.3 Cloud-based Internet of Things 200
        10.3.3.1 Importance of integrating cloud computing
                with Internet of Things network 201
    10.3.4 Software-defined networks 202
10.4 Open research challenges and issues in next-generation network 203
    10.4.1 Challenges and issues in 5G 204
    10.4.2 Challenges and issues in edge intelligence 204
    10.4.3 Challenges and issues in Cloud-based Internet of
        Things network 205
    10.4.4 Challenges and issues in software-defined network 206
10.5 Applications 207
    10.5.1 Intelligent healthcare 207
    10.5.2 Supply chain management 208
    10.5.3 Smart education 209
    10.5.4 Intelligent disaster management system 210
10.6 Conclusion and future scope 210
References 210

10.1 INTRODUCTION

Traditionally, telecommunication networks were at first used for "voice traffic," where a circuit-switching network was used to establish communication between sender and receiver. A circuit switching network is characterized by

DOI: 10.1201/9781003355946-10

reservation of bandwidth for the duration of the call. This reservation involves an initial call establishment phase during signaling messages and the release of the bandwidth in a call termination phase at the end of the call, although circuit switching worked well for voice data and imposed minimal information loss [1–3]. However, a circuit switching network suffers from several limitations. First, the circuit switching network results in inefficiency during the data busty condition [4–8]. Second, it is inflexible to accommodate data flows at different rates.

As an improvement to the circuit switching network, the packet-switched network has attracted worldwide attention. In a packet-switched network, making a connection is not required and it was idle for all other types of data except voice traffic [3–6]. Packet switching is the basis for Internet Protocol (IP) where data are grouped into variable-length packets. The packets are forwarded to their neighbor routers, and by looking up the address of the destination, they are again forwarded to the next hop [9]. It is continued until it reaches its target destination. A packet switching can lead to more efficient link utilization, and unpredictable queuing delays force network operators to operate their network [10–14]. However, a packet switching network is connection-less and thus not as reliable as circuit switching. In the recent few years, the Next-Generation Network (NGN) evolved as the latest evolution of the global communications networks. The general idea behind the NGN is ubiquity in that a network moves all data and services by encapsulating these into packets [1, 12]. Gartner defines NGN, as "the evolution and migration of fixed and mobile network infrastructures from distinct, proprietary networks to converged networks based on IP." NGNs represent a significant evolution toward greater reliability and security in corporate networks, as they incorporate the virtualized functions of Software-Defined Wide Area Networks (SD-WANs) and Secure Access Service Edge (SASE) to achieve more efficient, centrally managed network operations. NGN as a future network comprises a richer set of features that can provide robust services to the end users and meet the requirement of Industry 4.0 network service providers. Recently [15], with the increasing interest in emerging technologies, such as 5G, cloud, Internet of Things (IoT), edge, fog, and software-defined networking (SDN), a major question that needs to be addressed is how NGN can be incorporated with them. Therefore, in this study, we explored the application and future challenges of NGNs with the emerging technologies such as 5G, cloud, IoT, edge, fog, and SDN.

The remaining sections of this paper are structured as follows: the architecture of the next generation network is presented in Section 2. NGN enabling technologies are described in Section 3. In Section 4, open research challenges and issues are discussed. In Section 5, the application is introduced. Finally, the conclusion with a future research direction is presented in Section 6. Figure 10.1 provides the organization of this paper.

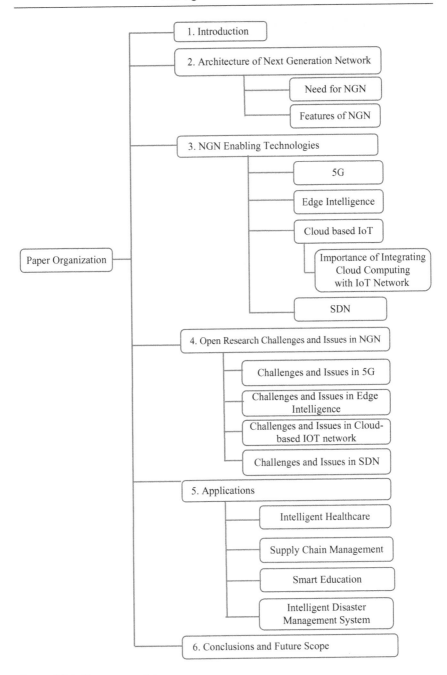

Figure 10.1 Structure of the paper.

10.2 ARCHITECTURE OF NEXT-GENERATION NETWORK

NGN is redefining the telecommunication networks. The general idea behind the NGN is ubiquity in that a network moves all data and services by encapsulating these into packets. NGN is a packet-based network that can provide services, including telecommunication services and can use multiple bandwidths and QoS-enabled transmission technologies [16–20]. The main feature of the NGN is the division of transport functions and services into two sections. With this division, services can be developed and offered by different companies. As an evolutionary technique, current IP networks suffer from lack of mobility, loss of transparency, scalability issues, protocol incompatibility, security issues, and all in all, protocols taking roles for which they were not originally designed [21]. Future web analysis comes as a square measure shooting up everyplace leading to new design styles and protocols. In Europe, analysis activities square measure primarily carried out the multi-year continental Framework Programme (FP), which covers a good variety of subjects, from ICT to energy, engineering, health, and so on. The present program is the seventh (FP7), which started in January 2007 and can expire in 2013. In Japan, the Akari project [22] – sponsored by the National Institute of Communication and Technology (NICT) – features a unit for the event of a brand-new spec following a clean-slate approach in what they decide as a brand-new generation network (NwGN) by 2015 [17]. In the US, the National Science Foundation (NSF) has been actively funded, which comes at intervals in the longer-term web style (FIND) framework, wherever clean-slate thinking has been a significant topic. Figure 10.2 describes the architecture of the NGN.

10.2.1 Need for next-generation network

Since its inception at the end of the 20th century, the requirements for the worldwide communication networks known as the Internet have changed dramatically. Based on its current trends, it is expected to be 100 times larger than what it is today. This means that information and communication technology (ICT) electricity usage will soar. The necessity to preserve energy may stifle the growth of the internet [23–25]. Another issue is security. Spam emails, denial of services, or DOS attacks have struck computer operations by attacking users with illegal software packets and garbage data. To address these growing patterns, appropriate software solutions are required. Furthermore, because new features are constantly added to the internet, it has serious structural flaws [26, 28]. If this trend continues, the network system will soon be unable to withstand the strain. This is the reason for developing new generation networks [27].

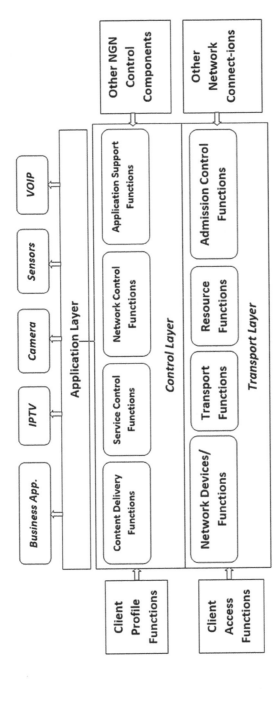

Figure 10.2 Next-generation networks (NGNs) architecture.

Table 10.1 Different features/parameters of the NGN network and its applicability

Parameters	NGN Network
Multimedia services	Yes
QoS-enabled	Yes
Network intelligence	Yes
Intelligent CPE	Yes
Underlying Transport Network	Packet
Service Architecture	Distinct
Integrated Control & Management	Yes
Service Reliability	High
Service creation	Systematic
Ease of use of services	High

10.2.2 Features of next-generation network

a) *Mobility*: SIP-based. Has mobility issues due to IP restrictions. The mobility support of the cellular network is also used by IMS. The ID/Loc decoupling is used by NGN-GSI [28] as shown in Table 10.1.

b) *Ubiquity*: Due to a lack of IP address space, traceability is constrained. Scalability of NAPT and other entities is necessary for IP ubiquity [28].

c) *Security*: IPsec-based. Suffers from traditional IP security constraints as well as new ones related to SIP.

d) *Generality*: The service stratum is detached from transportation resources. RACF provides limited network customization [29].

e) *RVWI*: NED support is practically nonexistent. Furthermore, it is unclear as to what extent the IP network can scale to meet NED's expected extraordinary growth.

f) *Information-centrism*: Traditional protocols such as HTTP, RTP, SMTP, and others are supported by OSA/Parlay and SIP gateways and servers [29–31].

g) *Service- centrism*: Services are orchestrated via SIP and its proxies. A very centralized strategy. SDPs (service delivery platforms) are based on SOA. The app-store model.

h) *Autonomy*: Almost all operations rely on proprietary management software, which necessitates daily human intervention [29–31].

10.3 NEXT-GENERATION NETWORK ENABLING TECHNOLOGIES

NGNs combine the capabilities of a variety of established and emerging technologies, including 5G, artificial intelligence (AI), edge intelligence, network softwarization, and data-plane programmability. In wireless communication and networking, NGNs promise ultra-high data speeds and low latency. AI and machine learning (ML) provide smart and autonomous services and applications [30–33]. NGNs provide a multitude of smart services and user-defined applications when combined with advancements in end-user devices. New state-of-the-art NGN management solutions are required as system complexity grows, and the volume of data transferred across networks grows exponentially.

End-users receive more reliable and efficient services and applications when cooperative and distributed management solutions are used. Furthermore, NGNs could be designed to accommodate the dynamic nature of network configuration and enable end-to-end system automation using distributed learning techniques. Federated learning (FL), deep reinforcement learning (DRL), and blockchain integration with NGNs, for example, can allow scalable, secure, and diverse services and applications. Furthermore, network intelligence could be implemented directly on programmable devices with the network core, thanks to data plane programmability [34–38]. An intelligent forwarding plane would allow for speedier network event response without relying on a time-consuming data-control plane exchange. In this chapter, we have categorized NGN-enabled technologies into three major categories given below:

a) Cellular network technology
   i.   5G
   ii. 6G
b) Cloud-related technology
   i.   Fog computing
   ii. Edge computing
   iii. Cloud-based IoT services
c) Computer network technology
   i.   Software dependent network (SDN)
   ii. Network slicing

10.3.1 5G

In the previous three decades, there has been a considerable expansion in wireless communication with the change from 1G to 5G [38, 39]. The major research objective of 5G is to meet high bandwidth and low latency requirements. 5G presents superior data rates, reduced expectancy time, increased quality of service (QoS), high dependability, high coverage, and services that are affordably accessible. There are three types of services provided by 5G, which are listed as follows:

a) *Enhanced mobile broadband (eMBB)*: It is a feature of 5G that allows consumer devices to take use of extraordinary network speeds, increased bandwidth, streaming of videos at UltraHD, moderate latency, virtual reality, and augmented reality (AR/VR) media, among other things.

b) *Massive machine communication/Massive machine type communication (MMC/MMTC)*: MMC is a sort of machine-to-machine communication across wired or wireless networks in which data production, information exchange, and actuation occur with little or no human intervention. It provides broadband and long-range communication with minimal power usage at a low cost. For IoT-based applications, MMC provides a high data rate service, and wider coverage through marginal device complexity through mobile carriers [38, 39].

c) *Ultra-reliable low latency communication (URLLC)*: It is one of the essential services offered by 5G. It delivers extremely high trustworthiness, low latency, and a fine QoS. URLLC is intended for on-demand real-time interactions such as autonomous driving, vehicle-to-vehicle (V2V) communication, smart grids, remote surgery, intelligent transportation systems, smart factories, and industry 4.0 [40].

5G is a cornerstone of the digital revolution; it outperforms all previous mobile generation networks. 5G is quicker than 4G and allows for remote control over a secure network with no delays. It has a maximum downlink capacity of up to 20 Gbps. 5G also provides support to the 4th Generation Worldwide Wireless Web (4G) [41] and is built on the IPv6 protocol. With exceptionally fast speed, high throughput, low latency, improved reliability and scalability, and energy-efficient mobile communication technology, 5G enables a limitless internet connection at your convenience, anytime, anywhere [42]. *6 GHz 5G* and *Millimetre wave* (mm Wave) *5G* are the two basic types of 5G. 6 GHz is a mid-frequency band that provides a great setting for 5G connection by bridging the gap between capacity and coverage. High bandwidth and enhanced network performance will be provided by the 6 GHz frequency. It provides continuous channels, reducing the requirement for network densification when the mid-band spectrum is unavailable, and it makes a 5G connection accessible to everyone at any time and in any location. mm Wave is a critical technology for 5G networks that need to be of high performance. 5G mm wave provides a wide range of services, which is why all network operators should include it in their 5G implementation plans. Many service providers have installed 5G mm wave, and their simulation results demonstrate that this spectrum is significantly less used. It offers ultra-wide bandwidth for the next-generation mobile network, as well as very high-speed wireless communication [38–42].

10.3.2 Edge intelligence

Edge intelligence, also known as edge-native AI [43–44], is a new technological paradigm that focuses on the seamless integration of AI, communication networks, and mobile-based edge computing. Edge intelligence lays the

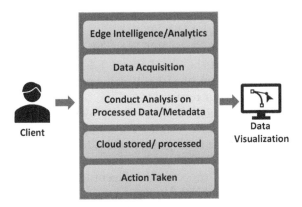

Figure 10.3 Edge intelligence/analytics framework.

groundwork for pervasive and faster AI integration in the next-generation wireless system by deploying a huge scale of decentralized mobile edge servers to execute AI-based processing and decision making closer to where the data and service requests are created [44]. The combination of PMN (private mobile networks) with edge intelligence is predicted to be critical in achieving the next generation of commercial applications. This is called IPN (intelligent private networks) and is used in certain industries like transportation systems, which can unleash a variety of use cases and key applications, allowing businesses to meet expanding demand. Edge intelligence is widely acknowledged as a key enabler for 6G to fully realize the potential of network intelligence [45]. Figure 10.3 shows the framework for edge intelligence or edge analytics.

Following are some of the advantages of edge intelligence technology:

a) *Providing information using low latency*: The problem of delay has plagued cloud computing and centralized systems. Capturing and transferring data to a central location, analyzing it, and replying takes time and is ineffective for near-real-time decision-making. The main benefit of edge intelligence is that it reduces latency, allowing for near-real-time actionable events and improving overall system efficiency. It allows you to detect a vacant parking place using camera video feeds and update the vacancy table without having to upload all the feeds to the cloud, set up a central server for video processing, and wait for the inputs. The edge device performs the overall task of identifying the car, parking place, and location of the vehicle, in an intelligent manner [40–46]. This allows cloud and centralized systems to focus on highly structured, context-rich actionable data rather than processing raw and irrelevant data. This reduces latency throughout the system, not just at the edge.

b) *Provides data storage using small bandwidth*: The bandwidth requirements for transmitting all the data collected by thousands of edge devices are extremely large in any IoT scenario. It will also expand at an exponential rate, as the number of these devices grow. Remote site locations may not have enough bandwidth to send data and analysis back and forth from the cloud server. Edge intelligence aids in the analysis and execution of tasks. It can save data, information, and action reports for later retrieval [46–47].

c) *Provides the linear scalability*: As IoT deployments expand, edge intelligence systems can scale linearly. The computing power of deployed devices is used in edge intelligence designs. It can handle the high load of deep learning and machine learning models. Edge devices share the principal load of executing intelligent operations, which relieves demand on centralized cloud systems.

d) *Supports operation at low costs*: Intelligent edges act on time-sensitive data locally, saving you a lot of cloud space while providing content-rich data to central systems. This lowers your operating expenses. Edge intelligence drives real-time actions for all connected IoT devices, allowing OT workers to deploy and maintain devices more efficiently [48].

10.3.3 Cloud-based Internet of Things

With the popularity of IoT, network researchers had predicted that in the future, computing most of the data trapped will come from computer-enabled things as compared to the one generated by people. The primary idea was to assign each thing a tag, which would act as an identifier in the network for communication. The cloud service delivery model can be used to provide computing resources for the deployed IoT applications. Here, each existing system consists of separate IoT infrastructure and computing resources. Also, it is challenging to extend deployed services, because for this solution, providers must make changes in all system layers [35–37]. Each time they deliver services to a new customer, they must repeat the same process of development and deployment to provide an isolated vertical solution. Due to such problems, this service delivery model is not much efficient. Figure 10.4 shows the cloud-based architecture for the IoT. As depicted in Figure 10.4, the IoT based on the Cloud is a far cry from the typical IoT, as it has the potential to develop and deploy IoT applications online with the help of the cloud. Based on the existing work proposed by [32], Figure 10.4 highlights the main components of Cloud Things Architecture and their importance for IoT. It also mentions the preferred protocols for networking with Things, Interacting with Things, and Integrating Things with the Cloud.

The cloud computing services, which play a significant role in the IoT network, are highlighted as follows:

a) Infrastructure as a Service (IaaS): It is a Cloud-based service that allows users to run their applications using Cloud hardware. It simplifies the

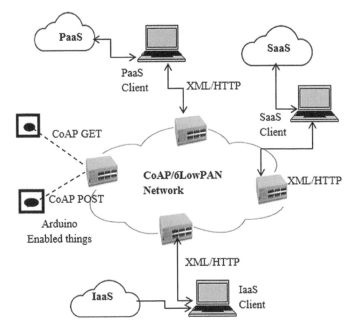

Figure 10.4 Cloud computing based IoT network architecture [53].

process of application development by wiping out the need for infrastructure development and hence reduces the overall costs. It interacts directly with things and offers storage for data captured by various sensors. It then processes and analyzes the stored data for future predictions. It offers Virtualization, Storage, Network, Load balancer, and firewall for easy development of Things Applications [32].

b) Platform as a Service (PaaS): It is a Cloud-based developer suite that provides service tools for developing an application for the IoT. These tools consist of application programming interfaces (APIs), databases, programming language, and application server, which provides an entire kit for the development and deployment to developers of IoT applications [35].

c) Software as a Service (SaaS): It is a Cloud-based operating portal that offers a set of cloud services for the deployment of IoT applications, and it also supports various services like data intelligence, things composition, and management of service subscriptions [37].

10.3.3.1 Importance of integrating cloud computing with Internet of Things network

Both Cloud computing and the IoT are growing technologies and have their features. If we consider a case study of any IoT application like Smart Home, we will come to know that many sensors and actuators are used, which generate a large amount of data and need large computation capabilities to process the data. IoT involves challenges of big data storage, heterogeneous hardware infrastructure management, integrated computing, security, privacy, and many more as discussed below [32–37].

    i. Sensors generate a huge amount of heterogeneous data that require large storing space, but utilizing embedded memory and memory cards in things is not sufficient. So, things lack storage resources.

    ii. Things also do not have ample computing resources to handle large applications for real-time processing of data, and to make overcritical decisions.

    iii. Things crave Web-based interfaces so that users can access and monitor things from anywhere and at any time. The only thing they require is high-speed internet.

    iv. Things crave Web-based platforms so that programming and deployment can be done without creating downtime.

    v. Things also crave on-demand use of IT resources in a scalable and economical way.

    vi. Things need to design in such a way that they are open to heterogeneous hardware and standards.

    vii. Things need to design in such a way as to ensure security and privacy during data exchange.

On the other side, Cloud can offer unlimited resources like storage and processing energy on demand, and it provides new services mentioned in Table 10.2, which will help in improving the service delivery of IoT.

10.3.4 Software-defined networks

The number of internet-connected gadgets has expanded dramatically in recent years. The IoT of today is being transformed into the vast IoT of

Table 10.2 Cloud IoT applications and related challenges

Applications \ Challenges	Security	Privacy	Performance	Reliability	Heterogeneity	Large scale
Pervasive healthcare	YES	YES	YES	YES	YES	YES
Smart homes	—	—	YES	YES	YES	—
Smart cities	YES	YES	YES	YES	YES	—
Video surveillance	YES	—	YES	YES	YES	—
Smart grid	YES	YES	YES	YES	YES	—

the future by increasing the number of linked devices to the internet. It is expected that within a few years, huge IoT devices and applications requiring data exchange and processing will necessitate a high transmission and computation capacity. Mobile networks in the 5G and above, on the one hand, are projected to meet some of these requirements by providing data rates of up to terabits per second. It will be a major enabler for huge IoT and developing task-critical applications that must adhere to severe latency limitations. The next generation of SDN combined with new cloud-related technologies such as edge computing and fog computing, can, on the other hand, play a key role in enabling and executing the aforementioned applications [49–50].

Traditional cloud computing, which included one or a few massive data centers was a potential data processing architecture a few years ago for storing and processing vast amounts of data and providing a variety of reliable and mission-critical services to customers with severe delay limits. These centralized data centers are not ideal for supporting new applications connected to future enormous IoT since they are typically located far away from end-users and cannot provide ultra-low latency and high bandwidth connectivity. Furthermore, typical cloud computing fails to meet needs of several projects of smart objects with mobility, such as geolocation [51].

Cisco created fog computing to address all these technical problems. Cisco expanded the typical cloud-enabled computing paradigm to the network edge with fog computing [49, 51]. Fog computing, in other words, expands cloud computing to the edge of networks to minimize latency delay by spatially dividing IoT application modules and enabling item portability [49]. SDN, on the one hand, can be coupled with fog computing nodes to make it even smarter, analytical, and effective [51, 52]. 5G and even beyond (i.e., 6G) has, on the other hand, been a vital source for huge IoT and enabling technologies [49–51].

10.4 OPEN RESEARCH CHALLENGES AND ISSUES IN NEXT-GENERATION NETWORK

In this section, we outline some of the research challenges and issues that need to be addressed in NGN and its enabling technologies. Some of the NGN challenges are listed below:

- Expandable failure management solutions are desirable since there are more devices to cover larger geographical locations and users, as well as more types of equipment [53].
- One of the major obstacles in NGN is providing real-time identity verification services so that when traveling is necessary, the user can be registered and allowed to switch networks on the fly [54].

- In the NGN context, data protection and internet security are two crucial components of security.
- Vehicular networks are another significant concern. Changing networks for a session with specific QoS demands will be a major difficulty [53–55].

10.4.1 Challenges and issues in 5G

- New revenue channels, on the one hand, from the latest smartphone experiences, apps, and solutions are offered with 5G. These emerging services and applications, on the other hand, impose a wide range of latency, performance, scalability, and access policies on the network [55].
- mmWave is significantly more difficult to construct than the low-frequency range, and RF professionals may need advanced training. These are not your typical surf breaks!
- Poor signal coverage and excessive reflection from construction materials are significant obstacles when planning for mmWave. In-building mmWaves necessitate an architecture redesign, with new antennas, fiber optics, and tiny cells all requiring to be deployed across an area for proper connectivity [56].
- Beamforming, a crucial component of 5G NR, allows for hyper information transmission but necessitates rising computation and input during the design phase. It is an effective instrument that necessitates a large amount of conceptual design [57].
- Because 5G is expected to empower advanced technologies such as self-driving cars and robotic healthcare implants, latency might prove disastrous. In these sectors, precise, well-designed 5G networks are crucial to reducing latency [58].
- The benefits that 5G offers need not be made minor. While most 5G infrastructure is inconsistent with current systems, expanding a system also necessitates upgrading antennae [59].

10.4.2 Challenges and issues in edge intelligence

- Edge data centers involve the configuration, installation, and operation of edge computing platforms. Numerous older devices limit processing capacity, and integrating modern external capabilities requires more CapEx.
- Because edge computing only uses a subset of data, a large amount of raw data is wasted. Otherwise, this squandered data could have been useful. Data segregation is a complex task for firms seeking to enhance productivity and minimize data loss [67–69].
- Because edge data centers are close to humans, a comprehensive physical security mechanism is essential to prevent any undesired security flaws.

- Remotely managing and supporting many edge data centers presents new problems such as IT troubleshooting, security protection improvements, and unifying maintenance and support across various spots [67–69].
- Choosing and installing the appropriate infrastructure components might be a difficult task. If not caught early enough, even the tiniest problem can spread to multiple installations. This might result in an inadequate or oversized UPS, as well as a lack of or extra rack space [67–69].

10.4.3 Challenges and issues in Cloud-based Internet of Things network

Integrating Cloud and IoT encourages the birth or enhancement of various applications that can have a great impact on one's life. In this section, we will discuss that apart from getting benefitted from the Cloud-IoT paradigm, these applications suffer from various challenges also shown in Table 10.2. In this section, the main challenges faced by IoT applications are mentioned. We then also focus on other issues that can be concerned with future work.

a) *Heterogeneity*: One of the main challenges in Cloud Things is heterogeneity among Things, operating systems, services, and platforms used for various applications. The heterogeneity of cloud platforms is a non-ignorable matter. But Cloud-based IoT platforms used for the deployment of IoT applications have solved the problem of heterogeneity to a great extent.

b) *Performance*: Applications related to Cloud Things often demand high-level performance and QoS at various levels, but it is not that easily achievable. The reason behind this is that it is very tough to obtain constant network performance to reach the Cloud. The performance of real-time applications is mainly affected due to poor networks. Usability can also be suffered by poor QoS [57–60].

c) *Reliability*: Reliability is of great concern when Cloud IoT is considered for mission-critical applications. Cloud Computing has overcome the challenge of reliability to some extent by offloading high computation needed tasks on the cloud and by providing unlimited resources on demand. But still, it generates issues like resource exhaustion [57–60].

Here, we come to know that the various issues of CloudThings need further research efforts like there is a need for proper standards of protocols, architectures, and APIs. Secondly, Energy Efficient sensing is a big issue in IoT, but with the adoption of Cloud technology, it is possible to use cloud resources on-demand. But more local activities that require computational power can be offloaded to the cloud, to save IoT device energy. Big Data is also a big challenge that requires research efforts. There is a need to focus on deep learning and new technologies to analyze a large amount of heterogeneous data. For the improvement of QoS, there is a need to work on Cloud Scheduling algorithms to handle task duplication to avoid failures. Security is still a major issue in CloudIoT that needs to be considered for improvement [57–60].

10.4.4 Challenges and issues in software-defined network

- Complete transition to SDN-based infrastructure can be difficult, particularly considering economic limitations. In the end, enormous SDN part installation and softwarization enabled tools are required for the cloud-fog system. It can make a full SDN setup more secure. As a result, these programs incorporate a layered architecture in which traditional and SDN-based systems, resources, routing protocols, services, and virtual environments are compatible and consented to meet the client's needs. Mixed SDN for fog computing emerges from this agreed-upon architecture amalgamation, where problems include optimal resource provisioning, upgrading networking protocols, and latency-aware scheduling. One of the stiffening consequences may be that a global regulator (i.e., root controller) cannot examine the network architecture or swap responsibilities inline as quickly as pure SDN deployed parts [51–54, 63].
- For the time being, a hybrid SDN-traditional IP network design is a viable option. Hardware expenditures are essential to completely adapt the network to SDN. As a result, network operators are eager to open with a hybrid SDN-IP network infrastructure. Then, there is the problem of gathering precise network structure and instructing devices that are not physically linked to the center. Separate installation of both kinds of devices, as well as assessing the setup validity and statistical choice of controller positioning near equipment, are additional issues. New SDN technologies enabling multi-layer, multi-vendor operations, ideally with some legacy compatibility via open APIs, should be intended to assist network operators in transitioning to the SDN network. Furthermore, SDN systems should ideally be built on a cloud-native software foundation to make use of elastically scalable cloud resources (CPU, memory, and connectivity) [51–54].
- Governments are likely to impose additional limits on network providers in the future to reduce carbon emission and privacy protection, both of which must be handled.
- The control plane, particularly the SDN controller, is the most vulnerable feature of SDN architectures, as the network is controlled by the SDN controller, which must be safeguarded. SDN resiliency support study (e.g., Da Silva et al. in [70]) classified them into several planes of the SDN architecture. Redundancy is the most traditional method of providing fault tolerance. The authors predicted three possible applications of redundancy in SDN: (i) protecting the SDN controller from

failures, (ii) protecting forwarding devices and communication links from link disruption, and (iii) protecting SDN applications from mis-configurations [54–63].

- Because the control plane is conceptually centralized and generally based on a single SDN controller, single point control channel failure is common. Using multi-controller topologies, however, the scalability of SDN can be improved. Multiple SDN controllers can be connected via west–east-bound APIs flatly or hierarchically [69]. However, in any service-oriented design, the controller placement problem is an NP-hard problem [67–70]. Furthermore, optimal design, load balancing, and demand nature conformed multi-controller placement are issues that must be overcome.
- In an SDN environment, the SDN controller selects how to transmit packets to create a dynamic network architecture that may be altered in milliseconds based on intents and flows. This makes it difficult to correlate defects and diagnose an SDN architecture, as information from physical nodes as well as rules implemented by the SDN controller must be correlated.
- The security and trust between SDN applications and controllers are some of the issues raised by SDN.
- The efficacy of SDN should be improved. The low efficiency of SDN in hybrid cloud-fog systems is due to large amounts of computational overhead caused by rules enforcement, overlapping network rules, and the memory-restricted capacities of OpenFlow-enabled devices.

Some of the issues listed above are for a specific sort of controller design. As a result, the challenges vary depending on the sort of controller design employed. A centralized controller suits corporations and data centers with a single administrator, whereas a heterogeneous environment, distributed, and, of course, hybrid controllers model function well for cloud-fog systems for the time being [70]. ML can be greatly utilized in the area of SDN and its application [61–66].

10.5 APPLICATIONS

This section provides some of the potential applications of NGNs. These applications include intelligent healthcare, supply chain management (SCM), cloud manufacturing, smart education, and intelligent disaster management. A few of these applications are discussed in the following sections.

10.5.1 Intelligent healthcare

By developing a health database local clinical information platform, smart or intelligent healthcare employs modern technologies of NGN to develop connectivity among patients and medical personnel, medical organizations, and medical equipment. Smart healthcare meets a patient's particular needs, such as monitoring blood pressure and glucose level, and supplies patients with individualized treatment with the help of specialists. Wearable technology, smart sensors, and other interactive fitness trackers can continuously capture the patient's healthcare data in real-time and save it in the cloud. The medical issues of patients can be evaluated using machine learning methods. These smart gadgets may connect, and if a doctor's supervision is required, this equipment can communicate the present state of the patient to the doctors and notify them to continue treatment. According to Haleen et al. [71], Industry 5.0 can serve a significant role in the development of individualized devices that can be customized to the patients' needs, which is a basic prerequisite in orthopedics. Researchers also propose that Industry 5.0 could aid in more specific medical procedures. The authors also highlight possible prospects of Industry 5.0 in the areas of medical training. Javaid et al. [72] investigated important capabilities in Industry 5.0 that could aid in the cure of Covid-19 sufferers. Experts discussed how critical empowering innovations in Industry 5.0, such as corobots, can aid in the care of patients without having to touch them. Investigators also indicated that robotic systems working with clinicians could assist in detecting and healing Covid-19 sufferers, lowering the chance of Covid-19 patients being exposed to front-line healthcare. Priadytmama et al. [73] advocated that assistive technology (AT), which was previously only available to disabled or handicapped persons, be made available to everybody to increase individual capabilities. Researchers indicated that emerging innovations in Industry 5.0, such as 3D printing, could aid in the widespread adoption of AT. Wearable AT, such as orthoses, limb prostheses, and exoskeletons, can be modified using the technologies to meet the geometry of the patient's body parts.

10.5.2 Supply chain management

Emerging innovations that support Industry 5.0, such as DT, cobots, 5G and beyond, ML [61–67], IoT [60], EC, and others, when combined with human intelligence and creativity, can assist businesses in fulfilling demand and producing individualized and customized occurs at a higher rate [78]. This enables SCM to incorporate mass customization, a major notion in Industry 5.0, into their industrial processes [74–77]. The SCM can be electronically replicated by employing DT, which includes warehouses, inventory positions, assets, and logistics. Industrial sites, providers, contractors, factories, transportation channels, distribution facilities, and client locations are all included in the DT. DT enables the SCM throughout its entire lifespan, from concept to installation and installation to services [79, 80]. DT may perceive actual information from IoT technology via emulating genuine

SCM systems. This statistic is used by cognitive computing, big data, and other technologies to estimate the issues experienced throughout various stages of SCM. As a result, companies can take proactive corrective efforts to mitigate losses and defects over various stages of SCM, allowing them to offer customized products to clients at a timely pace [74–77]. Liyanage et al. [78] suggested a DT-based strategy for evaluating the thermal performance of mango fruit during frozen shipping. They have also created a unique sensing gadget that simulates fruit to test the temperature model of the fruit pulp. The studies show how DT can provide details about fruit thermo-behavior across the supply chain. Such findings will aid the SCM sector in detecting where losses occur when transferring temperature-sensitive fruits and, as a result, preferred standpoint action to reduce losses. As a result, DT can assist in enhancing logistics and refrigeration practices to minimize inefficiencies and achieve a green supply chain. For the construction business, one researcher has presented a minimalist DT idea. Investigators glanced at the advantages of DT in lowering SCM costs in the building industry in this article. To enhance the SCM procedure in a more resilient manner, Marmolejo [79] designed a DT for the pharmaceutical industry. This technology was created by the researcher using solvers and simulator data analysis. The researcher has analyzed and studied various strategic plans for operations, supply, manufacturing, and product distribution operations of a a pharma firm.

10.5.3 Smart education

Learning is regarded as a basic requirement and the foundation of any country's reform efforts. Education evolves in response to changes in economy and culture, producing the important intellectual assets that firms will require in the ahead to prosper. In Industry 4.0, learning [73] was more technologically driven, focusing on diminishing manual intervention and prioritizing devices, whereas, in 5.0, the goal is to build harmony between unsupervised humans and computers. The combination of strong technology and effective experts will promote efficient, long-term, and ethical output. The job of Senior Automation Engineer will be introduced in Industry 5.0. This person focuses on machine interface and has competence in automation and AI. His work requires him to form opinions based on these aspects, which he should only do with education 5.0 abilities, which are the synthesis of technology, interaction, and management. Kent [80] aligned classical education to Industry 5.0 by addressing questions including, "Is formal education enough to instruct an employee?" Is it possible that a better education system is required? Their research turns the human interface issue into a cobot-coboters relationship, in which the coboter is a user who collaborates with the robot. This research also includes a business idea for cobots and coboters to collaborate on a given activity [73–80].

10.5.4 Intelligent disaster management system

A disaster is an unexpected, disastrous event that causes casualties or property, and its mitigation tactics are those that enable us to limit the disaster's repercussions. Catastrophe assistance is an important part of any business plan, but it only considers the near term. Because of the COVID-19 pandemic, numerous disaster recovery plans have been changed, perhaps ushering in long-term resilience as a policy that substitutes catastrophe mitigation techniques. Sukmono and Junaedi [81] recommended applying the fifth industrial revolution to disaster management, namely, the 7.0 magnitude earthquake that struck Indonesia in 2018. Their qualitative research demonstrated that Industry4.0's disaster recovery and management systems have weaknesses. Furthermore, combining people with AI and IoT can aid in the resolution of disaster-related challenges. Not just earthquakes, but also other crises such as pandemics, can be effectively controlled by bringing humans and intelligent machines together [81].

10.6 CONCLUSION AND FUTURE SCOPE

As we conclude, problems are at the heart of what drives research. In this regard, NGNs will be a powerful motivation. NGNs were briefly described in this study. Multiple networks are present now for numerous reasons such as telephony, data, and multiple kinds of video. Telecommunications, the world wide web, and wireless communications are all separate domains with their own rules and operations. The NGN is based on the concept of a single network that carries different kinds of data and offers assistance in the field of packets similar to those used on the world wide web. NGNs are frequently based on the IP. As a result, the shift to a NGN is sometimes referred to as an all-IP network (NGN). We provided an overview of NGN architecture along with the emerging need for NGN and its various features. We have also discussed the use of NGN using various emerging technologies such as IoT, cloud, edge intelligence, and SDN. The applications of NGN along with open research challenges and issues in NGN are also discussed.

REFERENCES

1 Hu, Yuxiang, Dan Li, Penghao Sun, Peng Yi, and Jiangxing Wu. "Polymorphic smart network: An open, flexible and universal architecture for future heterogeneous networks." *IEEE Transactions on Network Science and Engineering* 7, no. 4 (2020): 2515–2525.
2 Qiu, Tie, Ning Chen, Keqiu Li, Mohammed Atiquzzaman, and Wenbing Zhao. "How can heterogeneous internet of things build our future: A survey." *IEEE Communications Surveys & Tutorials* 20, no. 3 (2018): 2011–2027.

3 Yu, Quan, Jing Ren, Yinjin Fu, Ying Li, and Wei Zhang. "Cybertwin: An origin of next generation network architecture." *IEEE Wireless Communications* 26, no. 6 (2019): 111–117.

4 Kafle, V.P., M. Inoue, and H. Harai. "ID-Based New Generation Network research in AKARI Project." In *2010 9th International Conference on Optical Internet (COIN)*, pp. 1–3, 11–14 July 2010.

5 Khan, Manzoor Ahmed, Sebastian Peters, Doruk Sahinel, Francisco Denis Pozo-Pardo, and Xuan-Thuy Dang. "Understanding autonomic network management: A look into the past, a solution for the future." *Computer Communications* 122 (2018): 93–117.

6 Aoyama, T. "A New Generation Network — Beyond NGN." In *Innovations in NGN: Future Network and Services, 2008. K-INGN 2008. First ITU-T Kaleidoscope Academic Conference*, pp. 3–10, 12–13 May 2008.

7 Guo, Shaohua. "Study on the Age of the Internet Network Awareness of the New Generation of Migrant Workers." In *2014 7th International Conference on Intelligent Computation Technology and Automation (ICICTA)*, pp. 713–716, 25–26 October 2014.

8 Zhang, Zhishuo, Wei Zhang, Zhiguang Qin, Sunqiang Hu, Zhicheng Qian, and Xiang Chen. "A Secure Channel Established by the PF-CL-AKA Protocol with Two-Way ID-Based Authentication in Advance for the 5G-Based Wireless Mobile Network." In *2021 IEEE Asia Conference on Information Engineering (ACIE)*, pp. 11–15. IEEE, 2021.

9 De Nardis, Luca, and Maria-Gabriella Di Benedetto. "Mo 3: A Modular Mobility Model for future generation mobile wireless networks." *IEEE Access* 10 (2022): 34085–34115.

10 Eslamnezhad Namin, Mojtaba, Mehdi Hosseinzadeh, Nasour Bagheri, and Ahmad Khademzadeh. "A secure search protocol for lightweight and low-cost RFID systems." *Telecommunication Systems* 67, no. 4 (2018): 539–552.

11 Zhou, Yiqing, Lin Tian, Ling Liu, and Yanli Qi. "Fog computing enabled future mobile communication networks: A convergence of communication and computing." *IEEE Communications Magazine* 57, no. 5 (2019): 20–27.

12 Pop, Mădălin-Dorin, Jitendra Pandey, and Velmani Ramasamy. "Future Networks 2030: Challenges in Intelligent Transportation Systems." In *2020 8th International Conference on Reliability, Infocom Technologies and Optimization (Trends and Future Directions) (ICRITO)*, pp. 898–902. IEEE, 2020.

13 Gupta, Ishu, Preetesh K. Yadav, Sourav Pareek, Saif Shakeel, and Ashutosh Kumar Singh. "Auxiliary informatics system: An advancement towards a smart home environment." (2022).

14 Lee, Chae-Sub, and Dick Knight. "Realization of the next-generation network." *IEEE Communications Magazine* 43, no. 10 (2005): 34–41.

15 Olmedo, Vicente, Antonio Cuevas, Victor Villagrá, and José I. Moreno. "Next-Generation Grid Support over the SIP/IMS Platform." In *IP Multimedia Subsystem (IMS) Handbook*, pp. 149–172, 2018.

16 Sobin, C. C. "A survey on architecture, protocols and challenges in IoT." *Wireless Personal Communications* 112, no. 3 (2020): 1383–1429.

17 Alabady, Salah A., Fadi Al-Turjman, and Sadia Din. "A novel security model for cooperative virtual networks in the IoT era." *International Journal of Parallel Programming* 48, no. 2 (2020): 280–295.

18   McKinnel, Dean Richard, Tooska Dargahi, Ali Dehghantanha, and Kim-Kwang Raymond Choo. "A systematic literature review and meta-analysis on artificial intelligence in penetration testing and vulnerability assessment." *Computers & Electrical Engineering* 75 (2019): 175–188.

19   Circuit Switching Network (2022), Available on internet with this link: http://yuba.stanford.edu/~nickm/papers/UArch_Cam_Rdy.pdf, accessed on Feb 2022.

20   Circuit and Packet Switching Network (2022), Available on internet with this link: http://yuba.stanford.edu/~molinero/thesis/chapter.2.pdf, accessed on Feb 2022.

21   Al Ridhawi, Ismaeel, Safa Otoum, Moayad Aloqaily, Yaser Jararweh, and Thar Baker. "Providing secure and reliable communication for next generation networks in smart cities." *Sustainable Cities and Society* 56 (2020): 102080.

22   Alhammadi, Abdulraqeb, Mardeni Roslee, Mohamad Yusoff Alias, Ibraheem Shayea, and Abdullah Alquhali. "Velocity-aware handover self-optimization management for next generation networks." *Applied Sciences* 10, no. 4 (2020): 1354.

23   Next Generation Network ITU (2022), Available on internet with this link: https://www.itu.int/ITU-D/treg/Documentation/ITU-NGN09.pdf, accessed on Jan 2022.

24   ITU_NGN (2022), Available on internet with this link: http://www.hit.bme.hu/~jakab/edu/litr/NGN/Architecture/ITU_NGN_Module1.pdf, accessed on Jan 2022.

25   Shuja, Junaid, Kashif Bilal, Waleed Alasmary, Hassan Sinky, and Eisa Alanazi. "Applying machine learning techniques for caching in next-generation edge networks: A comprehensive survey." *Journal of Network and Computer Applications* 181 (2021): 103005.

26   Kadhim, Abdulkareem Abdulrahman. "5G and next generation networks." In *2018 Al-Mansour International Conference on New Trends in Computing, Communication, and Information Technology (NTCCIT)*, pp. 99–99. IEEE, 2018.

27   "Next generation network overview," http://www.techrepublic.com/blog/data-center/key-features-of-next-generation-networks/, accessed on Feb 2015.

28   Sultan, Kashif, Hazrat Ali, and Zhongshan Zhang. "Big data perspective and challenges in next generation networks." *Future Internet* 10, no. 7 (2018): 56.

29   Thantharate, Anurag, Cory Beard, and Sreekar Marupaduga. "An Approach to Optimize Device Power Performance towards Energy Efficient Next Generation 5G Networks." In *2019 IEEE 10th Annual Ubiquitous Computing, Electronics & Mobile Communication Conference (UEMCON)*, pp. 0749–0754. IEEE, 2019.

30   Vitturi, Stefano, Claudio Zunino, and Thilo Sauter. "Industrial communication systems and their future challenges: Next-generation Ethernet, IIoT, and 5G." *Proceedings of the IEEE* 107, no. 6 (2019): 944–961.

31   Sharma, Teena, Abdellah Chehri, and Paul Fortier. "Review of optical and wireless backhaul networks and emerging trends of next generation 5G and 6G technologies." *Transactions on Emerging Telecommunications Technologies* 32, no. 3 (2021): e4155.

32   Bhardwaj, A., and C. R. Krishna. "A container-based technique to improve virtual machine migration in cloud computing." *IETE Journal of Research*, 68 (2019): 1–16.

33 Minenna, Damien FG, Frédéric André, Yves Elskens, Jean-François Auboin, Fabrice Doveil, Jérôme Puech, and Élise Duverdier. "The traveling-wave tube in the history of telecommunication." *The European Physical Journal H* 44, no. 1 (2019): 1–36.

34 Orabi, Mariam, Raghad Al Barghash, and Sohail Abbas. "Dynamic Offloading in Fog Computing: A Survey." In *Proceedings of International Conference on Information Technology and Applications*, pp. 365–378. Springer, Singapore, 2022.

35 Bhardwaj, Aditya, and C. Rama Krishna. "Efficient multistage bandwidth allocation technique for virtual machine migration in cloud computing." *Journal of Intelligent & Fuzzy Systems*, vol. 35, no. 5, pp. 5365–5378, 2018.

36 Krishnan, Rajkumar, R. Santhana Krishnan, Y. Harold Robinson, E. Golden Julie, Hoang Viet Long, A. Sangeetha, M. Subramanian, and Raghvendra Kumar. "An intrusion detection and prevention protocol for internet of things based wireless sensor networks." *Wireless Personal Communications* (2022): 1–23.

37 Bhardwaj, A., & Krishna, C. R. (2019). Improving the Performance of Pre-copy Virtual Machine Migration Technique. In *Proceedings of 2nd International Conference on Communication, Computing and Networking*, pp. 1021–1032. Springer, Singapore.

38 Onwuegbuzie, Innocent, Samuel-Soma Ajibade, Taiwo Fele, and Sunday Akinwamide. "5G: Next generation mobile wireless technology for a fast pacing world." *Journal for Pure and Applied Sciences (JPAS)* 1, no. 1 (2022).

39 Agrawal, Reeya. "Comparison of different mobile wireless technology (from 0G to 6G)." *ECS Transactions* 107, no. 1 (2022): 4799.

40 Sharma, V., G. Choudhary, I. You, J.D. Lim, and J.N. Kim. Self-enforcing game theory-based resource allocation for LoRaWAN assisted public safety communications. *Journal of Internet Technology* 2 (2018): 515–530.

41 Agiwal, M., A. Roy, and N. Saxena. Next generation 5G wireless networks: A comprehensive survey. *IEEE Communications Surveys and Tutorials* 18 (2016): 1617–1655.

42 Salah, Ibrahim, M. Mourad Mabrook, Aziza I. Hussein, and Kamel Hussein Rahouma. "Comparative study of efficiency enhancement technologies in 5G networks-A survey." *Procedia Computer Science* 182 (2021): 150–158.

43 Niyato, D., and X. Yan. *Edge AI: Convergence of Edge Computing and Artificial Intelligence*. Springer, Singapore, 2020.

44 Wang, X., Y. Han, C. Wang, Q. Zhao, X. Chen, and M. Chen. In-edge Ai: Intelligentizing mobile edge computing, caching and communication by federated learning. *IEEE Networks* 33 (2019): 156–165. doi:10.1109/MNET.2019. 1800286

45 Asad, Syed Muhammad, Ahsen Tahir, Naveed Bin Rais, Shuja Ansari, Attai Ibrahim Abubakar, Sajjad Hussain, Qammer H. Abbasi, and Muhammad Ali Imran. "Edge intelligence in private mobile networks for next-generation railway systems." *Frontiers in Communication and Networks Journal* 2 (2021). doi: 10.3389/frcmn.2021.769299

46 Zhao, Y., W. Wang, Y. Li, C.C. Meixner, M. Tornatore, and J. Zhang. Edge computing and networking: A survey on infrastructures and applications. *IEEE Access* 7 (2019): 101213–101230.

47 Gupta, Umesh, and Deepak Gupta. "An improved regularization based Lagrangian asymmetric *v*-twin support vector regression using pinball loss function." *Applied Intelligence* 49, no. 10 (2019): 3606–3627.

48 Gupta, Umesh, and Deepak Gupta. "Lagrangian Twin-Bounded Support Vector Machine Based on L2-Norm." In *Recent Developments in Machine Learning and Data Analytics*, pp. 431–444. Springer, Singapore, 2019.

49 Xia, Wenfeng, Yonggang Wen, Chuan Heng Foh, Dusit Niyato, and Haiyong Xie. "A survey on software-defined networking." *IEEE Communications Surveys & Tutorials* 17, no. 1 (2014): 27–51.

50 Kirkpatrick, Keith. "Software-defined networking." *Communications of the ACM* 56, no. 9 (2013): 16–19.

51 Kreutz, Diego, Fernando MV Ramos, Paulo Esteves Verissimo, Christian Esteve Rothenberg, Siamak Azodolmolky, and Steve Uhlig. "Software-defined networking: A comprehensive survey." *Proceedings of the IEEE* 103, no. 1 (2014): 14–76.

52 Gahlot, Ayushi, and Umesh Gupta. "Gaze-based authentication in cloud computing." *International Journal of Computer Applications* 1, no. 1 (2016): 14–20.

53 Zhou, Jiehan, Teemu Leppanen, Erkki Harjula, Mika Ylianttila, Timo Ojala, Chen Yu, Hai Jin, and Laurence Tianruo Yang. "Cloudthings: A Common Architecture for Integrating the Internet of Things with Cloud Computing." In *Proceedings of the 2013 IEEE 17th International Conference on Computer Supported Cooperative Work in Design (CSCWD)*, pp. 651–657. IEEE, 2013.

54 Aloqaily, Moayad, Kobbane Abdellatif, and Feng Yan. "Special issue on internet of things: Intelligent networks, communication and mobility (AdHocNets 2020)." *Mobile Networks and Applications* (2022): 1–3.

55 Zikria, Yousaf Bin, Rashid Ali, Muhammad Khalil Afzal, and Sung Won Kim. "Next-generation internet of things (iot): Opportunities, challenges, and solutions." *Sensors* 21, no. 4 (2021): 1174.

56 Trifonov, Hristo, and Donal Heffernan. "OPC UA TSN: a next-generation network for Industry 4.0 and IIoT." *International Journal of Pervasive Computing and Communications* 7 (2021). DOI: 10.1108/IJPCC-07-2021-0160.

57 Raimundo, Ricardo Jorge, and Albérico Travassos Rosário. "Cybersecurity in the internet of things in industrial management." *Applied Sciences* 12, no. 3 (2022): 1598.

58 Gunathilake, Nilupulee A., Ahmed Al-Dubai, and William J. Buchanan. "Internet of Things: Concept, Implementation and Challenges." In *Internet of Things and Its Applications*, pp. 145–155. Springer, Singapore, 2022.

59 López, César, Ignacio Lacalle, Andreu Belsa, Zbigniew Kopertowski, Carlos E Palau, and Manuel Esteve. "Reviewing SDN Adoption Strategies for Next Generation Internet of Things Networks." In *Smart Systems: Innovations in Computing*, pp. 619–631. Springer, Singapore, 2022.

60 Haghnegahdar, Lida, Sameehan S. Joshi, and Narendra B. Dahotre. "From IoT-based cloud manufacturing approach to intelligent additive manufacturing: Industrial Internet of Things—An overview." *The International Journal of Advanced Manufacturing Technology* (2022): 1–18.

61 Singh, Deepika, Anju Saha, and Anjana Gosain. "wCM based hybrid pre-processing algorithm for class imbalanced dataset." *Journal of Intelligent & Fuzzy Systems* Preprint (2021): 1–16.

62 Singh, Deepika, Anju Saha, and Anjana Gosain. "Predicting Classifiers Efficacy in Relation with Data Complexity Metric Using Under-Sampling Techniques." In *Proceedings of Second Doctoral Symposium on Computational Intelligence*, pp. 85–92. Springer, Singapore, 2022.

63 Singh, Deepika, Anjana Gosain, and Anju Saha. "Weighted k-nearest neighbor based data complexity metrics for imbalanced datasets." *Statistical Analysis and Data Mining: The ASA Data Science Journal* 13, no. 4 (2020): 394–404.

64 Gupta, Umesh, Deepak Gupta, and Mukesh Prasad. "Kernel Target Alignment Based Fuzzy Least Square Twin Bounded Support Vector Machine." In *2018 IEEE Symposium Series on Computational Intelligence (SSCI)*, pp. 228–235. IEEE, 2018.

65 Gupta, Umesh, and Deepak Gupta. "Least squares large margin distribution machine for regression." *Applied Intelligence* 51, no. 10 (2021): 7058–7093.

66 Yadav, Sapna, Richa Mishra, and Umesh Gupta. "Performance Evaluation of Different Versions of 2D Torus Network." In *2015 International Conference on Advances in Computer Engineering and Applications*, pp. 178–182. IEEE, 2015.

67 Hassan, Najmul, Kok-Lim Alvin Yau, and Celimuge Wu. "Edge computing in 5G: A review." *IEEE Access* 7 (2019): 127276–127289.

68 Cao, Keyan, Yefan Liu, Gongjie Meng, and Qimeng Sun. "An overview on edge computing research." *IEEE Access* 8 (2020): 85714–85728.

69 Pham, Quoc-Viet, Fang Fang, Vu Nguyen Ha, Md Jalil Piran, Mai Le, Long Bao Le, Won-Joo Hwang, and Zhiguo Ding. "A survey of multi-access edge computing in 5G and beyond: Fundamentals, technology integration, and state-of-the-art." *IEEE Access* 8 (2020): 116974–117017.

70 Batista, José Olimpio Rodrigues, Douglas Chagas da Silva, Moacyr Martucci, Regina Melo Silveira, and Carlos Eduardo Cugnasca. "A multi-provider end-to-end dynamic orchestration architecture approach for 5G and future communication systems." *Applied Sciences* 11, no. 24 (2021): 11914.

71 Maddikunta, Praveen Kumar Reddy, Quoc-Viet Pham, B. Prabadevi, N. Deepa, Kapal Dev, Thippa Reddy Gadekallu, Rukhsana Ruby, and Madhusanka Liyanage. "Industry 5.0: A survey on enabling technologies and potential applications." *Journal of Industrial Information Integration* 26 (2022): 100257.

72 Madsen, Dag Øivind, and Terje Berg. "An exploratory bibliometric analysis of the birth and emergence of industry 5.0." *Applied System Innovation* 4, no. 4 (2021): 87.

73 Maddikunta, Praveen Kumar Reddy, Quoc-Viet Pham, B. Prabadevi, N. Deepa, Kapal Dev, Thippa Reddy Gadekallu, Rukhsana Ruby, and Madhusanka Liyanage. "Industry 5.0: A survey on enabling technologies and potential applications." *Journal of Industrial Information Integration* 26 (2022): 100257.

74 Garrido-Hidalgo, Celia, Teresa Olivares, F. Javier Ramirez, and Luis Roda-Sanchez. "An end-to-end internet of things solution for reverse supply chain management in industry 4.0." *Computers in Industry* 112 (2019): 103127.

75 Pal, Kamalendu. "Information Sharing for Manufacturing Supply Chain Management Based on Blockchain Technology." In *Cross-Industry Use of Blockchain Technology and Opportunities for the Future*, pp. 1–17. IGI Global, 2020.

76 Ben-Daya, Mohamed, Elkafi Hassini, and Zied Bahroun. "Internet of things and supply chain management: a literature review." *International Journal of Production Research* 57, no. 15–16 (2019): 4719–4742.

77 Lee, K., P. Romzi, J. Hanaysha, H. Alzoubi, and M. Alshurideh. "Investigating the impact of benefits and challenges of IOT adoption on supply chain performance and organizational performance: An empirical study in Malaysia." *Uncertain Supply Chain Management* 10, no. 2 (2022): 537–550.

78 Maddikunta, Praveen Kumar Reddy, Quoc-Viet Pham, B. Prabadevi, N. Deepa, Kapal Dev, Thippa Reddy Gadekallu, Rukhsana Ruby, and Madhusanka Liyanage. "Industry 5.0: A survey on enabling technologies and potential applications." *Journal of Industrial Information Integration* 26 (2022): 100257.

79 Marmolejo-Saucedo, Jose Antonio, Margarita Hurtado-Hernandez, and Ricardo Suarez-Valdes. "Digital Twins in Supply Chain Management: A Brief Literature Review." In *International Conference on Intelligent Computing & Optimization*, pp. 653–661. Springer, Cham, 2019.

80 Doyle-Kent, Mary. "Collaborative robotics in industry 5.0." PhD diss., Wien, 2021.

81 Junaedi, Fajar, and Filosa Gita Sukmono. "University students behavior in searching and disseminating COVID-19 online information." *Jurnal Aspikom* 5, no. 2 (2020.

Index

Note: Pages in *italics* refer figures.

A

architecture
of delay tolerant networks, 105
of IoT, 119

B

Babies' movement detection, 67
Berkeley media access control (B-MAC),
150–151
Bluetooth, 150
Bluetooth low energy (Bluetooth LE),
148–149
Blynk mobile application, 72, 73,
77–78, 84
breadboard, 71, 75

C

causes of indoor air quality
problems, 47
challenges and issues in 5G, 204
Cloud-based IoT, 197
cloud security vulnerabilities, 93
clustering system, 153
communication protocols, 148
comparison of existing steganography
tools, 186
computation cost analysis, 138
constant monitoring in the Crib by
using Internet of Things
(IoT), 67

D

DASH7, 148
data-based protocols, 153
data integrity, 133
delay tolerant messege based overlay
architecture, 104
design issues in communication
protocol, 149
design of transmitter, 74
digital signatures in network
security, 30

E

ECC algorithm, 34
edge intelligence, 198
elliptic curve cryptograph (ECC), 121
embedding algorithm, 180
equation of elliptic curve
cryptography, 121
execution of Diffie Hellman encryption
algorithm, 35
extraction algorithm, 181

F

features of NGN, *193*
FL applications in healthcare, 7
flat network system, 153
fuzzy based dynamic release of
healthcare datasets
(FUZZY-DP), 4, 13

fuzzy-logic, 2
    applications in healthcare, 7
    techniques in medical domain, 4
fuzzy logic applications in healthcare, a
    review based study, 7

G

GARUDA, 162
gateway management table, *111*
gossiping, 155

H

HomeCHEM project, 51
hybrid routing, 152

I

IEQ index scoring system, 49
implications and benefits of fuzzy logic
    in healthcare industry, 7
importance of integrating cloud
    computing with IoT
    network, 201
indoor air pollution study, No, Co,
    CO2, 51
indoor air quality
    carbon monoxide and carbon
        dioxide (AEN 125), 52
    and coronavirus disease, 51
    parameters, 48
intelligent disaster management
    system, 210
intelligent healthcare, 207
internal arrangement of border
    gateways, 108
Internet of Things (IoT), 116
    applications, 117
    applications of wireless sensor
        networks, 163
    in healthcare, 5
    in monitoring the health, 5

K

key generation ECC algorithm, 34

L

layered architecture of delay tolerant
    network, 105–106

layer information table, 108
LEACH algorithm, 36
leading carbon monoxide sources, 45
location-based protocols, 154
low energy adaptive clustering
    hierarchy (LEACH), 150

M

mutual authentication, 133
    phase, 127

N

need for layered security, 90
network security, 29
neuro-fuzzy system (NFS), 4
NGN, 203
    enabling technologies, 193
node arrangement of delay tolerant
    network, 105
NodeMCU ESP8266, 71

O

open source IPv6 automation network
    (OSIAN), 148

P

path selection and scheduling, 104
privacy, 133
proactive routing, 152

R

random oracle model security, 136
reactive routing, 152
real environment design, 80
regions and border gateways, 104
resource-constrained IoT devices, 115
routing protocols, 52
RSA algorithm, 35
RTSP IP camera application, 73

S

SDN, 206
security in wireless sensor networks, 29
security requirements, 133
self-organizing medium access control
    for sensornets (SMACS), 149

sensor media access control
        (S-MAC), 151
sensor protocols for information via
        negotiation (SPIN), 155
smart education, 209
software-defined networks, 202
specification and the measurements, 47
steganography, 171
structure of fuzzy logic, 2
supply chain management, 208
system flowchart, 75

T

technological impact on Covid-19
        pandemic, 45
temperature and humidity sensor
        (DHT11), 71

threshold air pollution values, 50
threshold thermal comfort values, 50
transmission control protocols, 159

U

ultrasonic sensor, 70
usage of blockchain in cloud, 93

W

wireless sensor network routing
        protocol approaches, 153

Z

Zigbee, 148